Spiritual Mestizaje

A BOOK IN THE SERIES
Latin America Otherwise:
Languages, Empires, Nations

EDITED BY
Walter D. Mignolo, Duke University
Irene Silverblatt, Duke University
and Sonia Saldívar-Hull, University
of Texas, San Antonio

· ·

Spiritual Mestizaje

RELIGION, GENDER, RACE, AND NATION IN
CONTEMPORARY CHICANA NARRATIVE

Theresa Delgadillo

DUKE UNIVERSITY PRESS | DURHAM AND LONDON | 2011

© 2011 Duke University Press
All rights reserved.

Printed in the United States of America on
acid-free paper ∞

Designed by April Leidig-Higgins
Typeset in Garamond Premier Pro by
Copperline Book Services, Inc.

Library of Congress Cataloging-in-Publication Data
appear on the last printed page of this book.

IN MEMORY OF

Amalia Martínez Delgadillo

Contents

About the Series

Latin America Otherwise: Languages, Empires, Nations is a critical series. It aims to explore the emergence and consequences of concepts used to define "Latin America" while at the same time exploring the broad interplay of political, economic, and cultural practices that have shaped Latin American worlds. Latin America, at the crossroads of competing imperial designs and local responses, has been construed as a geocultural and geopolitical entity since the nineteenth century. This series provides a starting point to redefine Latin America as a configuration of political, linguistic, cultural, and economic intersections that demands a continuous reappraisal of the role of the Americas in history, and of the ongoing process of globalization and the relocation of people and cultures that have characterized Latin America's experience. Latin America Otherwise: Languages, Empires, Nations is a forum that confronts established geocultural constructions, rethinks area studies and disciplinary boundaries, assesses convictions of the academy and of public policy, and correspondingly demands that the practices through which we produce knowledge and understanding about and from Latin America be subject to rigorous and critical scrutiny.

Acknowledgments

My gratitude to those who accompanied me in this project is immense.

Identifying an origin for this work is difficult. In some ways, it began years ago in an independent study with Alberto Rios, comparing the spiritual perspectives represented in the work of Leslie Marmon Silko and Rudolfo Anaya. In other ways, it began with my introduction to liberation theology in the activist movements of the 1980s. Another beginning was in graduate school, with a group of passionate and fierce peers and amazing mentors. And yet another origin for this work was in my mother's bedroom, before her altar and her images of Nuestra Señora de Guadalupe and the Virgin Mary. This is why my gratitude is immense: because so many have shaped it and me.

For the critical questions and comments that prompted me to read again, think again, write again, I am deeply grateful to Sonia Saldívar-Hull, Valerie Smith, Rafael Pérez-Torres, Raquel Rubio Goldsmith, Mary Pat Brady, Elizabeth Lapovsky Kennedy, Ana Ortiz, Carl Gutiérrez-Jones, Jim Lee, Joanna Brooks, Sarah Deutsch, Lucila Ek, Yvonne Yarbro-Bejarano, Alvina Quintana, Richard Yarborough, Cecilia Corcoran, Maurice Stevens and the anonymous reviewers of this work in manuscript form.

For conversations and work shared, conference experiences enriched, especially on questions of religion and spirituality, and the pushes and nudges that undoubtedly fueled this work I thank Miroslava Chávez-García, Mark Quigley, Norma Mendoza Denton, Laura Briggs, Ana Ochoa O'Leary, Miranda Joseph, Andrea Romero, Daniel Cooper Alarcón, Ron Carlson, Kay Sands, Cordelia Candelaria, Rosa Linda Fregoso, Laura Pérez, Teresita Aguilar, Marisela Chávez, Grace Huerta, Constance Razza, Norma Cantú, Anne Martinez, Mario Ascencio, Priscilla Ybarra, AnaLouise Keating, Michele Habell-Pallán, José David Saldívar, Sara Ramirez, Victoria Sanford, Lara Medina, Lydia Otero, Karen Mary Davalos, Irene Lara, Louise Roth, Frances Aparicio, David Carrasco, Timothy Matovina, Orlando Menes, Tammy Ho, Luz Calvo, Catriona Esquibel, Alma López, Beretta E. Smith-

Shomade, Khanh Ho, Ellie Hernandez, Dalia Kandiyoti, Norma Alarcón, Tracy Curtis, Ernesto Chávez, Lynn Itagaki, Scott Stevens, Alma Lopez, Yolanda Lopez, Larry LaFountain, Amalia Malagamba, and John Phillip Santos.

I owe very special thanks to the authors who so generously answered my questions and shared their thoughts on spirituality in literature and film: Denise Chávez, Kathleen Alcalá, Lourdes Portillo, Norma Cantú, and Demetria Martínez.

Two very special groups of women, whom I met during the preparation of this manuscript at the Latina Women's Spiritual Quest in Mexico City in 2005 and 2006, shared their commitment, passion, knowledge, encouragement, and activism with me, providing inspiration that influenced this work in many ways. It was my good fortune to share the experience of the quests with each of them, especially Sister Anita De Luna in 2005. Her knowledge, skill, patience, and depth of commitment to the advancement of Latinas is much missed in this world.

I was the recipient of two fellowships that provided the gift of intellectual community to feed this work and the gift of time with which to complete it. Thank you to the Center for Chicano Studies at UCSB, where I was in residence in 2001–2, and to the Rockefeller Foundation for supporting my fellowship there. My thanks to those who made this an especially rewarding experience, including Carl Gutiérrez-Jones, Anne Elwell, my fellow postdocs Naomi Quinonez and Paul Lopez, and Laura Furlan, who provided excellent research assistance. I was fortunate to have many colleagues at UCSB who encouraged this work and shared their insights, including María Herrera-Sobek, Yolanda Broyles-González, Chela Sandoval, and Jonathan Inda. I benefited from attending the religious studies colloquia there as well as events organized by the Departments of Chicano/a Studies and English. During 2005–6 I was the recipient of an Andrew Mellon/Woodrow Wilson Career Enhancement Fellowship, which allowed me time to work on this project at a critical moment and through which I met many outstanding scholars whose critical engagements sharpened my skills and work. I remain indebted to the entire community of Mellon/Wilson fellows and extend a special thanks to the participants in the 2005 conference, fellows and mentors alike, who offered me helpful feedback on this project, especially Gloria González-López, Jennifer Brody, Rafael Pérez-Torres, and Ondine Chavoya. For arranging a much-needed workspace for me during the fellowship period and for library privileges, intellectual community, and friendship, I thank Gregory Jay, Jane Gallop, Kristy Hamilton, and Kim Blaeser. For amazing research assistance during the later years of this project, I especially thank Kara Jacobi, Scott Smith, Taiko Hoessler, and Rashelle Peck.

For assistance with research expenses, I am grateful to the Friends of Women's Studies at the University of Arizona, the College of Humanities at the University of Arizona, the Institute for Latino Studies at the University of Notre Dame, the College of Arts and Sciences at Notre Dame, and the College of Humanities at Ohio State University. This project benefited from the administrative assistance of several people at these three universities, including Lynn McCormack, Lori Wilson, Shu-Wen Tsai, and students who willingly engaged these materials and ideas with me in the classroom; thank you all. This work owes much to the conversations, debates, and experiences at each university and would not have been the same without my participation in these different cultures.

From our very first conversation about this manuscript several years ago at an American Studies Association Conference until his recent retirement, Reynolds Smith has been a supportive and encouraging editor. Thank you, Reynolds, for your expertise and interest and for all your work to bring this book to publication. My thanks also to Sharon Torian, editorial assistant at Duke University Press, for her care in shepherding this book through the initial stages of the publication process. Valerie Milholland and Gisela Fosado deserve thanks for taking over in the editorial process upon Reynolds's retirement, and Rebecca Fowler for additional editorial assistance, and Nancy Zibman for the index. I have made every effort to treat the works discussed here with the respect they deserve and to provide readers with an accurate, engaging, well-organized book, but any errors that remain are my responsibility.

Amalia Martínez Delgadillo, who taught me so much about the power of spiritual commitment, the agency of religious participants, and respect for the views of others, passed away during the preparation of this work, but not without encouraging me to persevere. She had looked forward to the day when she would see my book in print, so this moment is bittersweet. I am eternally grateful for my life with her, for all she taught me, all she gave me, all she pointed me toward.

For the love, shared experiences, encouragement, and conversations that made my life richer and my work better, I remain grateful to the entire Delgadillo family—father, sisters, brothers, in-laws, nieces, nephews, great-nieces, great-nephews, cousins, aunts, and uncles, especially Elena and Rosemary. You are my blessings.

Spiritual Mestizaje

1   *A Theory of Spiritual Mestizaje*

Nuestra alma el trabajo, the opus, the great alchemical work; spiritual
mestizaje, a "morphogenesis," an inevitable unfolding. We have
become the quickening serpent movement. — Gloria Anzaldúa[1]

A new mestiza consciousness cannot be achieved without it,
yet "spiritual mestizaje" is named only once in Gloria Anzaldúa's seminal
work *Borderlands/La Frontera* (1987). As the epigraph demonstrates, the
term is synonymous with transformative genesis in Anzaldúa and closely
associated with the figure of the serpent, a creature much maligned in the
Christian tradition, but often sacred and revitalizing in indigenous worlds.
This metaphorical description locates spiritual mestizaje at the center of
Anzaldúa's autobiographical, historical, theoretical, and poetic text about
personal and social transformation at the U.S.-Mexico border. Here the
writer *works* her own experience of spiritual, social, emotional, and intellectual journeying to theorize the significance of the U.S.-Mexico border
in the creation and potential of the Chicana subject, particularly the queer
Chicana subject. In this work, Anzaldúa develops a theory and method of
spiritual mestizaje capable of guiding the Chicana subject toward a heightened consciousness of justice that is also an embodied one. This state is one
out of which the new paradigms of social relation that Anzaldúa imagines
might be enacted. What is this powerful and life-changing process named
spiritual mestizaje? It is the transformative renewal of one's relationship to
the sacred through a radical and sustained multimodal and self-reflexive
critique of oppression in all its manifestations and a creative and engaged
participation in shaping life that honors the sacred. My work examines the
significance of this critical mobility, lived and imagined at the border, as a
key critical intervention in recent scholarship.

Anzaldúa's innovative theoretical contributions and her instantiation of
new narrative forms have been widely influential in studies of subjectivity,

consciousness, language, spirituality, gender, religion, sexuality, literature, history, feminism, activism, culture, and cultural change. Born of the U.S.-Mexico border, *Borderlands/La Frontera* has been received throughout the hemisphere and the world as a text that addresses new global realities, advancing our understanding of many aspects of the cross-cultural exchange increasingly characteristic of contemporary society. Her theory of spiritual mestizaje, however, remains underexamined, prompting my interest in fleshing out its place in *Borderlands* and *This Bridge We Call Home*, and considering it in relation to other theories and theologies that pair mestizaje with spirituality.[2] The shape and significance of this process in Anzaldúa's work are the subject of this chapter; subsequent chapters will enlarge upon spiritual mestizaje in an analysis of eight Chicana narratives that enter into the space opened by Anzaldúa's queer, feminist, and border theorizing on spirituality. These narratives include both fictional and documentary texts that are significant for the forms they invent, the arts they employ to tell particular stories, and their meaning in the world outside of the text. My discussion of them derives from my interest in the imaginative use of language and narrative technique and the social practice of imagination—what some would call literature's political unconscious and others would call its ability to speak to us about our worlds.[3] In these fictional and documentary narratives, to imagine spiritual mestizaje is in some ways to enact it. This participation in the creation of new forms of consciousness—a route toward new ways of thinking and being in the world—is not unique to Chicana literature and film, but the narratives themselves are beautifully unique and compelling.

Anzaldúa's instantiation of a new narrative form—*autohisteoría*—in *Borderlands/La Frontera* also merits further examination, particularly as it converges with and differs from the Latin American *testimonio* form. Since both forms factor into the theory and method of spiritual mestizaje, this analysis is a necessary step in the creation of a framework for reading what occurs in Chicana texts that engage religion and spirituality. The Chicana narratives that I will address include Denise Chávez's *Face of an Angel* (1994), Demetria Martínez's *Mother Tongue* (1994), Norma Cantú's *Canícula* (1995), Judith Gleason's and the Feminist Collective of Xalapa's *Flowers for Guadalupe* (1995), Lourdes Portillo's *Señorita Extraviada* (2001), and Kathleen Alcalá's borderlands trilogy: *Spirits of the Ordinary* (1998),

The Flower in the Skull (1999), and *Treasures in Heaven* (2000). A *Borderlands* ethos emerges in these texts in their testifying, historicizing, critiquing, and imagining of the past, present, and future on the U.S.-Mexico border. The spiritual realm and spiritual work figure centrally in that ethos and in each of these narratives. Indeed, as contemporary texts, these novels and films speak to the growing "spiritual inventiveness" that many have observed in contemporary society.[4] My discussion of these texts begins with those that imagine the nexus of religion, gender, race, nation, and sexuality in individual contexts, then moves to those that imagine this nexus in the register of the communal, and ends with those that focus on these intersections in broader social contexts. Taken together, this selection of Chicana narratives portrays a spiritually pluralist borderlands that is also (of course, since this is what pluralist societies demand) the site of difficult negotiations.

Throughout this work, I employ terms that require a critical caveat, specifically the terms *religion* and *spirituality*, especially when used in relation to indigenous rituals and beliefs. "Religion," as Tomoko Masuzawa notes, exists as a Christian and Western category of thought and social relations that is widely imposed upon societies for which the term holds no meaning or is retroactively applied to societies in the past that bear no resemblance to Christian or Western society.[5] Talad Asad illuminates the mechanisms by which "religion" has become a prevailing concept in the West for categorizing certain kinds of human behavior or social relations and for furthering the presupposition that religion is universal, but differs from place to place in values, rituals, and symbols. Asad argues that this approach has obscured the relationship between religious discourses and relations of power as well as the ways that religion overlaps with contemporary national identity in the West (through his discussion of the British government's response to the *fatwa* against Salman Rushdie).[6] In some respects, "spirituality" is similar, and shares origins with "religion"; however, the former has entered the contemporary lexicon as a signifier of non-Western belief and life systems and non-institutional or organic forms of engagement with nonmaterial realities.[7] Therefore, in this book I generally employ the term *religion* to refer to organized, institutionalized, traditional religions in Western thought and the term *spirituality* to refer to non-Western and non-institutional forms of relation to the sacred.

Queering Spirituality

In *Borderlands* spirituality informs the theorization, in the narrative section, and imagination, in the poetry section, of the psychic, intellectual, emotional, discursive, and material components of a process that can shift the borderlands from a world of "isms" to a more just order. Anzaldúa emphasizes the development of a spiritually informed critical awareness and its employment rather than the achievement of a prescriptive consciousness. This unique and radical contribution to feminist thought departs from the search for resolution to the conflict of gender, sexuality, and institutional religions.[8] More importantly, it insists not on epistemic privilege but on unceasing epistemic inquiry.

Spirituality denotes, on one hand, a connection to the sacred, a recognition of worlds or realities beyond those immediately visible and respect for the sacred knowledge that these bring and, on the other hand, a way of being in the world, a language of communication and interrelation embodying this understanding and one's response to it. A transculturative process, Anzaldúa's spiritual mestizaje demands the recognition, assessment, and critique of the paradigms that, woven together, have colonized the borderlands and the Americas. Queering spirituality creates a vehicle for the mestiza body and self to combat and surpass oppressions. The *Borderlands* perspective begins to disentangle the religious, racial, gender, sexual, and national conceptions—where, for example, one's ethnicity determines one's religion, or one's religion determines one's sexuality—that have contributed to this colonization. Because intellect and rationality, psyche and spirit, and the body and the material are subject to these paradigms, and interrelated, spiritual mestizaje involves all of these spheres in the reconfiguration of individual and collective social relations and subjectivities. For Anzaldúa, spirituality is distinct from organized religion and describes both an ethics of recognizing multiple ways of knowing and a specific acceptance of a nonmaterial sacred realm present in the world. A multilayered text, *Borderlands* works its way through these varied discourses, centering the negotiations that Anzaldúa's queer Chicana self and body must engage and thereby advancing a theory of Chicana subjectivity rooted but not fixed in the experience and epistemology of the U.S.-Mexico border and of queer Chicana feminists.

The many scholars and readers who have found in Anzaldúa's theory of the borderlands a paradigm through which to think about other encounters, literary or material, between divergent cultures have drawn from the powerful ability of *Borderlands* to address both the conditions and conceptions specific to the border between Mexico and the United States and its ability to represent in microcosm, in the age of globalization, the conditions of the world and its peoples. Writing about the ways in which *Borderlands* has been received, Yvonne Yarbro-Bejarano observes that some readings of this theory of difference ignore the specific conditions, histories, and identities that the text addresses—the very difference it asserts—and cautions against such "appropriative readings" whether they come from those seeking to theorize and understand difference across borders or from those working to understand identity in a postmodern context. Yet Yarbro-Bejarano rightly situates *Borderlands* as a work that "exemplifies the articulation between the contemporary awareness that *all* identity is constructed across difference and the necessity of a new *politics* of difference to accompany this new sense of self."[9] Chela Sandoval places the work's theory of differential consciousness alongside the work of Frantz Fanon, Cherríe Moraga, Jacques Derrida, Roland Barthes, Emma Pérez, and Trinh T. Minh-ha in an analysis that brings these varied perspectives into conversation.[10] The two levels of work in *Borderlands*—the elaboration of a specific difference and a more abstract theory—remain tightly interwoven throughout the text and apply to the cultivation of new levels of consciousness about the material, social, and conceptual frameworks through which we define ourselves. In Anzaldúa's work, and here, consciousness is not confined or limited to the mind/rational, but is instead an awareness that can be experienced in varied modes. *Borderlands* and the other Chicana narratives under discussion in my project must also be situated within an evolving body of Chicana feminist work and queer Chicano/a literature from 1969 to the present that began in small community and academic publications and now garners international attention and includes national and international publications.[11] For that earlier generation of Chicana feminists, a confrontation with prevailing religious systems was necessary to the project of securing gender equality, and their efforts reverberate here and in other Latino/a feminist writing, art, theorizing, and activism.

Many have commented on the elision of lesbianism in *Borderlands*, the failure to recognize both the text's grounding in queerness and the work it does in situating Chicano/a queerness at the center of transformative thought and action, which, indeed, remains an oversight in many assessments of Anzaldúa's work. As a theoretical work, Anzaldúa's *Borderlands* might be read as visionary or utopian; what both perspectives recognize in her theory is the emphasis on future possibilities. The aspect of *Borderlands* that remains still in the shadows, and that this book engages, is its spirituality, which is not unconnected to its queerness or its forward-looking perspective.

The Serpent Movement of Spiritual Mestizaje

Spirituality informs every aspect of the work that *Borderlands* performs with respect to subjectivity, epistemology, and transformation, including its consideration of inherited and invented practices honoring the sacred, recollection of home-centered religious rituals and healing ceremonies, descriptions of out-of-body experiences, research on and contemplation of the significance of indigenous deities, and exploration of love, compassion, and justice in addressing social inequalities. In this light, it is plain that Anzaldúa does not employ the unique term *spiritual mestizaje* to designate a particular practice or belief, but instead names and theorizes a critical mobility through which one might gain a new mestiza consciousness. In *Borderlands*, she states:

> As a *mestiza* I have no country, my homeland cast me out; yet all countries are mine because I am every woman's sister or potential lover. (As a lesbian I have no race, my own people disclaim me; but I am all races because there is the queer of me in all races.) I am cultureless because, as a feminist, I challenge the collective cultural/religious male-derived beliefs of Indo-Hispanics and Anglos; yet I am cultured because I am participating in the creation of yet another culture, a new story to explain the world and our participation in it, a new value system with images and symbols that connect us to each other and to the planet. *Soy un amasamiento*, I am an act of kneading, of uniting and joining that not only has produced both a creature of darkness and a creature of light, but also a creature that questions the definitions of light and dark and gives them new meanings.

We are the people who leap in the dark, we are the people on the knees of the gods. In our very flesh, (r)evolution works out the clash of cultures. It makes us crazy constantly, but if the center holds, we've made some kind of evolutionary step forward. *Nuestra alma el trabajo,* the opus, the great alchemical work; spiritual *mestizaje,* a "morpho-genesis," an inevitable unfolding. We have become the quickening serpent movement.[12]

The terms employed to describe spiritual mestizaje—alchemy, morpho-genesis, unfolding, serpent—underscore its status as a critical process. Made possible by or a consequence of the particular terms of Anzaldúa's identi-fication as a mestiza in the previous paragraph, it is also a collective move-ment, the "I" of the first paragraph above yields to the "we" of the second paragraph. In contrast to the notion that Anzaldúa maps a particular journey applicable only to other individual journeys, this shift from indi-vidual to collective perspective indicates that this critical mobility ideally enjoins others in its processes and perhaps achieves greater force through this intensification. It also practically recognizes that the transformations it enacts or foresees might exceed the individual frame, creating necessary collectivities. Her discussion here challenges exclusionary paradigms of nation, ethnicity, race, gender, and sexuality with the very terms that ap-pear to authorize them, signaling a project of renewal that also requires resignification.

In *Borderlands* Anzaldúa's spiritual mestizaje begins with the recog-nition of her social location at the border and her contemplation of the identities and histories that have defined that site. She quotes William H. Wharton invoking the support of God against the supposedly savage and superstitious Mexicans in Texas to signal that an interrogation of compet-ing religious systems in the borderlands forms a key part of her study. Her investigation raises questions, challenges, and doubts and leads Anzaldúa, as she describes it, to leave family and culture to explore her individual ex-perience in light of previously suppressed knowledge, which includes the history of indigenous spirituality and the suppression of Indian women. In this process, her body is not only the site of experience but also the re-pository of knowledge, which can only be fully deciphered in tandem with research and contemplation. Writing becomes both an intensely physical, bodily process of decolonization and an examination of the imprint of ideologies and religions on the physical self. It is perhaps the intensity of this discovery, of the way that our physical presence in the world, our very bodies, are shaped by oppressive discursive paradigms that creates the rupture that leads Anzaldúa, and others following in her path, into the Coatlicue state. Coatlicue, the goddess of life and death, names the site of death and rebirth in spiritual mestizaje, a metamorphosis that opens the way to acts of interpretation, or what Chela Sandoval terms "meta-ideologizing."[13] And these acts of interpretation become the bridge to a new consciousness that is enacted through speaking and writing. Yvonne Yarbro-Bejarano links this to ancient indigenous beliefs and values when she notes, "Anzaldúa uses the nahual notion of writing as creating face, heart, and soul to elaborate the idea that it is only through the body that the soul can be transformed."[14] In *Borderlands*, spiritual mestizaje brings the interconnection of these aspects of self and being into play, and strongly suggests a cyclical quality to the making and remaking that it denotes.

Anzaldúa returns to the process that unfolds in *Borderlands* in her later work, offering the concept of *nepantla* to describe more generally the challenge posed in spiritual mestizaje and offering the concept of *conocimiento* as an "overarching theory of consciousness." In *This Bridge We Call Home* Anzaldúa states: "I use the word *nepantla* to theorize liminality and to talk about those who facilitate passages between worlds, whom I've named *nepantleras*. I associate *nepantla* with states of mind that question old ideas and beliefs, acquire new perspectives, change worldviews, and shift from one world to another." Nepantla here remains dynamic—"question," "acquire," "change," "shift." In the closing essay of the collection, she states: "*Nepantla* is the site of transformation, the place where different perspectives come into conflict and where you question the basic ideas, tenets, and identities inherited from your family, your education, and your different cultures." Anzaldúa appears to reserve the words *nepantla* and *nepantleras* to refer to active engagement in a stage of spiritual mestizaje in contrast to *spiritual mestizaje*, which names a process that she theorizes as both a historical and contemporary methodology of renewal.[15] Through discussion of her personal experience with family religious practices, reflections on her spiritual inheritance, historical research on Guadalupe, and exploration of her relationship to indigenous goddesses, she identifies spiritual mestizaje in history, and herself as an heir of prior spiritual mestizajes.[16] By examining her, and others', continued vulnerability to subjection and silencing, estrangement from self, and alienation from community and environment authorized by religious discourses circulating in tandem with notions of normative gender and sexuality and exclusionary paradigms of race and national citizenship, Anzaldúa initiates the negotiations that signal her contemporary spiritual mestizaje.

Regard for the sacred circulates throughout Anzaldúa's work. As an editor of *This Bridge Called My Back* she collects writings by women of color, many of them addressing spirituality and its intersections with other aspects of subjectivity, while in *This Bridge We Call Home* she includes many essays that address spirituality by "women and men of different 'races,' nationalities, classes, sexualities, genders, and ages."[17] In the latter work, Anzaldúa's contributions emphasize an ethical, compassionate commitment to justice and the work of building alliances as necessary to the development of new spiritual and political visions. Here, spiritual mestizaje expands into the seven stages of conocimiento that Anzaldúa describes in her essay "And Now Let Us Shift." Conocimiento echoes spiritual mestizaje and represents, perhaps in keeping with the ethos of *This Bridge We Call Home*, a rewriting of the process for a broader audience. In making the core of her theory of spiritual mestizaje available to all in the seven stages of conocimiento, she enacts the work of bridging, that is, of "attempt[ing] community" so that this work "is not just about one set of people crossing to the other side; it's also about those on the other side crossing to this side."[18] That Anzaldúa would willingly engage in this revision of her ideas speaks to her intellectual humility and depth of commitment to social justice.

As in spiritual mestizaje, entering into the seven stages of conocimiento sharpens critical consciousness, restores connections within the self severed by oppressive ideologies and leads to a more profound appreciation of both the ineffable and one's present relations. It too is a continual, cyclical, epistemic inquiry. The soul/spiritual remains central in conocimiento, including the passage through nepantla toward a different way of living. Her emphasis on the materiality of spiritual practice as well as the interrelation between body, spirit, and psyche draws from her study of indigenous knowledge and is the foundation of her theory for a way of being in the world as opposed to a way of getting through the world—in Marcus Embry's words, an epistemology rather than an eschatology. Embry states:

The combination of Freud with Olmecs, of psychoanalysis with a Native American cosmology, illustrates Anzaldúa's sense that religion is an epistemology rather than an eschatology, and that the pagan symbols of serpents and animal bodies and souls, *tonos*, are directly related to bodily emotion and desire—fear and elation flooding her body—the site of her construction, oppression, and resistance.[19]

The metaphor of the serpent therefore works to evoke the pre-Christian, the earth, the animal and human linked, regeneration, body, knowledge, and mobility.

Anzaldúa's subjection to and resistance of colonial religious paradigms happen in her body, psyche, and intellect, hence the importance of her childhood on the U.S.-Mexico border and the physicality of her transformation. She initiates a decolonial project in the very action of engaging all aspects of her being in unmaking her subjection. In an interview originally published in 1991, Anzaldúa states:

> We're corporeal. We occupy weight and space, three-dimensionally. We're not some kind of disembodied thought energy. We're embodied in the flesh so there must be a purpose to this stage we're living in, to this corporeal body which we lose when we die and which we don't have before we're born. The things that we really struggle with and need to work out we need to work out on the physical plane.[20]

In this statement, she underscores her view of spirituality as epistemology and the multiple sites such a view engages.

A Critical Mestizaje

The term *spiritual mestizaje* contrasts with other kinds of mestizaje and alters the standard or traditional use of the term, which has been largely, though not exclusively, used to designate racial mixture, and when used to describe other phenomena has often retained an unmarked racial framework. The Chicano movement thought of mestizaje as a racial or cultural phenomenon, using it both to designate the particular racial formation of Chicano/as and to acknowledge the previously denigrated indigenous cultural inheritance of Chicano/as. Yet this conception, while working to engage mestizaje as a critique of notions of racial and cultural purity against which an emerging Chicano movement positioned itself, tended to enshrine in mestizaje and the mestizo a static, nationalist, binary, and patriarchal subject. *Borderlands* effects a further, valuable transformation of the term by breaking it free of these limitations.

Repeatedly, *Borderlands* joins the discourses of race and culture when it discusses mestizaje, indicating how strongly she reads race as a social formation rather than biology. The "new mestiza consciousness" she proposes is not automatically produced by this racial formation but exists as a possibility if the mestiza subject consciously engages the process of spiritual mestizaje to create a new perspective from which to speak, act, and move. Nonetheless, reading *Borderlands* requires us to consider mestizaje and its varied meanings. Rafael Pérez-Torres notes that

> within Chicana/o critical discourse, mestizaje has been used to articulate multiple and relational identity positions. Critical mestizaje embodies the struggle for power, place, and personhood arising from histories of violence and resistance. As vying social discourses have produced Chicano/a identities and cultural formations, so too have they given rise to a series of different significances ascribed to the mestizo.[21]

Norma Alarcón's observation that mestizaje worked to "racially colligate a heterogeneous population that was not European" in the "Mexican nation-making process," while in the United States the term had merely signaled non-white until its reclamation by Chicano/as, adds to our awareness of the contrasting uses of this term on each side of the border.[22] In our lexicon mestizaje has shifted from a term that erases indigenous ancestry to one that claims it, from one that signals only racial mixture to one that celebrates cultural hybridity, from one that bespeaks narrow nationalism to one, as in Anzaldúa, that dismantles that striving. *Borderlands* joins in this reconsideration and reconfiguration of mestizaje and its designation of "spiritual mestizaje," in particular, opens up the possibility for analyzing mestizaje as a process in ways that make this term critically productive in the articulation and analysis not only of Chicano/a literature and culture but of hemispheric cultural exchange.

In *Borderlands* Anzaldúa asks: "Which collectivity does the daughter of a dark-skinned mother listen to?" Even as she reconceptualizes mestizaje from a static (Chicano warrior) to a transformative (living in the crossroads) state of consciousness in her groundbreaking work, Anzaldúa's query foregrounds the dangerous ideological terrain that must be crossed by those who refuse a singular subjectivity. She historicizes the concept by evoking key narratives in the formation of a Mexican national identity and its influence on the development of a Chicano identity in the latter half of the twentieth century. In considering the narrative of conquest, she creates a mother figure who, as "dark-skinned," might be Indian or black. Indeed, Anzaldúa thoughtfully and explicitly recognizes the African diaspora in the Americas as part of the cultural inheritance of Chicana/os. This figure is mother not to a male nation but, instead, to a mixed-blood daughter. The daughter's confusion over her allegiances suggests that Anzaldúa's mother will neither assume self-effacement nor accept erasure. By posing a different kind of question than that previously asked, Anzaldúa transforms the originary narratives she calls forth. In suggesting that we might read mestizaje as an ongoing process which places contradictory demands on the subject, *Borderlands/La Frontera* dismantles a conception of mestizaje that at best subsumes and at worst ignores the multiple diasporas and migrations of the Americas and their impact on both Mexican and Chicano/a subject formations.[23]

Although *Borderlands* invokes José Vasconcelos's notion of the cosmic race, of the mestizo as the ultimate and desired racial subject, a mixture of all races, Anzaldúa's theory of a mestiza consciousness does not suggest a positivistic fusion nor the "eventual hybrid homogeneity" brought about by "generalized miscegenation" that, for example, Richard Rodríguez proposes.[24] Instead, Anzaldúa revises a key narrative of the Chicano/a movement of the 1960s and 1970s—the story of mestizaje that informs a resistant Chicano/a racial and ethnic identity—into a living, ongoing process that requires a more comprehensive assessment of the elements that inform it. Since El Plan Espiritual de Aztlán, to be Chicano/a is to be aware of one's mixed racial and ethnic heritage—Spanish and Indian—and, especially, to turn back the marginalization of Indian and Mexican peoples. For the new mestiza, a mixed racial identity creates the possibility for multiple alliances rather than a singular and nationalist embrace of a common heritage.

Indeed, the term that Anzaldúa employs to designate the critical and conscious process of transformation in all aspects of being—spiritual mestizaje—requires us to further differentiate among types of mestizaje. In *Borderlands* spiritual mestizaje exists in contrast to racial mestizaje, or interracial mixing; material mestizaje, or the syncretic fusion of varied cultural elements;[25] and historical mestizaje, or the events, movements, and conditions in the Americas through which diverse peoples and cultures were forged, frequently forcefully, into new nationalities and subjectivities. The new mestiza consciousness does not designate the subject "naturally" produced by racial, material, or historical mestizajes but instead the framework capable of transforming the conditions of mestiza and borderlands existence. Accordingly *Borderlands* reserves the term *spiritual mestizaje* to designate the critical mobility that can create new mestiza consciousness. Anzaldúa's use of the term is distinctive in that, for her, it designates a process rather than a product, one that corresponds to the shifting that her autohisteoría recounts.[26]

In the paragraph leading up to the assertion of spiritual mestizaje, Anzaldúa defines herself as a mestiza, reasserting the pejorative, derogatory meaning of mestizo/a as a marginal, half-breed, uncultured body over the celebratory enshrinement of mestizo/a identity in a move that cracks the sexist, nationalist, and racist encodings of the term. She then declares her willingness to create a new culture. *Borderlands* thereby distances itself from both Chicano and Mexican nationalist projects that police sexuality and gender as Anzaldúa reopens the terms *mestizo/a* and *mestizaje* for interrogation based on their historical meanings. Since the mestizo/a subject has historically been the disenfranchised, marginal, and impure, Anzaldúa claims that space outside of the center and asserts it as the space from which new cultures and identities emerge, a process to which she emphatically subscribes, although in the contemporary situation with a different set of cultures:

> So, don't give me your tenets and your laws. Don't give me your lukewarm gods. What I want is an accounting with all three cultures—white, Mexican, Indian. I want the freedom to carve and chisel my own face, to staunch the bleeding with ashes, to fashion my own gods out of my entrails. And if going home is denied me then I will have to stand and claim my space, making a new culture—*una cultura mestiza*—with my own lumber, my own bricks and mortar and my own feminist architecture.[27]

The work of that creation, the work of transformation initiated by the recognition of herself, of oneself, as a reclaimed mestiza subject is the ongoing work of spiritual mestizaje, and it involves the critical reexamination of received religious instruction, the recognition of the multiple spiritual traditions that inform life on the borderlands, and the ability to imagine new ways of both apprehending and honoring the sacred in daily life. It recognizes spiritual pluralism in the palimpsest of the borderlands and undertakes an investigation of it. Anzaldúa's hope for an "evolutionary step forward" may appear to signal a teleological conception, but I read this instead within her emphasis on movement rather than hierarchy as ongoing vigilance attentive to the religious pluralism of the borderlands, the imposition of orthodoxies, the genocidal elimination of indigenous spiritualities, and historical erasure.

Spiritual Mestizaje and Religious Studies

Anzaldúa's conception of spiritual mestizaje has influenced, inspired, and entered into dialogue with others seeking to understand Chicana/o, Latina/o, and Latin American spiritualities. Her work has also prompted many to embark on their own journeys of spiritual mestizaje and to give voice to their own situations of nepantla. David Carrasco notes that Anzaldúa "perceives our shared but complex reality as a borderlands that is at once geographical, political, ethnic, gendered but also profoundly mythic," while Luis D. León characterizes the *Borderlands* paradigm of border crossing as a key element of a religious poetics that opens the door to "new religious innovations."[28]

There are particular historic reasons that Anzaldúa's spiritual mestizaje resonates so widely, dating back to the complexity of the negotiations between the religious systems initiated with conquest and the interrelationship that emerged, during conquest, between religious doctrine and the determination of those fit for citizenship, or even humanity. The incorporation of vibrant racial, cultural, and religious minorities into newly forming nations and the legacy of religious institutional organization along national, racial, and gender lines have exerted influence on the shape of religiosity and spirituality in the Americas that continues to reverberate today. This hemispheric context for Anzaldúa's spiritual mestizaje is shared by those who study religion in the Americas, and it figures, in some way, in any examination of new religious and spiritual phenomena, beliefs, and practices in the Americas. This history makes Anzaldúa's work on spirituality important for religious studies and theology, particularly Chicano/a and Latino/a, feminist, and women-of-color religious and spiritual studies. A closer examination of her influence on and difference from existing studies of Chicano/a and Latino/a religion and theology is therefore in order.

In theorizing spiritual mestizaje as a process directed toward the creation of new ways of being in the world, *Borderlands* speaks to issues that have been significant in Chicana/o and Latina/o religious studies, including religion and social justice, popular religiosity, material mestizajes in religious ritual, and the relationship of individuals to religious institutions. Several contributions in the field of Latino/a theology openly claim the influence of *Borderlands* in developing new paradigms for the fuller inclusion of Latino/as into existing religious communities. Christian theologians inspired by or in dialogue with Anzaldúa's work have advocated greater Chicano/a and Latino/a representation in religious leadership, institutions, and communities; offered Chicano/a and Latino/a readings of spiritual phenomena in the Americas; and explored other avenues for Christian denominations to become more responsive to Chicano/a and Latino/a needs. Several Christian scholars have written about religious cultural mestizaje among Chicano/as and Latino/as, particularly in popular religiosity, and theorized forms of Chicano/a and Latino/a religious consciousness. The continuance of indigenous beliefs and practices under Christianity—which from one side appears as syncretism and from the other side as enculturation[29]—and how these inform a particularly Chicano/a or Latino/a religiosity have been important areas of inquiry in this field. For others, Chicano/a and Latino/a religious inheritance and identity are intricately tied to the histories and processes evoked in Anzaldúa.[30] Many working in Chicana and Latina religious studies, and Latina feminist theologians in particular, explicitly cite Anzaldúan reconceptions of indigenous and Christian aspects of Guadalupe and of Chicana spirituality more generally, as well as elements of her theorization of spiritual mestizaje. Chicana and Latina feminist theologians also align themselves with Anzaldúa's respect for and love of women.[31]

We might read the work of some Chicano/a and Latino/a religious studies scholars and theologians as enacting the spiritual mestizaje that Anzaldúa theorizes in *Borderlands* from within the space of their own denominations or religious traditions, critiquing aspects of the tradition in which they find themselves and working to embody and write about an alternative for Chicano/as and Latino/as from within those religious institutional settings. In contrast, Anzaldúa's spiritual mestizaje is a process through which she seeks new spiritual formations. She does not claim a dominant religious tradition as her own, but instead grounds her theory in the long history of alternative and home-centered spiritualities that characterizes life in the borderlands—a history she evokes by recalling her childhood and the words of her older female relatives. Her spiritual mestizaje involves a reexamination and critique of Catholicism, a tradition in which her connections to her own body as a woman and lesbian and her connections to the mythic and spirit world remain taboo.[32] Though she would undoubtedly be supportive of those engaged in dialogues with traditional religious denominations to eliminate the discrimination against and silencing of gays and lesbians and to incorporate women, particularly Chicanas, more fully in religious organizations, her own path was another.[33] In contrast to the work of most Latino/a theologians or Latino/a feminist theologians, Anzaldúa does not seek to reform the dominant religious traditions. Instead she works to forge new ways of being in the world. Understanding the difference between particular Latino/a theologies and Anzaldúa's theory is vitally important to my reading of Chicana narratives, as it is to reading Chicano/a literature more generally, and for that reason it is useful to recall the specifics of the different proposal that Anzaldúa voices and theorizes in her spiritual mestizaje.

Contemporary Feminist Spiritualities

Another perspective on the relationship between mestizaje and spirituality emerges from among Chicana feminists who retain some identification with the Catholic Church, or who recognize that other Chicanas do, and yet increasingly lean toward the creation of new spiritual communities of healing that may take inspiration and knowledge from indigenous worldviews.[34] As Ana Castillo in *Massacre of the Dreamers* states:

> We have unearthed the ways of our Mexic Amerindian ancestors preserved by our mestizo elders, most often, women, in the form of curanderismo.
>
> However, women must be cautious about our sources for spiritual

regeneration. Even as we select from our Mexica (Nahua) and Christian traditions, it is only we today, who ultimately can define what is needed to give us courage.[35]

The critical inquiry that is spiritual mestizaje remains relevant for women who draw from multiple spiritual traditions, as Castillo notes, blending them into particular forms of mestizo/a spirituality. The historic presence of curanderismo in the borderlands, the knowledge of the Americas it represents, and the way that many aspects of this kind of spiritual healing dovetail with growing ecologically driven interests in homeopathy and organic and natural food supplies makes it especially significant in contemporary Chicana spirituality.[36] Eastern spiritual traditions, Islam, and Judaism—including the mysticism of Kabbalah—are also significant for Chicana/o communities. Randy Conner, a long-time collaborator of Gloria Anzaldúa, has addressed the multiple spiritual traditions that Anzaldúa studied, revealing how her spiritual journey surpassed the borders of Christian and Nahua spiritualities to explore Eastern contemplative practices, Kabbalah, and Santería, and how she eventually moved toward an earth-centered spirituality.[37] Among the plural spiritual traditions of the borderlands, curanderismo and Kabbalah register alternative, non-dominant spiritual knowledge and leadership in Chicana narratives.

Anzaldúa's conception of spiritual mestizaje, and her critical examination of religion and spirituality as these intersect with the material effects of normative categories of race, gender, sexuality, and nation, have resonated profoundly among those who also identify as women-of-color scholars and activists, many of whom are involved in feminist spiritual communities. Her work, like that of Toni Cade Bambara, Louise Erdrich, Toni Morrison, and Maxine Hong Kingston, to name a few, is deeply preoccupied with women's spirituality, particularly in non-Western spiritual traditions. Indeed, situating Anzaldúa among spiritual, feminist, women-of-color activists, scholars, and writers, many of them queer, including Audre Lorde, Cherríe Moraga, bell hooks, the many contributors to both *Bridge* collections, and the writers and filmmakers examined in this book, recognizes this as a school of thought in its own right, in contrast to the elision of this spirituality in the broader frameworks of feminists, liberals, progressives, and racial and ethnic civil rights organizations and academics. For those women who have shared in the vision and practice of a liberatory and holistic spirituality in tandem with social justice work, usually drawing from alternative spiritualities rather than mainstream religions, Anzaldúa's work has been either an example of déjà vu or pivotal in opening another spiritual path.

AnaLouise Keating, a leading and long-time scholar of Anzaldúa's work, initiates a discussion of feminist spiritual perspectives based on Anzaldúa's work in *Entre Mundos/Among Worlds: New Perspectives on Gloria E. Anzaldúa*. Keating describes Anzaldúa's faith in this way: "Deeply spiritual and intensely political, she believed in human beings' basic decency and potential wisdom. . . . Despite the racism, sexism, homophobia, and other forms of rejection she experienced throughout her life, she maintained her faith in people's ability to change."[38] Keating notes that, throughout her work, Anzaldúa grounds herself in an "experientially-based epistemology and ethics" while emphasizing the importance of spirituality in eliminating social injustice.[39] Recognizing the fluidity of the new mestiza consciousness as well as the "transcultural and transgendered" aspects of Anzaldúa's mestizaje, Keating embraces Anzaldúa's visionary method and views, especially her articulation of how differently "culturally inscribed bodies" may yield distinct knowledges, and constructively compares Anzaldúa's work to that of third world women's testimonials.[40] In locating Anzaldúa among other self-identified women of color whose literary, cultural, and activist work encompasses the spiritual, and whose spirituality, directed toward just ways of being in the world, incorporates multiple influences, Keating recognizes how her work with and about Anzaldúa has allowed her to fully embrace her own previously denied spirituality.

Echoing Keating's feminist and spiritual appreciation for Anzaldúa's work, M. Jacqui Alexander writes: "You taught us that our politics would not be effective without a spiritualized consciousness. *Conocimiento*."[41] For Alexander, gaining this awareness is itself a political act, and she declares, "We are not born women of color. We *become* women of color." The requirements of this conscious joining include the desire and willingness to, as she says, "become fluent in each other's histories," in contrast to a containment within our particular histories that may feed divisiveness.[42] Alexander's spiritual mestizaje confronts the colonial histories of dominant religions as well as the postmodern secularism that dismisses non-Christian spiritual systems as "bad tradition."[43] Like Keating, Alexander consciously and intentionally follows the path opened by Anzaldúa, allowing herself to recognize Mojuba and Voudou, the African-based spiritualities that had been always present in her life, and even more importantly, allowing her spirituality to exist within her academic work, "becom[ing] open to the movement of Spirit in order to wrestle with the movement of history," as she describes it.[44]

Border Memories

Anzaldúa's theorization of her journey and its stages is grounded in her personal and family experience. The stories she recounts—of working in the fields, of farming, of childhood spiritual experiences, of a neighbor who did not conform to gender expectations, of being schooled out of her language, and more—represent broader collective experiences and, therefore, take on the force of a testimonio. Anzaldúa names these types of narratives "autohisteorías—the concept that Chicanas and women of color write not only about abstract ideas but also bring in their personal history as well as the history of their community."[45] In *Borderlands* she remembers the narratives, practices, and beliefs by which she and others in her border community constituted themselves, critically engaging the aesthetic and material consequences of that formation and its embedded values. Through recollections, critiques, and choices that are often viscerally felt or experienced in her body, she creates a more just mythos and proposes reconfigured communities. Remembering allows her to apprehend multiple collectivities where previously she saw only one monolithic culture and people on the U.S.-Mexico border. Yet she is also recounting a personal and communal history of struggle. In its combination of two forms, the testimonio and the theoretical text, autohisteoría emerges as a new genre that shares some continuity with the testimonio form in the Americas. The individual and collective story through which a new consciousness can be theorized is brought to light through memory. The new mestiza consciousness is not an essentialist, inherited one, but a critical one that, as Yvonne Yarbro-Bejarano notes, is consciously produced.[46]

The first page of *Borderlands/La Frontera*, representative of the first chapter, situates the work concretely in an actual physical location: the U.S.-Mexico border. Yet it also suggests the multiple origins, languages, histories, and voices that inform Anzaldúa's understanding of that border. As the Chicana feminist and literary critic Norma Alarcón notes:

> These borderlands are spaces where, as a result of expansionary wars, colonization, juridico-immigratory policing, and coyote exploitation of émigrés and group-vigilantes, formations of violence are continuously in the making. These have been taking place as misogynist and racialist confrontations at least since the Spanish began to settle Mexico's (New Spain) "northern" frontier of what is now the incompletely Anglo-americanized Southwest. Subsequently, and especially after the end of the Mexican-American War in 1848, these formations of violence have been often dichotomized into Mexican/American, which actually have the effect of muting the presence of indigenous peoples yet setting the context for the formation of "races."[47]

Borderlands acknowledges this frontera history and reality as it seeks to un-make the dichotomy that marginalizes Indian, Chicano/a, and Mexicano/a people.

The title of her chapter, "The Homeland, Aztlán/El otro México," with its combination of English, Nahuatl, and Spanish, invokes the polyvalence of being Chicano/a, but the bold lines between the languages on the page remind us of the geographic, historic, linguistic, and national divides that have created the border as a site of the "violent clash" mentioned in her opening poem. The opening of *Borderlands* combines excerpts from a song by Los Tigres del Norte, two scholarly studies on indigenous peoples of the Americas, and Anzaldúa's poem about standing at the U.S.-Mexico border, suggesting that while history informs her exploration, equally important are the popular sentiments expressed in song and her own voice—each a different form of memory or, in this case, counter-memory.[48] The lyrics of Los Tigres del Norte, referencing their displacement from Mexico, simultaneously invoke a past when the Southwest *was* Mexico and suggest another space, one where Anzaldúa resides and which she also seeks to recreate: "The other Mexico that over here we have constructed / the space that has been national territory."[49]

Remembering historicizes the ground where the discourses of race, ethnicity, religion, and gender are intertwined in the inter-American formation of Chicana subjects. In her text and in other Chicana narratives, time and again memory rather than history (an official record from which women are often absent) nurtures a spiritual mestizaje attentive to the constraints of nation, race, and norms of gender and sexuality.[50] This becomes apparent as Anzaldúa moves from citations of the history of Spanish and Anglo American conquest and colonization to individual and family memories of life on the border, experiences not captured or recorded in history:

> In the fields, *la migra*. My aunt saying, "*No corran*, don't run. They'll think you're *del otro lao*." In the confusion, Pedro ran, terrified of being caught. He couldn't speak English, couldn't tell them he was fifth generation American. *Sin papeles*—he did not carry his birth certificate to work in the fields. *La migra* took him away while we watched. *Se lo llevaron.* He tried to smile when he looked back at us, to raise his fist. But I saw the shame pushing his head down, I saw the terrible weight of shame hunch his shoulders. They deported him to Guadalajara by plane. The furthest he'd ever been to Mexico was Reynosa, a small border town opposite Hidalgo, Texas, not far from McAllen. Pedro walked all the way to the Valley. *Se lo llevaron sin un centavo al pobre. Se vino andando desde Guadalajara.*[51]

Anzaldúa's memory of the voices and facial expressions in this scene and the information garnered later join with her mother's and grandmother's voices at other points in the first chapter to offer testimony of a border experience where terror, displacement, and shame are imposed. From personal and intimate to grand continental narrative of the peopling of the Americas, *Borderlands* weaves these stories together in a way that places migration and mobility at the core of hemispheric existence, creating a counter-memory that contests the supposed "illegality" of some humans. According to George Lipsitz:

> Unlike historical narratives that begin with the totality of human existence and then locate specific actions and events within that totality, counter-memory starts with the particular and the specific and then builds outward toward a total story. Counter-memory looks to the past for the hidden histories excluded from dominant narratives. But unlike myths that seek to detach events and actions from the fabric of any larger history, counter-memory forces revision of existing histories by

supplying new perspectives about the past. Counter-memory embodies aspects of myth and aspects of history, but it retains an enduring suspicion of both categories.[52]

The multiplicity of stories in the first few pages of *Borderlands* suggests both revision and suspicion in that a new story of the border emerges, but one that no single voice can adequately or entirely convey. Attentive to the myths, rituals, and stories of the border and the Americas, Anzaldúa evaluates each. In offering her memories and those of family and friends as testimony to the history and experience of the U.S.-Mexico border, Anzaldúa makes the border's inhabitants not merely informants but knowledgeable subjects—a critical shift in status.[53] Moreover, as knowledgeable subjects, they are engaged in making community out of their cultural inheritances.

The opening pages of *Borderlands* suggest, in keeping with testimonio and autohistoría, that Anzaldúa's memories are also group memories. Yet these are not memories that are merely "accessed" as if they exist in a data bank. They must be excavated and worked in writing; they must become embodied.[54] In this way they become the substance out of which new communities and spiritualities emerge. The preservation and repetition of personal memories owe much to the fact that they are collectively significant.[55] Maurice Halbwachs explains, "Each impression and each fact, even if it apparently concerns a particular person exclusively, leaves a lasting memory only to the extent that one has thought it over—to the extent that it is connected with the thoughts that come to us from the social milieu."[56] The circulation of individual stories within a collectivity, therefore, adds to the coherence of the group, akin to the contribution of "episodic memories" to the construction of "semantic memory" or social knowledge.[57] The contemporary practice of oral history recognizes this relation between individual and social memory without overlooking the content, motives, factuality, and form of memory stories.[58] Anzaldúa's treatment of memory is in consonance with contemporary oral histories—revealing the interrelation between the individual and the collective in the telling.

In accounting for the way in which she is racialized on the northern side of the border she calls into question who is native and who is alien, asks whether migratory movements can be illegal, and invokes the multiple collective border memories. She wants us to see the way that the border functions, and has functioned, as home to many who are excluded from national projects. In doing so, she explores how the nation on each side of the border perpetuates itself through the disciplinary regulation of collective memory. Halbwachs describes this as the social need "to erase from its memory all that might separate individuals, or that might distance groups from each other. It is also why society, in each period, rearranges its recollections in such a way as to adjust them to the variable conditions of its equilibrium."[59] Anzaldúa's invocation of alternative collective memories plays a critical role on the road to reconfigured communities that might include her and the collectivities to which she belongs.

In an interview originally published in 1995, Anzaldúa elaborates on the significance of collective memory to her own identity:

> For me, identity is a relational process. It doesn't depend only on me, it also depends on the people around me. Sometimes I call this "el árbol de la vida." Here's el árbol de la vida [while drawing] y tiene raíces y cada persona is her own árbol. Y estas raíces son la raza—the class you come from, the collective unconscious of your culture and aquí tienes a little body of water I call "el cenote." El cenote represents memories and experiences—the collective memory of the race, of the culture— and your personal history. . . . The tree of your life is embedded in the world, y este mundo es el mundo de diferentes gentes. . . . Identity is not just what happens to me in my present lifetime but also involves my family history, my racial history, my collective history.[60]

Throughout Anzaldúa's oeuvre, including the development of spiritual mestizaje as theory and method, nepantla as the liminal space of crossing, and conocimiento as an "overarching theory of consciousness,"[61] memory work figures prominently for precisely the reasons that she articulates. This relational aspect of memory is one that M. Jacqui Alexander also adopts, placing it in the service, as Anzaldúa does, of making social change. Alexander says:

> What brings us back to remembrance is both individual and collective; both intentional and an act of surrender; both remembering desire and remembering *how* it works. Daring to recognize each other again and again in a context that seems bent on making strangers of us all. Can

we *intentionally* remember, all the time, as a way of never forgetting, all of us, building an archeology of living memory, which has less to do with living in the past, invoking a past, or excising it, and more to do with our relationship to Time and its purpose?[62]

In *This Bridge Called My Back*, women of color give voice to long-suppressed concerns, and in *This Bridge We Call Home*, women and men from diverse backgrounds and social locations consider the work of coalition and alliance building that lies ahead.[63] In the latter work, Anzaldúa's spiritual vision opens itself to these possibilities and guides an ever-wider circle of *caminantes*. Memory work here will, of necessity, go beyond the experience and history of the U.S.-Mexico border, but it continues to inform the cultivation of awareness in Anzaldúa's theory of conocimiento, a process that, like spiritual mestizaje, embraces the materiality of the body, the presence of the intellect and psyche, and the grace of the spirit.

Indigenous Goddesses

In her remembrance of pre-Columbian Indian societies, of colonization and conquest, and her tracing of a Chicana, Indian, woman's, queer spiritual history—one interrupted by repression and often silenced—Anzaldúa addresses the way that politics and gender interact with religious and mythological narratives and symbols. She recognizes that, for her and for other mestizas, Indian ancestry runs through Guadalupe and, in part, through Catholicism. However, her view of Guadalupe differs from a strictly Christian one in that she sees Tonantzin, Coatlicue, Coatlalopeuh, and Cihuacoatl—the indigenous female deities of what is now Mexico—in Guadalupe. Critical of both Aztec and colonial Catholic splitting of the "good" (virgin, mother) female deity from the "bad" (powerful, life-giving, destructive) female deity,[64] Anzaldúa recognizes Guadalupe as a representative of the spiritual mestizaje that she inherits as a Chicana and a Mexicana, a figure that represents survival and resistance against subjugation:

> *Mi mamagrande Ramona toda su vida mantuvo un altar pequeño en la esquina del comedor. Siempre tenía las velas prendidas. Allí hacía promesas a la Virgen de Guadalupe.* My family, like most Chicanos, did not practice Roman Catholicism but a folk Catholicism with many pagan

elements. *La Virgen de Guadalupe*'s Indian name is Coatlalopeuh. She is the central deity connecting us to our Indian ancestry.[65]

As Yvonne Yarbro-Bejarano notes, Anzaldúa's excavation of indigenous female deities, rather than signaling a desire for a romantic, Indian past as was often promoted through the cultural nationalism of the Chicano movement, deconstructs such desires by revealing the gendered tensions, displacements, and violence of that past.[66] In the quoted passage she highlights the nondoctrinal religious practices of family and community, beliefs and rituals that suggest both a hybrid spirituality and a historical process of spiritual mestizaje through which folk Catholicism takes life. Central to this pantheon is the female deity. Anzaldúa's work expands the male-centered, early Chicano movement's interest in indigenous cultures, specifically Mexican indigenous cultures, while it also continues the Chicano movement's abiding interest in Mexican culture and history as formative of Chicano/a subjectivity. The latter has been understood as the biculturalism and bilingualism of the movement, but we might also read it as the transnational impulse present in the Chicano movement, by necessity, from its inception.

The rediscovery of Mexico's indigenous past was new not only to Chicano/as in the 1960s and 1970s but, in some ways, to Mexico and the world beyond, since it was a period both of significant archaeological finds in Mexico and of the emergence of research and analysis about Mexico's indigenous civilizations that sought further understanding of gender and sexuality in the organization and spirituality of native peoples.[67] Anzaldúa acknowledges the paradigm shifts these archaeological finds engendered when she recounts her first view of the newly discovered figure of the mutilated Coyolxauhqui in Mexico City in 1972.[68] An understanding of female deities and figures, let alone gender and sexuality, in Mexico's indigenous history was never a given, but instead a task to be undertaken, and Anzaldúa, too, participates. The rewriting in *Borderlands* of a Chicano/a indigenous past to include sacred female figures contests the limitations of a Chicano nationalist identity and attempts to heal, to (re)member the Chicana body, to give back to the "maligned and abused" Chicana, Indian, woman, queer body her sexuality, spirit, and mind, a project also of the Chicana narratives under discussion here. Norma Alarcón engages the

(handwritten marginalia at top: "mo' street K. Not me Protestant way when we hide in our house and read the bible to each other")

work of Paula Gunn Allen and Gloria Anzaldúa in describing the work of reappropriating "the" native woman:

> The native woman has many names also—Coatlicue, Cihuacoátl, Ixtacihúatl, and so on. In fact, one has only to consult the dictionary of *Mitología Nahuátl*, for example, to discover many more that have not been invoked. For many writers, the point is not so much to recover a lost "utopia" or the "true" essence of our being, although, of course, there are those among us who long for the "lost origins," as well as those who feel a profound spiritual kinship with the "lost"—a spirituality whose resistant political implications must not be underestimated, but refocused for feminist change. The most relevant point in the present is to understand how a pivotal indigenous portion of the mestiza past may represent a collective female experience as well as "the mark of the Beast" within us—the maligned and abused indigenous woman. By invoking the "dark Beast" within and without, which has forced us to deny, the cultural and psychic dismemberment that is linked to imperialist racist and sexist practices is brought into focus.[69]

In *Borderlands*, reconnecting Guadalupe to the indigenous goddesses reclaims her from those that uphold her as a figure of docility and subordination. In contrast to beliefs that "encourage fear and distrust of life and of the body," Anzaldúa remembers the Virgen de Coatlalopeuh in Guadalupe, the forgotten "symbol of the dark sexual drive, the chthonic (underworld), the feminine, the serpentine movement of sexuality, of creativity, the basis of all energy and life."[70] Anzaldúa's new image of the divine, or her new mythos, is one capacious enough to include the impure, mestizo/a, queer women and men for whom there is no room in dominant religious traditions.

Writing La Lupe

Anzaldúa's reclamation of Guadalupe/Coatlalopeuh resonates in the works of many Chicano/a writers each of whom offers a unique perspective on the past and present significance of Guadalupe in Chicano/a spirituality and culture. While some texts embrace Guadalupe the mother, few if any endow her motherhood with qualities of submission and self-sacrifice. In other texts, Guadalupe represents a connection to an indigenous heritage or to a female ancestry, a shared belief and experience, or simply the power-ful presence of the divine in daily life. In Chicano/a literature, therefore, the meaning of Guadalupe is not a preconceived given but instead is imag-ined through the very act of writing La Lupe, creating a Guadalupe whose divine presence is rich with meaning, who continually gives birth to new formations, and who is an intimate friend and confidante. Literature that creates a new Guadalupan imagery in this way parallels the popular reli-gious practices and devotions to Guadalupe that have existed for centuries and continue throughout the hemisphere in home altars, crafts, art, pil-grimages, and songs.[71]

In the short story "Mericans," published in a collection titled *Woman Hollering Creek and Other Stories* (1991), Sandra Cisneros's child narrator, Michele/Micaela, accompanies her Mexican grandmother and two broth-ers to Tepeyac, the sacred site of Guadalupe's appearance. There, she expe-riences her grandmother's pious devotion, "armies of penitents" in proces-sion, her brothers' play, and wandering tourists, discovering her connection to each but also her difference from each: she will not be a quiet, self-sacrificing, pious woman, nor an underling to her brothers, nor an Ameri-can who assumes that all other Americans are white. Instead, Michele/Micaela arrives at a sense of herself as a "Merican," which is at once both an identity and a historical condition that situates her in the borderlands.[72]

The terrifying newness of the concept of Merican, spoken into being at Tepeyac, is grounded in the historical and theological significance of Guadalupe as the embodiment of divergent social, cultural, and religious systems. Anzaldúa notes that Guadalupe appeared "on the spot where the Aztec goddess, *Tonansti* ('Our Lady Mother'), had been worshiped by the Nahuas and where a temple to her had stood."[73] Tepeyac, of course, has great significance for both Catholic theology and Mexico as the site of the miracle of Guadalupe's appearance in the Americas. Many Catholic Latina/o theologians have described the site and Guadalupe as embodying the cultural memory of Nahua and Spanish cultures or as inaugurating a new religious culture,[74] while historians of religion such as Jacques Lafaye and D. A. Brading have traced the significance of various Guadalupe nar-ratives in the formation of criollo and mestizo subjectivities, the Church in New Spain and colonial and independent political economies.[75]

Tepeyac, therefore, exists as a social space with historical, theological, and symbolic significance for the emergence of Americas out of conquest and encounter. This creation has been viewed as one that embodies mixture, fusion, syncretism, or hybridity, each term suggesting a different understanding of and relationship to the history, theology, and cosmology linked to the site. Mary Pat Brady, discussing how Cisneros's story "Mericans" conveys Michele/Micaela's "hybridized sense of place," notes that this knowledge of place and history gives strength to Chicana recreations of Guadalupe.[76]

It is, indeed, through Michele/Micaela's focus on Tepeyac and the palimpsest of the site that the story can speak or assert Merican, a term that offers up, in Anzaldúan terms, Michele/Micaela en route to a new mestiza consciousness. In this story Michele/Micaela moves among the microspaces of the church, where her grandmother prays for everyone in the family and scolds Micaela; the outside plaza, where her brothers tell her, "*Girl*. We can't play with a *girl*. *Girl*," yet incorporate her in their play as a subordinate; and the side of the church, where Anglo tourists happen upon the children and mistake them for Mexicans.

The designation Merican, spoken by Junior in identifying himself and his brother and sister to the tourists, becomes a new subject position—not Mexican and not American but somewhere in between. The terrifying and liberating statement with which Michele/Micaela ends the story, "We're Mericans, we're Mericans, and inside the awful grandmother prays," aptly conveys her contradictory senses of distance from and belonging to each of the three different social formations, making Tepeyac, yet again, a site of cross-cultural encounters and the emergence of new cultures.[77] The story's new mestiza consciousness lies precisely in its critical ability to articulate the divisions that could fragment Michele/Micaela, and the acquisition of that knowledge is both terrifying and liberating for the young girl.

Cherríe Moraga's *Loving in the War Years* (1983) addresses the literal and metaphoric barrier between herself and Guadalupe in this way:

> The first time I went to the Mexican basilica where el retrato de La Virgen de Guadalupe hovers over a gilded altar, I was shocked to see that below it ran a moving escalator. It was not one that brought people up to the image that we might kiss her feet; but rather it moved people along from side to side and through as quickly as possible. A moving sidewalk built to keep the traffic going.

What struck me the most, however, was that in spite of the irreverence imposed by such technology, the most devout of the Mexican women—las pobres, few much older than me—clung to the ends of the handrailing of the moving floor, crossing themselves, gesturing besos al retrato, their hips banging up against the railing over and over again as it tried to force them off and away. They stayed. In spite of the machine. They had come to spend their time with La Virgen.

I left the church in tears, knowing how for so many years I had closed my heart to the passionate pull of such faith that promised no end to the pain. I grew white. Fought to free myself from my culture's claim on me. It seemed I had to step outside my familia to see what we as a people were doing suffering.[78]

For Moraga (and for Micaela, the fictional character), Guadalupe exerts a pull. She tugs at the soul and the body, but she joins women together in a community of suffering—a model of female submission, self-sacrificing motherhood, and pleading devotion that Moraga flees. Moraga's tears mark a return to Guadalupe, like the women battling the barriers around the image, yet with a difference, for her suffering is not that of submission to poverty, others, and male dominance, but instead suffering over the limitations imposed on women. Moraga's journey toward a different appreciation of Guadalupe takes her away from the immediate familial and cultural understandings of Guadalupe, allowing for the further development of a critical awareness she describes as a separate physical space—a "step outside"—that echoes Micaela's action of leaving the church.

In another Cisneros story, a character is able to establish an intimate correspondence with Guadalupe only because her vision and understanding of Guadalupe has expanded, similar to Moraga's. "Little Miracles, Kept Promises" unfolds in the form of a series of prayers offered up to varied saints and holy figures and shows us Chayo writing a note of thanks to Guadalupe, beginning with the familiar and affectionate address "Virgencita." In offering her prayer and thanks, Chayo says:

Virgencita de Guadalupe. For a long time I wouldn't let you in my house. I couldn't see you without seeing my ma each time my father came home drunk and yelling, blaming everything that ever went wrong in his life on her.

> I couldn't look at your folded hands without seeing my *abuela*
> mumbling, "My son, my son, my son . . ." Couldn't look at you without
> blaming you for all the pain my mother and her mother and all our
> mothers' mothers have put up with in the name of God.[79]

For Chayo, as for Moraga, reconciliation with Guadalupe grows from her understanding of the palimpsest of Tepeyac, a knowledge that enables her to reclaim Guadalupe from the gendered readings of her as the model of female self-abnegation cloaked as mercy. The intimacy of Chayo's address to Guadalupe suggests a renewal, with difference, of her relationship to Guadalupe and the divine.

Pat Mora plays on the pseudo-intimacy and spectacle associated with daytime talk-show television, largely aimed at a female audience, in her poem "Consejos de Nuestra Señora de Guadalupe: Counsel from the Brown Virgin," which is included in the collection *Agua Santa/Holy Water* (1995) in a special subsection titled "Cuarteto Mexicano: Talk Show Interviews with Coatlicue the Aztec Goddess, Malinche the Maligned, the Virgin of Guadalupe and La Llorona: The Wailer." Playful and visionary, the poems in "Cuarteto Mexicano" are literally at the center of the collection, suggesting the poet's sense of the centrality of origin stories, yet they also, in postmodern feminist fashion, recreate the revered, holy, and iconic figures of Mexican women and of the Mexican nation as contemporary talk-show participants.

In "Consejos de Nuestra Señora," Guadalupe addresses her audience as "hijas," a form of familiar and affectionate address as well as an indicator of familial relationship. In the opening stanza of the poem, Guadalupe speaks: "You seem surprised that I've appeared. / You gape like Juan Diego as I hovered in a cloud / that December morning above dry Tepeyac. Mortals lack faith / and imagination, fear flying. Hijas, be unpredictable."[80] Her words reveal the gap between the common tendency to see her as fixed and immobile, a perception perhaps fueled by her authoritative installation at Tepeyac as well as the prevalence of statuary depicting her, and the accepted narrative of her apparitions. By pointing to that gap, the poem seems also to challenge, even if playfully, skepticism of modern-day apparitions. With wit and wisdom, Guadalupe recasts her seemingly passive and subordinate presence into patience for the right conditions for social, and perhaps heavenly, change, telling her audience: "I raise neither my voice nor eyes— / yet. Bodies, even celestial, are creatures of habit." The "yet" and the reference to heavenly habits suggest an awareness of her status as a woman whose truths must be tactfully spoken, but when spoken they will upset the heavens. The speaker here evokes the varied registers through which Chicanas move and speak.[81]

In the next stanza, the Brown Virgin quietly subverts the dominant readings of her dress and image by asserting that "consistent trappings can release us for internal work."[82] In Mora's "Cuarteto Mexicano," Guadalupe becomes a powerful woman negotiating her status, condition, and gendering. The poem ends on a lighthearted note that reverses the association of Guadalupe with passivity by making her the agent of transformation through grace when she counsels, "Hijas, silence can be pregnant. My voice rose like a beam / of sunlight, entered Juan. Remember, conceptions, / immaculate and otherwise, happen. He knelt, full of me."[83]

Ana Castillo's essay "Extraordinarily Woman" also embraces a vision of a powerful Guadalupe, one whose giving of love and life exists side by side with the power of death embodied in the figure of María Guadaña.[84] The essayist's suggestion that "perhaps they are two faces of the same coin, a two-headed goddess like Coatlicue,"[85] contributes to the reclamation of Guadalupe's origins in indigenous belief systems as a figure of power rather than meekness. Castillo elsewhere suggests that the Virgen de Guadalupe, as the successor to Tonantzin and Coatlicue, can be freed from a subordinate role to assume a primary position as a model of female strength.[86]

Her connection to conquered native nations also makes Guadalupe an important ally of both indigenous and working-class people. Luis Alfaro's performance piece "The Doll" narrates the story of a working-class Los Angeles Latino family held together by their faith in La Lupe.[87] For the performer Alfaro, a small Virgen de Guadalupe doll, purchased during one of the family's many overnight trips to Tijuana, paradoxically represents the transience and challenges of the everyday for the family as well as their enduring faith. The Guadalupe doll, when plugged in, would "turn and bless all sides of the room."[88] The doll moves from Tijuana to their Los Angeles home to their tia's second-story flat during her battle with cancer, gets burned in a house fire, is rescued from the debris, and is finally claimed by Alfaro's brother as a target for BB gun practice. When the speaker later meets and falls in love with an Anglo man who also owns a rotating Our Lady doll, their union is blessed by the grandmother, who sends them a crate of grapes and whose refrain, repeated at the conclusion of each episode in the narrative, later consoles him over the loss of that love: "M'ijo, *Blood is thicker than water, family is greater than friends, and that old Virgin, Our Lady, she just watches over all of us.*" This refrain of the grandmother ironically punctuates each travail, each hardship, each challenge faced by the family and its various members, conveying a sense of the paradox the family embraces: Guadalupe is a sign of both change and enduring, loving presence for all.[89]

These varied representations of Guadalupe perform important work. A body of literature infused with the multilayered religious imagination of the Americas, Chicana/o literature often imaginatively addresses the many disparities that haunt us. It asks readers to join in this act of reimagination. In fiction, creative essays, poetry, and drama, Chicana/o authors have created a Lupe who dwells in the streets of Tijuana and talks on television, a Lupe who understands why a young woman might not be prepared to become a mother, a Lupe who moves with us from burned-down house to crowded apartment, a Lupe who accompanies those in struggle against narrow and discriminatory norms governing gender and sexuality, a Lupe whose power and grace are felt daily and intimately. As is the case for Anzaldúa, these renewed visions of Our Lady of Guadalupe originate in an examination of Guadalupe's Mesoamerican roots and meanings and in a woman-centered popular religiosity that is critically conscious of paradigms of gender, ethnicity, sexuality, and race.

Autohisteoría and Other Narrative Forms

The transnational perspective of *Borderlands/La Frontera*, which reads the U.S.-Mexico border as the site of Chicano/a interpellation by two different nations and cultures, suggests that its mestiza feminist vision might also have hemispheric resonances. Echoing José Martí's call that "the history of America, from the Incas to the present, must be taught inside out,"[90] Anzaldúa insists that we "root ourselves in the mythological soil and soul of this continent."[91] A more complete knowledge of the Americas—its histories, struggles, and peoples—forms a critical component of the new mestiza consciousness that *Borderlands* imagines as a conversation among the hemisphere's inhabitants: "we need to know the history of their struggle and they need to know ours."[92]

The personal and collective memories that infuse Anzaldúa's text map the contours of life in the borderlands, *how* its subjects know as well as *what* they know. Anzaldúa's narration of these memories reveals the construction of both individual and collective knowledge and the critical evaluation of that knowledge in theorizing borderlands consciousness and the possibilities for change. This makes Anzaldúa's term for her narrative—autohisteoría—the most apt. It shares with the Latin American literary genre of testimonio the narrative re-creation of a subaltern individual experience of marginalization and struggle that is a collective experience, and within that experience is embedded a critique of dominant society whose impact upon the reader is that of awakening consciousness or inspiring solidarity. Nonetheless, autohisteoría departs from testimonio in its making, theorizing, and critiquing action as it advances new paradigms and conceptions for understanding cross-cultural encounters and for actively shaping their outcomes. Several of the novels and documentary films discussed here reference the testimonio as a genre influencing their production, yet they also frequently go beyond testimonio to engage in autohisteoría, producing new meanings and possibilities out of their imagined and documentary narratives of Chicana lives.

Sonia Saldívar-Hull identifies the invocation and adaptation of the testimonio form in Chicana feminist and literary theory in the United States as an expression of solidarity with third world women. This feminism on the border, as she names it, conscious of both geopolitics and gender politics, strategically seeks to insert itself within a "global literary history" through the use of the testimonio form.[93] Saldívar-Hull's analysis sees the link between testimonio and Chicana narrative not only in their generic similarities but in their shared enactment of the inseparability of gender, race, and class concerns; the capacity of narrative to theorize; and the intimate connection between activism and literary enterprise.[94] Doris Sommer suggests that key features of women's testimonios include an exploration of subject formation that recognizes difference within networks of relationship as well as multiple subjectivities, critique of gender privilege, and most importantly, the substitution of the metaphoric "I" of heroic autobiography with the metonymic "I" of testimonio.[95] These analyses reveal echoes of autohisteoría in testimonio, and vice versa, marking a hemispheric frame for women's narratives. Important distinctions between the positions and testimonios of Latin American male guerrilla leaders, Latin American female community leaders, and Chicana writers who only recently gained access to higher education and publishing cannot be overlooked. Similar caution applies when ascribing unlimited privilege to Chicana narratives in the context of social stratifications in the United States. Instead, this brief comparative discussion of points of convergence and mutual influence suggests that we foreground a transnational context for understanding the emergence of new genres and new forms of fiction that both speak from particular social locations and speak across borders in an attempt to explore the possibilities for social transformation in the Americas.[96]

This reading also requires another acknowledgment, one that goes beyond the discussion of narrative form, for today Chicano/a and Latino/a and especially Chicana and Latina literature still suffers under a critical (though sometimes loving) gaze which reads influence as imitation, engagement with popular culture for kitsch, paratextual marketing as text, and appeal among Latino/as as indicative of low literary value. Another concern is the degree to which Chicana and Latina fiction might be read as sociology or anthropology or might form part of a capitalist publishing enterprise that reproduces desires for exotic Others. Indeed, the "popularity" of Chicana and Latina fiction appears to have inspired anxiety about who or what is being represented and how, as well as who is reading it and how, while its increasing incorporation into the literature curriculum in schools and universities appears to have inspired another set of concerns about its literariness. These are not trivial matters. Scholars of Chicano/a and Latino/a literature challenge a too-easy consumption of this literature, demanding instead that we attend to both its particularities and its contexts. If, despite the existence of informed criticism, these works are read by some as a confirmation of exotic Others, predatory macho males, loose Latina women, or dysfunctional, poor Chicano/a families, then that another, and bigger, problem is afoot, one that goes beyond academia. One context, however, that we ignore at great peril is the daily violence—discursive, material, and physical—directed against Chicano/as, Latino/as, and immigrants from Latin America as well as intra-group violence against women. The fact of the violence and the history of the violence—which animate, in part, what Ramón Saldívar terms the *difference* of Chicano literature—cannot be ignored.[97]

The Chicana novels and documentary films addressed in this book unfold in varied forms, as autohisteoría, testimonio, fictional testimonio, or just plain fiction—particularly historical fiction. I use the term *fictional testimonio* to designate fictions that present themselves as testimonies, such as *Face of an Angel, Mother Tongue,* and *The Flower in the Skull.* In this way, these texts experiment with language and form to address violence in the borderlands.[98] *Mother Tongue* also engages and critiques the romantic novel while *Face of an Angel*'s metafictional elements use multiple literary conventions to create language that can adequately address violence. Both novels, in mapping shifts in the consciousness of their protagonists, provoke reformulations of the paradigms that govern their protagonists' lives. *Canícula* also employs fictional testimonio, working with mini-chapters, vignettes, and photographs to create a text that is at once an individual and a collective story. The documentary films *Flowers for Guadalupe* and *Señorita Extraviada* are marked by their use of collaborative methods in creating cinematic testimonios about the forms of violence that poor women face in the Americas. Two books in the Alcalá trilogy do not fall into the categories of autohisteoría, testimonio, or fictional testimonio. Instead, *Spirits of the Ordinary* and *Treasures in Heaven* are novels of historical fiction set in the borderlands of the nineteenth and early twentieth centuries and centered on the Catholic and Jewish Carabajál family, especially the mother, Estela Carabajál, as they negotiate the shifting ground of religious (in)tolerance, national identity, gender, and sexuality.

Remembering, in these narratives, is also simultaneously a moment of critical analysis, for rarely are any of these remembrances free of the sharp edge of critical assessment. In contrast to Rigoberta Menchú, who appears already in possession of an awareness at the moment of narrating her journey toward it, the fictional Mary/María of *Mother Tongue* (1994) presents readers with her vulnerability to dominant discourses and her effort to work through them while *Face of an Angel* (1994) situates its naïve protagonist, Soveida, amid the gender-stratified, marginalized collective of working-class Chicano/as in New Mexico—among whom and with whom she finds her way. Mary/María's reflective tone in *Mother Tongue* colors her remembrance, which comprises most of the novel. In her frequently satirical and humorous telling in *Face of an Angel*, Soveida does not merely reaffirm the unified resistance of the ethnic or class group, but instead deflates the pretensions of a male-centered collective that silences and abuses women while refocusing the testimonial voice on the story of an often invisible collective within a collective—Chicanas. The varied registers and multiple discourses through which these narratives work, as well as the contradictions of the particular social locations that their characters and participants inhabit, truly resonate with Anzaldúa's call to embrace a multiply defined subject.[99]

Here, spiritual mestizaje yields partial insights gradually, sometimes allowing for reconfigurations of normative gender and sexuality, on other occasions creating greater awareness of overlapping national and religious ideologies, and even, at times, facilitating border-crossing solidarity and transnational feminist alliances. Chapter 2 examines two fictional testimonios, *Face of an Angel* by Denise Chávez and *Mother Tongue* by Demetria Martínez, that feature Chicana protagonists engaged in writing accounts of their lives that are also chronicles of their spiritual mestizaje or journey toward a new mestiza consciousness. The working-class waitress Soveida in *Face of an Angel* and the solidarity activist turned writer María in *Mother Tongue* are caught up in ideologies and traditions that limit, even endanger them, but they work to reclaim the spiritual and sexual agency they initially lack. In *Mother Tongue*, María grapples with her critique of Catholicism and her desire for inclusion in spiritual community; however, in *Face of an Angel*, Soveida becomes aware of the subordination and violence imposed on her by the convergence of religious and ethnic discourses authorized by the Guadalupe and Malinche dyad. Overcoming these "metaphoric controls," as Alarcón names them, presents a central challenge for each character and forms a significant part of the journey that each undertakes.[100] Both novels take place near the U.S.-Mexico border, a setting that informs each novel's concern with the multiple cultures and populations that inhabit the borderlands and the disparities and inequalities engendered by the region's history.

In chapter 3 my analysis focuses on the construction of women's spiritual communities en la frontera in one fictional autobioethnography, *Canícula: Snapshots of a Girlhood en la Frontera* (1995) by Norma Cantú, and two documentary testimonio films, *Flowers for Guadalupe/Flores para Guada-*

lupe (1995) by Judith Gleason and the Feminist Collective of Xalapa and *Señorita Extraviada* (2001) by Lourdes Portillo. Each of these works creates a frontera or transnational space of spiritual communion among women: in the novel by recalling the significance of popular religious practices, beliefs, and spiritual community in linking families and communities despite a border, and in the films by documenting the voices and stories of women involved in the movement to forge a transnational feminist spiritual community in order to combat isolation, violence, exploitation, dispossession, racism, sexism, and genocidal misogyny. Chapter 4 examines three novels by Kathleen Alcalá—*Spirits of the Ordinary* (1998), *The Flower in the Skull* (1999), and *Treasures in Heaven* (2000)—that trace the encounters among competing religious traditions in the borderlands in the stories of the Catholic Quintanilla Navarro family, the Crypto Jewish Caraval/Carabajál family, and the Opata family of Chiri/Hummingbird. The trilogy begins in the latter half of the nineteenth century and ends in the late twentieth century and explores the history and the lasting legacy of religious and political conflicts in the borderlands. The novels move back and forth between Mexico and the United States with particular emphasis on the shared repression of women, Jews, and indigenous peoples and the cross-cultural alliances that some characters are able to effect in attempting to create more just social relations. In chapter 5, I explore the relationship between Anzaldúa's work and postcolonial scholarship, particularly with respect to religious and spiritual formations, and consider some of the obstacles that remain to the models of scholarship and activism left to us by Anzaldúa.

In each of the narratives under examination here, whether testimonio, fictional testimonio, or historical fiction, memory feeds spiritual mestizaje—that work of recognition, assessment, rupture, and transformation of individual and collective consciousness that sees itself in respectful relation to the realm(s) of the divine. The critique offered in these novels and films owes much to the way that Chicana/o literature and culture often offer strong contrasts to dominant cultural norms.[101] Laura E. Pérez terms this "the tenacious, socially and economically overdetermined biculturality" of Chicano/a cultural practices, which also makes them "heterogeneous and conflictive, *with respect to both Chicana/o and dominant U.S. culture*."[102]

These narratives represent several versions of spiritual mestizaje; yet, in each one, we witness the radical and sustained critique of oppression that is intellectual, spiritual, embodied, and psychic as it unfolds. This does not happen without confronting the fears and blocks of the Coatlicue state—figured differently in each text—but it does eventually lead to an original and engaged involvement in creating a life that honors the sacred. The assessment of religious tradition that occurs in this process opens the way toward new spiritual formations and a new mestiza consciousness. In some cases, this seems like the beginning of a new spiritual practice and community, and in others it appears simply as the ability to remake one's relation to and understanding of religious tradition for contemporary times.

2 *Bodies of Knowledge*

"To Tell another person about what was done to your body in the name of politics is a frightful act of intimacy, risky beyond sex."[1]

"I remembered how Eloisa took control that night. How an Off Night became an On Night. How, once again, I was shown that beyond the work was the value of the person working."[2]

Denise Chávez's *Face of an Angel* (1994) and Demetria Martínez's *Mother Tongue* (1994) imaginatively portray the sometimes funny, often difficult, life-altering journey toward a new mestiza consciousness of working-class Chicanas. Although both novels appear to center on the romantic lives of their protagonists—Soveida humorously chronicles her relationships with men while María recalls a passionate love affair—these relationships are only one facet of the characters' searches, as borderlands inhabitants, for greater spiritual and sexual agency, a quest that brings them into conflict with their own religious backgrounds as well as prevailing norms of gender and sexuality in their families, communities, and towns. The spiritual mestizaje of these characters takes them to new understandings of the sacred, critical insight, psychic peace, and passionate commitment to social justice. In Anzaldúa's lexicon, these characters are *caminantes*—those working for a more just society who create the bridges, alliances, and awareness necessary for change through their work. Their compassion, and then activism, figures in their journeys of spiritual mestizaje.

The choice to write a fictional testimonio suggests that something more than fiction is at stake, raising the interesting prospect of fictional texts staging an intervention in contemporary discourses of religion, nation, spirituality, race, ethnicity, gender, and sexuality. Thematically, the novels address their setting in the U.S.-Mexico border region by explicitly engaging questions of cross-border solidarity with Mexican and Salvadoran women and men. They also resist the traditional narrative arc toward a crowning, climactic epiphany, replacing it instead with a different momentum in a series of smaller epiphanies that unfold over the course of each narrative, guiding the individual narrator-protagonist along the path toward new forms of awareness.

Both novels acknowledge the birth of the Chicana feminist movement in their story lines: in *Mother Tongue* the brief missives from Mary/María's Aunt Soledad represent the struggle and wisdom of that earlier generation, and in *Face of an Angel* a feminist and ethnic consciousness emerges among the working people of the small town of Agua Oscura. These narrative elements situate the texts within a broader, historical feminist movement of Chicanas, one well-documented in Alma M. García's *Chicana Feminist Thought: The Basic Historical Writings*, that emerged from many local struggles. In the 1960s and 1970s, discussions about feminism flourished in colleges and universities, arenas from which Chicanas had previously been excluded. Chicana writing of the era appeared in journals dedicated to Chicano/a literature and politics, state college publications, community newspapers, and even early Chicana community feminist journals.[3] The precursors to Chicana literary production in the 1980s and beyond, including the novels under discussion here, these local publications demonstrate the almost immediate efforts of Chicanas newly admitted to academic, political, activist, and intellectual circles to create writing communities around issues of importance to them, particularly the convergence of gender, racial, and ethnic concerns. In making use of the literary forms available to them, Chicana feminists brought a literary movement of their own into being, one that *Face of an Angel* and *Mother Tongue* participate in and, within their pages, metafictionally represent.

As the essays in the García collection reveal, earlier Chicana feminists engaged in a lively debate regarding the role of religion in Chicana lives.[4] Some questioned the religious institutions and doctrines that contributed to the subordination of women and the devaluation of women's sexual and social agency.[5] Others recognized and explored Chicana agency within religious communities, while yet others took up the study of indigenous spirituality or researched religious foremothers who were active in shaping spiritual life (such as Sor Juana Inés de la Cruz). Many demanded that religious institutions become more responsive to their communities.[6] The concern with religion that surfaces repeatedly in these early movement texts indicates that it impacted the socialization of women in particular, and therefore a specifically Chicana feminism had to engage the religious traditions, histories, practices, and beliefs of Chicanas, a task that Gloria Anzaldúa furthers in *Borderlands/La Frontera*. As works of fiction, *Face of an Angel* and *Mother Tongue* imagine characters whose vitality is restored by their critical negotiation of the social and economic inequalities they and others face, and the religious cultures that have long held sway in their lives.

The domestic sphere figures prominently in these novels—narratives that present an imagined, first-person, spoken and written testimonio addressed to a listening or reading audience. In each text, the home, understood as the sphere of women, shifts over time from a site of containment or delusion to one of feminist spiritual praxis. If, as Daphne Spain notes, "the home is the spatial institution containing the least amount of socially valued knowledge," then these narratives, in representing the Chicana home as a site of significant learning, insight, and activism, generate a new perspective on domestic knowledge.[7] They also reveal how the home or domestic space interrelates with Chicana labor, historical agency, communities, and bodies, disrupting the artificial dichotomy that links female, domestic, and private as distinguished from male, civic, and public. In both works, the narrators/protagonists gradually acquire awareness of their interpellation by dominant discourses, an awareness necessary for the task of social transformation. *Face of an Angel* and *Mother Tongue* end not with the incorporation of their Chicana protagonists into the status quo, nor with their radical disruption of it, but instead with open-ended transformations of the central characters who, at the novels' end, are poised to take their journeys in new directions.

Consciously learning about previously obscured indigenous beliefs and practices, especially the feminine divine, as an aspect of their own mestiza histories contributes to the spiritual renewal that Soveida and María achieve. In *Face of an Angel*, Oralia Milcantos, Soveida's grandmother's lifelong aide and domestic worker, is a source of knowledge for Soveida. For María in *Mother Tongue*, who feels alienated from the religion and church that is her ancestral inheritance, a new spirituality emerges from multiple sources, including her collaboration with Aunt Soledad, an unorthodox Catholic; her engagement with Eastern mysticism; her participation in a

Protestant pacifist community; and her introduction to Salvadoran religiosity. In both texts, the central characters experience an estrangement from themselves that can only begin to be remedied through a reclamation of their sexuality and the acquisition of an awareness of the conditions shaping their subjectivity, particularly the historically thorny nexus of race, gender, and religion.

In *Mother Tongue* María's sense that there exists a little-known women's spiritual history out there, just beyond her grasp, and her hunger for it surface throughout the narrative—in architectural observations, brief notes from Soledad that she saves, readings, and prayers. This is part of her attraction to her Aunt Soledad's house, which she shares with José Luis, a refugee from El Salvador, and which she describes as a place that holds the fragrance of refugee women cooking in the morning "before North Americans bundled them off to other houses."[8] María intuitively understands that Soledad can inform her spiritual mestizaje with knowledge of curanderismo and popular religiosity and opportunities for praxis in the refugee movement. María, therefore, eagerly enters into Soledad's house, literally and metaphorically, to pursue her journey.

Soveida, in *Face of an Angel*, learns about the sacred, healing, and the divine from Oralia Milcantos, her grandmother's servant, cook, and companion, who also guides and heals Soveida throughout her life. As an adult, Soveida recalls the numerous occasions she received the gifts of Oralia's tenderness, wisdom, domestic skills, and herbal healing knowledge, weaving Oralia's story into a narrative that includes the stories of Dolly, her mother; Mamá Lupita, her grandmother; Milia, her mentor and co-worker; Petra, her co-worker; and Chata, her house cleaner, among others. Following the death of Soveida's second husband, Oralia counsels Soveida to rely on "la diosita, the Guadalupe," and performs a limpia for Soveida, demonstrating the hybrid spirituality she practices.[9] The many women's stories that make up Soveida's narrative reveal a collective experience as they also explain how the child Soveida came to be Soveida the waitress, writer, and mother. Nonetheless, Oralia's story is singled out when Soveida makes her the subject of her oral history term paper in Chicano studies (which appears as a text within the text complete with professor's comments and grade). Soveida's term paper codifies her appreciation of Oralia as a person, an indigenous woman, a healer, and a domestic worker. Her professor chides her for what he considers to be an emotional, non-analytical paper, and his comments indicate that Soveida has not sufficiently internalized the role of the interrogating researcher who culls facts and information from a subject that the researcher then interprets. But this "shortcoming" suggests that Soveida does not seek to speak for Oralia, much less provide the "grand sweep," as her professor prompts. On the contrary, her oral history, like *The Book of Service* she is engaged in writing throughout the novel, recognizes the individual agency and subjectivity of the women she writes about.

The value and power of these alternative understandings of the sacred (whose origins may not be entirely knowable due to histories of conquest, displacement, and migration) for women's journeys become manifest in Soveida's engagement with Oralia Milcantos and María's relationship with Soledad. Within the framework of the borderlands, these narratives enact an imaginative partial recovery and recirculation of indigenous knowledge that function as countermeasures to hegemonic interpellation rather than as a nostalgic yearning for premodern simplicity.[10]

Gender, Body, and Spirit:
Denise Chávez's *Face of an Angel*

In this novel the narrator and central protagonist, Soveida Dosamantes, a waitress at the popular Mexican restaurant El Farol in the small New Mexican town of Agua Oscura, recounts her life from childhood to anticipated motherhood. Soveida's narrative conveys the life of a woman in the process of coming into full possession of her body, intellect, and soul. Soveida's story grounds itself in family history without either reifying the traditional family or limiting itself to the telling of an individual life. Instead, *Face of an Angel* portrays several working-class Chicana characters. In the first chapter, "A Long Story," her grandmother Lupita tells Soveida:

> Even *you* have a story to tell. Tell it while you can, while you have the strength, because when you get to be my age, the telling gets harder. The memories are the clothes in your closet that you never wear and are afraid to throw out because you'll hurt someone. But then you realize one long day, m'jita, that there's no one left to hurt except yourself. . . . And then you wake up suddenly with a mouthful of cenizas, nothing but ash.[11]

Lupita's words are a call to speak ("tell") what might otherwise remain hidden or unknown out of fear, embarrassment, or misplaced concern. As these opening pages suggest, speaking is a central concern in the novel, which is manifested in its form as well as its content. The act of "giving voice to those who cannot speak," which Elizabeth Coonrod Martínez identifies as an element of Latina literature, breaks the silence and intervenes to end the continued victimization of women.[12] Lupita's caution becomes Soveida's action.

Soveida's narrative reveals the degree to which the silence about women's lives is an "unnatural" one, as Elaine Hedges and Shelly Fisher Fishkin suggest, that derives from "being born into the wrong class, race or sex, being denied education, becoming numbed by economic struggle, muffled by censorship, or distracted or impeded by the demands of nurturing."[13] Similarly, Kate Adams suggests that the silence imposed on women is not easy to reverse:

> For the North American woman of color, writing in the face of such forces means recognizing that her "silences" are, in some sense, *meant to be*: what Olsen has called "the overwhelmingness of the dominant" requires and depends on her silence; what Audre Lorde has called structures "defined by profit and linear power" actively discourage her coming to voice.[14]

Soveida's journey toward overcoming this silence requires her to interrogate those structures wherever they appear, writing not just her story but a collective one, as she openly declares: "I speak for them now. Mother. Father. Brother. Sister. Cousin. Uncle. Aunt. Husband. Lover. Their memories are mine. That sweet telling mine. Mine the ash."[15]

Her reclamation of ash in this context carries multiple meanings, as does the word itself. Ash is the "solid residue left when combustible material is thoroughly burned," a recoverable substance after a fire; it is "ruins," the worthless rubble or the still-standing, damaged artifact; it is the "remains of the dead human body after disintegration," the physical link to dead ancestors; it is a symbol of "grief, repentance, or humiliation," of which there is plenty in this novel.[16] Yet ash is also an agent of cleansing: in the right amounts, it purifies water so that it can be used for human consumption—drinking, cooking, washing—without causing harm.[17] The meanings of ash reinforce both Lupita's words and Soveida's project, suggesting a counter-point between the narrator and structures of gender, family, religion, community, and race.[18] Soveida's declaration "I speak for them now" might seem a gesture at self-effacement, but instead asserts her voice in shaping a narrative based on her social location, memory, perceptions, and imagination. In claiming the power to create the story that comes with speaking, her narrative takes the form of a fictional testimonio.

Testimonios inherently reject the notion of "private" pain, instead publicly attesting to the individual pain, misery, oppression, and heroism resulting from inequalities or specific circumstances.[19] For René Jara, the testimonio is an unavoidable "jolt to the collective consciousness . . . that breaks down the distinctions between public and private as it brutally dismantles the soothing stories provided by the state."[20] While Soveida's fictional testimony does not directly challenge the state, as do many Latin American testimonios, it exposes violence against women in the home and workplace and the insidiousness of narratives aimed at pacifying women. In doing so, it creates the story of a marginalized subject whose speaking and writing enact the resistance of both the individual and a group.[21] Soveida's direct appeal in the body of her manuscript, *The Book of Service*, to the character of the young waitress, Dedea, to create a life different from the one assigned to women suggests the influence of testimonio thematically. In a brilliant shift on the testimonio—which frequently employs the mediation of an "as told to" editor—*Face of an Angel* places the reader in the position of listener and mediator, with the attendant demands of those roles.

With their origins in religious discourse as a form of bearing witness, observes Laura Rice-Sayre, testimonios emphasize moral law and human rights, thereby circumventing the reauthorization of positive law, especially since that law often represents "the received ideas of powerful groups of men at particular times."[22] Testimonio's adoption by Chicana writers indicates a desire to bear witness to Chicana lives, and to do that as part of a project that emends religious doctrines, forms, and discourses that contain women. Testimonio becomes a pattern for these narratives precisely because of its religious as well as ethical and political significance.

Soveida's self-reflexive critique takes particular aim at the beliefs, values, and behaviors that have perpetuated the silence of the women in her family. Her dislike for her grandmother Lupita's whispered attempts to silence and ostracize Mara, Soveida's cousin, rather than take Lupita's son Luardo (and Soveida's father) to task for sexual abuse emerges as a key tension.[23] In contrast to Lupita and Dolores, who seek to read Mara out of the family history, Soveida includes Mara and critiques the lies that Lupita and Dolores spread, especially those that have perpetuated their collective submission to the men in the family.[24]

In this context, the statement, "I speak for them now" is loaded with complications. I propose to read Soveida's declaration as an example of what Tey Diana Rebolledo describes when she speaks of the dual functions that Chicana writing undertakes: to mediate between temporalities and cultures and to testify about Chicana experiences and histories.[25] This testimony, Rebolledo suggests, is both personal and collective, and it often includes the names and stories of "mothers, grandmothers, sisters, aunts, friends."[26] Soveida's narrative does not distance itself from these other voices, but places itself among them, in this way becoming representative of the collective and of an age that Miguel Barnet argues is a feature of the novel testimonio.[27] For Soveida, the collective is not only female-identified but inclusive of both men and women; hence, she tells us, the "stories begin with the men and always end with the women."[28] Her statement alludes to both women's secondary status and the difficulties of mediation that she confronts—a "culturally explosive" negotiation, as Alvina Quintana terms it, in the service of constructing a new sense of self.[29]

Parody and Satire in the Making of the Fictional Testimonio

Face of an Angel's parodic and satiric eruptions are distinctive in that the novel departs from the gravity of form on which it patterns itself.[30] It is perhaps the sharpness of *Face of an Angel*'s critique of gender asymmetry that calls forth humor to mitigate that critique. Although the novel opens with a family history, the satiric edge to Soveida's genealogical account calls into question its patriarchal underpinnings. Here and elsewhere, *Face of an Angel* repeatedly mocks the behaviors, practices, and beliefs that contribute to social and economic inequalities. As Guillermo E. Hernández notes:

> In comedy those who are marginal are subjected to ridicule or abuse, but this debasement serves principally to amuse by reinforcing established norms, given that comic figures, as inoffensive beings, do not

challenge the values and symbols of the status quo. The satiric attack, in contrast, has a primary purpose to ridicule and invalidate the normative principles and interpretations upheld by victims who are portrayed with scorn. Consequently, the satirist frequently is perceived as a subversive whose art represents an opposing, incompatible, and overwhelming evaluative norm that challenges the legitimacy of cherished normative values and figures.[31]

This subversion, readily apparent in Soveida's narrative, manifests a running critique that contributes to her spiritual mestizaje.

While Soveida adopts the point of view of her great-grandfather Manuel Dosamantes Iturbide, her grandfather Profetario Dosamantes, and her father, Luardo, in telling their stories, hers is not a romantic family history nor a sober one. She satirizes the pretensions, conventions, behaviors, and ideologies that guide their lives, including the "secret" second families of Profetario Dosamantes and Biterbo Loera and the long-standing practice of her adult male ancestors marrying teenage girls. Readers hear about her father Luardo's fetishization of women's bodies and Biterbo Loera's and Luardo Dosamantes's violence against women and children. Her great-grandfather Manuel rejects a woman because she is "dark-skinned, flat-chested" while the woman he marries is "blond-haired and blue-eyed." The nostalgic family tale of the enterprising great-grandfather Manuel and the ideal Mexican family he creates reverberates with the racial ideology of whitening, or *blanqueamiento*. Soveida's tone in relating this history is self-consciously ironic, distancing herself from it by marking the difference between what she hears and what she knows as in this excerpt:

> I never knew my great-grandfather Manuel Dosamantes. Nor did I really know my grandfather Profetario very well. To me he was a blustery man, big as the sky, always yelling at my grandmother Lupe. He was a man who lived under the yoke of his father Manuel's perfectly balanced life. Profetario was a rascal, living with two wives, two families. The Dosamantes name fit him, eternally split between two lovers.[32]

While a romantic family story has obviously been passed down to her, Soveida declares that she "never knew" those on whom the story centers, and to the degree that she did, they did not appear to fit the story, prompting her to question rather than perpetuate the nostalgic family yarn. Soveida's irony and satire dismantle an oppressive insistence upon idealized narratives of the Chicano family.

These strategies surface throughout the novel, for example when Soveida humorously mocks her fellow church member María Estefanita's act of religious witness, a dedication to Christ prefaced by a long list of material items that María lacks yet clearly desires. This mockery turns into biting satire in her description of the "exorcism" performed upon her by Raúl Rojas, Brother Michael Trainor, and Rosarío Rojas of the Traveling Prayer Team, whose misplaced and self-serving commitment to saving souls is reflected in the grotesqueness of their appearance to Soveida, as well as the thinness of their healing powers.[33] *Face of an Angel* makes generous use of various types of humor and language play. Soveida's first encounter with Jester, the bad-boy boyfriend from the wrong side of town, hilariously pokes fun at the Mexican custom of nicknaming everyone and everything—often with brutal honesty—by quoting Jester's hurried appeal for help:

> "Tell Beliso to call Tía Pepa. Tío Nati got some fingers cut off on the farm. Chipi can't pick him up at the hospital because Fernie took off with the car.
>
> Maybe Tin or Pollo could do it."
>
> "Could you repeat that?"[34]

Soveida plays the "straight man" in this exchange, unable to follow Jester's request because it is peppered with too many nicknames—a humorous exaggeration that plays with ethnic customs without rejecting them. In this case, the scene's humor is rather mild.[35] *Face of an Angel* frequently indulges in this kind of comedy, poking fun, from within, at particular customs, rituals, or practices that will remain in place, such as the penchant for nicknames. The novel's satire, however, appears to be reserved for that which perpetuates inequality. While some critics suggest that satire and parody inevitably convey nostalgia for ideal norms or an idealized past,[36] *Face of an Angel*, time and again, questions that desire and deconstructs inherited norms.

Women's Work

El Farol is arguably the principal sub-setting of this narrative and in it readers learn a great deal about women's work. At the restaurant, Soveida enjoys community with a group of working women who help her to grow in strength, self-awareness, and professionalism: Milia Ocana, who guides her in the work of waitressing and eventually passes on the job of head waitress to Soveida; Eloisa Ortiz, the tough, dedicated, and talented cook at El Farol; and Bonnie Larragoite, the savvy business manager. The experience of work makes it possible for Soveida to see and identify with women more generally, including Oralia, her mother's domestic helper, and Esperanza "Chata" Vialpando, the cleaning woman who helps Soveida tend to her own house, but also the women of her own family—Mara, Dolly, and Lupita. The narrative's focus on communities of working women develops in the section titled "Powers," additionally identified in the text by the image of a milagrito in the shape of a hand. In contrast to other employers of domestic labor, Soveida joins Chata in the work of cleaning her house and is guided by Chata's expertise in household maintenance and her "no-nonsense," "unafraid" approach to work, epitomized in her strong and fearless hands.[37] Soveida values Chata's work and person by describing her as "a woman in a state of grace," that is, a woman who has come to self-awareness through her own work and life journey, who knows herself and her work and who is full of practical common sense, not flighty idealism.[38]

Chata's description of the many obstacles and indignities that she encounters as a domestic worker brings another segment of the border workforce into focus. In her study of domestic labor, *Maid in the U.S.A.*, Mary Romero observes: "domestic workers are disproportionately women of color. Domestic service cannot be separated from America's history and the capitalism that produced and continues to maintain a gender-stratified and racially hierarchical labor market."[39] Romero's work challenges previous analyses of domestic work in which the disregard for this labor (even, it is claimed, by those who perform it) leads to its low status. Instead, she suggests that the gap between domestic labor and other occupations in terms of rights and benefits more centrally affects its status.[40]

Despite the existence of some labor laws that cover domestic work, few people are aware of them and, therefore, most people consider it a private matter.[41] According to Hondagneu-Sotelo, the widespread perception of domestic work as "something other than employment" because it frequently requires caring, or because it replaces the unpaid labor of mother or wife, continues to impact pay, working conditions, and employer-employee relations.[42] In contrast to the maternalism of old, strict boundaries are the new norm for relations between employers and employees in domestic service as most employers seek to limit personal contact with domestic help while most of the Latina immigrants who perform this work, notes Hondagneu-Sotelo, "*want* social recognition and appreciation for who they are and what they do."[43] *Face of an Angel* imagines this recognition in creating communities of working women who come to see and treat each other as allies in a common struggle, removing domestic work from the category of "private arrangements" and placing it on par with Soveida's public employment as a waitress. The work issues that Chata and Oralia face mirror those of real household workers, including multiple demands of employers, lack of privacy, low wages, parental unwillingness to support the authority of a domestic worker over their children, and abusive or violent behavior. Interestingly, food is an important issue for live-in nannies and housekeepers, and the frequency with which employers deny domestic workers food or regulate their food intake provokes much uneasiness for employees,[44] an issue that *Face of an Angel* represents in Chata's critique of employers who don't feed her in contrast to Soveida's willingness to share meals with her. However, the racial divide between largely Anglo employers and Mexican or Mexican American women in the research contrasts with the intra-ethnic and intra-racial divide that *Face of an Angel* addresses. Chata describes "las americanas" as providing better working conditions than those offered by Mexican or Mexican American households, where she is treated as a "Mexican" by people who have forgotten that they, too, are Mexican.[45] The privilege of citizenship and class exerts a powerful force in the mistreatment of immigrant domestic labor, and the novel does not ignore this in its critique of the discourses and material realities that shape life on the border.

Labor stratification in the fictional Agua Oscura, located near Juárez, appears to echo Romero's observations about the readily available pool of inexpensive labor at the border that makes it possible for even apartment dwellers to employ a housekeeper.[46] The transnational domestic workforce readily available to inhabitants of the region since the 1970s has spread throughout the United States, but principally in cities where large wage gaps exist, and one of the more common scenarios generated by economic globalization is that of the immigrant domestic worker tending to the households and children of families in wealthier nations. Instead of creating greater or stronger bonds of sisterhood among women brought together

in this economic exchange, the situation has perpetuated mistress-maid relations among women with differing access to opportunity and wealth.[47]
According to Patricia Zavella, "Chicanos have remained in the bottom
strata of the working class for more than a century."[48]

This examination of Romero's, Hondagneu-Sotelo's, and Zavella's work,
rather than demonstrating how closely the work world of *Face of an Angel*
accurately portrays the work situation of Mexicans and Chicanas, instead
suggests that the novel's imaginative creation of a workplace and work life
is concerned with telling a story of Chicana labor in the United States that
remains at the margins even in the twenty-first century. This fictional testimonial centers on Chicana working-class labor in the twentieth century
by chronicling Soveida's entrance into the work world; her desire for and
struggle to enjoy decent working conditions, a living wage, and respect; and
her ongoing negotiation of familial and social roles. At the end of the book,
Soveida remains a waitress. Hers is not a narrative of upward mobility out
of the working class—and her unwillingness to idealize that upward mobility is evident in her satiric barbs about J. V. Velásquez, Ph.D.—but one
that oscillates between the accumulation of knowledge and awareness of
her condition as a brown-skinned, working-class woman on the border and
her corresponding actions to transform her conditions of life.

Service: Domestic and Commercial

In a confrontation with idealized notions of women's service, Soveida
writes *The Book of Service: A Handbook for Servers*, which she describes in
this way: "It's about service. What it means to serve and be served. Why is
it that women's service is different from men's?"[49] This guidebook, written
for the younger waitress Dedea and the next generation of waitresses at El
Farol, becomes a lens for the consideration of service from a working-class
vantage point. The alternative "service creed" that it offers distinguishes between service and submission to power; valorizes physical, intellectual, and
emotional awareness; sees the multiple subjectivities of those who serve;
conveys advice on negotiating gender norms in personal and work lives;
and suggests that its readers contribute the stories of their own personal
journeys to the ongoing collective story of "service." Soveida condenses the
knowledge she has gained through years of work into *The Book of Service*,
representing the restaurant workplace into a site of learning and teaching

as well as doing, and providing a fuller reckoning of the worker as subject rather than merely as paid labor. This aspect of the novel offers a corrective to the dehumanization of workers in the service industry. As a fictional handbook for waitresses, *The Book of Service* appears as a humorous contrast to real-life texts such as *Your Maid from Mexico* that emphasize subservience, resignation, and ingratiation in the performance of household duties.[50] Published in 1959 for employers of domestic labor, *Your Maid from Mexico* states:

> By taking our place in the home and doing many of our jobs, you can give us free hours to do the things we enjoy—playing golf, sewing, playing the piano, attending club meetings, or working at a job we like.
>
> Remember, as you learn new skills day by day, you are not only learning how to become a better wife and mother yourself, but you are learning to support yourself and your family in a worthwhile career in case you must be the breadwinner.[51]

Soveida's manual, in contrast, values both the labor and the personhood of waitresses, offering advice on how to negotiate the demands of the occupation and exert control over the conditions of labor. Like the novel of which it is a part, the manual chronicles the experience of a Chicana working-class server encountering the assumptions and expectations of others about her and their actions toward her. She opens it with the declaration: "As a child, I was imbued with the idea that the purpose of life was service. Service to God. Country. Men. Not necessarily in that order, but lumped together like that."[52] Throughout, Soveida dismantles this particular triad by critically comparing her religious and family training in service with her experience as a desiring working-class Chicana. Her service credo severs the tie between service and subordination that appears to have been imbibed by the women in her family. Instead, it places women on par with men, equally deserving of service but also honored, as individuals, for the service they provide. *The Book of Service* aligns itself with the desire expressed in Cherríe Moraga's *Loving in the War Years* to overturn the popular belief that "you are a traitor to your race if you do not put the man first."[53] It wryly conveys the sense of self, the self-care, and the assertiveness necessary to really serve, rather than the self-effacement or conformity often associated with service, especially women's service. In *Face of an Angel* labor as service does not underwrite the further exploitation of workers but rather recognizes the worker. Soveida imbues work with a holy purpose, a grace that inheres in work well done, respect for the worker, and the self-respect of the worker. This re-definition staged in *The Book of Service* elevates waitressing and disrupts the view of minority workers as mere menial laborers:

> "After all these years, what have you learned that you didn't already know before? I mean, can you tell me, Soveida, what does waitressing have to do with life. Real life?"
>
> "You're hopeless, Mara."
>
> "So what are you telling me, Soveida? Nothing has changed."
>
> "Is that it?"
>
> "Things haven't changed. They never will."
>
> "Maybe someday they will, Mara. Then we won't have any minorities. People won't think because you're black you'll get a job cleaning offices, or because you're Latino you'll clean bathrooms, or because you're young you'll work in fast-food restaurants, or because you're old you'll sweep the hallways."
>
> "Oh yeah? I don't think so. As long as there is life, there'll be slaves like Oralia and Chata, and the other one, what's her name?"
>
> "Tere? Oh, Mara, you're wrong. They're not slaves, they're women who serve. There's a difference. You just don't get it."[54]

Where Mara sees only poor, unfortunate victims, Soveida sees subjects. Her effort to influence how workers, and especially women workers, are read is offered not in the service of glorifying domestic or service work but in altering it so that the most marginalized are not continually relegated to it under the worst conditions.

What does writing a novel about writing a book about service signify? This metafictional aspect of *Face of an Angel* layered upon the framework of a fictional testimonio poses for readers, on multiple levels, the issues of voice versus silence and the problematic of language infected by oppressive class, gender, racial, and sexual norms.[55] *The Book of Service* is only one among several fictional subtexts in the novel; some of the other texts include a prayer missal, a childhood autobiography, and term papers for a Chicano studies class. The novel's repeated representation of the act of writing in texts embedded within the text effects an unavoidable contrast among the discourses through which Chicana subjects are figured, fore-grounding this as a critical framework for reading the novel. The fictional self-reflexivity of *Face of an Angel* contributes to the sense of unfamiliarity the text creates for its readers, undercutting an easy (and thoughtless) consumption. Grounded in the borderlands yet entirely imagined, Chávez's novel heightens the critical awareness of its readers.[56]

Milagritos and Body

In *Face of an Angel* Soveida moves from uncritical obedience to prevailing religious and gender norms—norms that, in effect, render her a subject without a body—to a fuller, critical awareness of her spiritual and material self. Divided into nine sections, each marked by the visual image of a milagrito and a rank in the celestial hierarchy of angels, her testimony represents this journey in chronological order, as a series of life lessons through which she is formed. The first section is titled "Angels," which is the lowest rank, and each of the remaining sections bears the name of the succeeding level, with one exception: archangels, principalities, powers, virtues, dominations (not dominions), thrones, cherubim, and seraphim. Each section of the novel is also adorned with the image of a different milagrito, a small amulet that is often affixed to an altar or figure of a saint and that comes in various shapes, often parts of the body. The physicality of the milagrito and its use as an object that represents a prayer of gratitude for the gift of bodily integrity—a leg healed, an arm restored, an eye granted vision again—or a plea for God's intercession (a leg that needs healing, and so on) further the novel's emphasis on women's bodies. Each image of a milagrito marks a stage in remembering women's bodies and in restoring Soveida's body to her. Together, the celestial hierarchy and the images of milagritos map the narrative journey. The milagrito images, therefore, function as part of the narrative rather than as mere decoration. Common at religious shrines on both sides of the border, they represent a transnational popular religious practice. This structuring device melds the discourses of institutional and popular religiosity in mapping Soveida's spiritual and physical journey.

Face of an Angel's engagement with religious discourse unfolds throughout the novel; varieties of religious expression are represented, but the book is largely grounded in the particular religious tradition of Catholicism. Soveida's reevaluation of her religious upbringing joins her imaginative exploration of alternative religiosities and leads her to develop a new spiritual praxis. Her retrospective reassessment of her childhood religious training includes a consideration of the religious perspectives expressed by those around her, the ceremonies in which she participated, and the understandings she gained or arrived at in the course of these events. Religious ceremony and gender socialization appear mutually constitutive in the first section of the novel as Soveida recalls how she and her cousin Mara were trained to compete for the titles of First Communion Angel, Queen of the Bazaar, attendant at the May Day crowning, and Spring Dance Queen. These events in Agua Oscura, New Mexico, in the 1950s represented a strict policing of the virgin-whore dichotomy and instilled in the girls a preoccupation with purity as the events demonized their sexuality; Soveida recalls the era as one in which a "shame . . . had been inflicted on us." As her narrative continues, the multiple sources of its perpetuation become gradually clearer.

In this context, the milagritos signal the reconstitution of the dismembered female body—perhaps a contemporary reconstitution of Coyolxauhqui.[57] The figure of an ear that accompanies the first section, "Angels," suggests listening and storytelling—that is, what has been passed down. This section focuses on Soveida's parents and grandparents as well as her own approach to storytelling. The milagrito image of a kneeling and robed woman in prayer, which marks the second section, indicates a woman alone in communion with God but also honoring, submission, a burden to bear—that is, the lessons conveyed by Soveida's religious training. The next seven sections are designated by milagrito images of a foot, hand, heart, mask, leg, face, and house.

Interposed between the sections marked by the mask and the face is the leg, the "Thrones" section, which is characterized by tales involving women's desire, such as Soveida's attraction to a married man, or women seemingly paying the consequences for their desire, such as Mara's tale about her father's abandonment of them and her mother's horrific death. Ailments abound in these stories and are, for Soveida, the physical manifestation of a spiritual and emotional lack that prevents women from caring for themselves sufficiently. These tales provide another piece of the knowledge and praxis that Soveida seeks, one that involves the integration of spirit and body—not an easy task for a character whose grandmother counsels her to take the veil in order to escape the sexual demands of men and whose

Angels

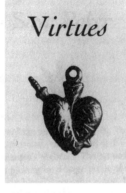
Virtues

Powers

Principalities

Archangels

mother represses her own sexual desire while she faithfully accompanies her husband to porn shows and clubs. *Face of an Angel* concurs with Cherríe Moraga's observation on the reciprocal relationship between spiritual and sexual freedom:

> Women of color have always known, although we have not always wanted to look at it, that our sexuality is not merely a physical response or drive, but holds a crucial relationship to our entire spiritual capacity. . . . Simply put, if the spirit and sex have been linked in our oppression, then they must also be linked in the strategy toward our liberation.[58]

The novel makes the connection that Moraga proposes in its attention to the female body and the many descriptive details of biological and gendered

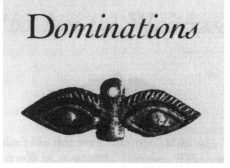

1–9. Milagrito images and titles for each of the nine sections of *Face of an Angel* by Denise Chávez.

bodily experience—including menstruation, sex, pregnancy, and vaginal infections as well as the cosmetics, clothing, and underclothing that contribute to the performance of gender and sexuality. These descriptions both reveal the physical costs of these norms and call attention to their performativity, critically interrogating each in the course of constructing a new subjectivity.[59]

While familial relationships, childhood experiences, and communal tales contribute to shaping Soveida's understandings, perhaps the most important arena of learning and growth for her is the workplace. It is in the workplace that Soveida's knowledge, values, and understandings undergo the test of experience; and it is in the workplace that she begins to bridge the split between body and spirit. As Soveida explains in *The Book of Ser-*

vice, waitressing requires knowledge of the self in relation to the demands of others and knowledge of one's physical limits and desires. At the conclusion of the novel, Soveida's grandmother Lupita, who has led a life largely cut off from her own body, and her mother, Dolores, who has led a life of denial of her own body, join Soveida in the reclamation of their bodies and sexual desires.

The milagrito of the face and the novel's title strongly suggest identity, personhood, wholeness, and grace, yet Soveida's path toward more thoughtfully constructed versions of these does not follow a neat, linear progression from fragmented to whole, feet to head, or lowly to superior, despite its chronology. The milagrito images that adorn the sections of the novel do not correspond to a straight path either, although the titles following the celestial hierarchy of angels are linear. The novel thereby opens a gap between the meanings of the visual and of the literary, which prompts us to consider the significance of this contrast. What work do these milagrito images do in the text? W. J. T. Mitchell suggests we can read the graphic realm or "virtual visuality" of literature in its "images, figures, inscriptions, projections of the space" or in the "heavily descriptive," or ekphrastic, aspects of texts.[60] Mitchell therefore suggests: "literature becomes not just a temporal art . . . but also a spatial art, involving the projection of virtual spaces, places, and landscapes."[61] As readers, we enter into these virtual spaces through the textual descriptions offered. In this case, we inhabit Agua Oscura, New Mexico, as Chávez has constructed it. The graphic images of milagritos included in the text perform a double function: remembering/imagining and projecting space. Literally, they display a part of the body as the site of story or memory, and figuratively, they represent the space of the altar where prayers are offered. We might then read these graphics in *Face of an Angel*'s as the suggestion of an alternative sacred space.[62] For as David Carrasco notes, "in the religious imagination a sacred place can be anywhere there is a revelation of the spiritual resources and destiny of a people."[63] *Face of an Angel* does not pretend it is a sacred text, but the milagritos convey the idea that the encounter with the sacred is not limited to any one place or time, that it occurs in the everyday. Furthermore, if, as Mitchell suggests, "the really foundational moment of visual culture . . . is *the seeing of other people and the experience of being seen*, what Lacan called the field of the 'eye and the gaze' and the domain of the scopic drive,"[64] then *Face of an Angel*'s use of the milagritos as tokens that make prayer, spiritual communion, and the sacred visible is of a piece with its rich descriptive detail and overarching concern with the acts of both seeing and being seen (especially how women are seen and not seen in its pages). The novel thereby investigates the conjoined visual, literary, and discursive construction of gendered subjectivities and spiritualities.

Recognizing the ways that the visual spurs memory and imagination, we can read the spiritually themed graphics of the novel as reminders of religious devotion and spiritual connection through which we experience both the presence and the promise of the divine.[65] However, the order of angels corresponds to dominant Christian theology while the milagrito images depicting human bodies, everyday events, or ordinary things belong to the popular religiosity of Mexicans and Chicano/as, a transnational spiritual practice. The incorporation of a popular religious practice, or religiosity from below, in such a prominent way directs our attention to the novel's engagement with spiritual mestizaje as well as its representation of Mexicano/a and Chicano/a religiosity.[66] The recognition that milagritos are "so much [a] part of Mexican culture" and that they represent "the prayers we send into the world" is offered by Chávez as a key reason for her inclusion of the images in the novel. She also notes that these sometimes come in the form of bottles of alcohol, ears of corn, cars, houses, or any number of ordinary things.[67] Chávez's choice echoes that of other Chicano/a artists and writers who have frequently reworked the spiritual symbols, icons, images, and practices of pre-Columbian, Mexicano/a, and Chicano/a cultures in the creation of new cultures, aesthetics, and spiritualities and in envisioning subaltern subjectivities.[68] Carrasco views this ability to draw from the past as "a special gift of the religious imagination that allows people . . . [to] make a world meaningful, give it a standing center, and provide for social and spiritual renewal."[69] The inclusion of the milagritos, suggestive as they are of non-institutional spiritualities, contributes to the spiritual mestizaje represented in and by *Face of an Angel* by staging a union of body/spirit and projecting a virtual space for new spiritual formations.

Fashioning a New House

Over the course of the novel, Soveida moves from uncritical and idealized acceptance of received religious knowledge and its parallel in the adherence to gender norms that constrain women, through unsatisfying and heart-breaking relationships with men who are dependent upon women serving them, to the development of her own physical and intellectual power as a working woman, and the beginnings of a new kind of community, epito-mized in the makeover of her grandmother Lupita's house for herself with the assistance of her mother, Dolores; her house cleaner, Chata; and Lupita. The coming to consciousness that *Face of an Angel* narrates accepts mul-tiple subject positions—worker, believer, woman, Chicana—and the ability to link these as critical to a Chicana feminist consciousness. Perhaps this is one reason that the seraphim, which are six-winged creatures, work as a signifier of this new awareness.

Each section of the novel marks the journey toward a feminist under-standing of experience and the consequent effort, as Ralph Rodriguez sug-gests, to "imagine new lines of connection."[70] Revising Cherríe Moraga's notion of the need to "[make] familia from scratch / each time all over again,"[71] Rodriguez proposes that we scratch familia, that is, that what is called for is to "trouble our own understandings of what we take family to be, never blindly accepting preconceived notions of what *familia* is."[72] Soveida's journey includes moments of insight that further the develop-ment of a new mestiza consciousness as well as the redeployment of this consciousness in continued transformation—her spiritual mestizaje. In this process, the angels signal not the achievement of a stage or an "arrival" but instead, according to Chávez, the company throughout her journey of those "beings who guard and protect us."[73] The section titles, therefore, refer to Soveida's spiritual helpers. Accordingly, the final two sections of the novel, "Cherubim" and "Seraphim," mark not narrative closure but the spiritual and social awakenings that make transformation possible. When Soveida observes that Luardo, her father, "taught me what love was through his lovelessness, and what loyalty was, and yes, trust, through his lack of both," she indicates that her journey has, in many ways, been one of unlearning.[74]

The three principal female characters in this novel, Soveida, Dolores/ Dolly, and Mamá Lupita, ultimately renounce the ideal of womanhood that their fathers, husbands, and priests uphold. This includes a renewed commitment to each other, one that had been previously eclipsed by their adherence to a patriarchal authority that kept them apart and "looking the other way" when the men in their lives caused harm.[75] Each woman also experiences a renewed relation to the sacred. For example, Mamá Lupita, a deeply religious woman (she goes daily to Mass, paints her house blue in honor of the Blessed Mother, makes pilgrimage to the Basilica of Guadalupe), develops an interest in studying women in the Bible, but more importantly, rejects her earlier racism. Dolores becomes Dolly, a woman freed from an oppressive tradition of subservience to men to pursue her interests and desires. Soveida's transformations unfold gradually through her work, education, and family relations. The final scenes of the novel featuring her domestic rearrangements mark these shifts with reference to material changes, such as the commemorative plate of Pope John Paul's visit to Mexico that she places in the "donate to charity" box or her decision to paint her new home in shades of purple, white, blue, and turquoise in the fashion of her ancestors.[76] Soveida's renewed relation to the sacred is perhaps most evident in her description of the landscape around her:

> The yard was still, except for the growing song of the cicadas. Thunder rumbled in the distance, and lightning cracked the sky behind the Lagrimas. I could smell rain. I would sit outside and await its approach. Surely it would come and nourish the yellow and blue desert flowers in the sand, the white yucca flowers by the side of the winding road, the ocotillo's red-tipped tendrils waving to the seemingly empty sky, the nopal's sweet, blood-red fruit.[77]

In this observation, Soveida turns away from fear and toward the beauty and grace of her place in the world. Finally, the unexpected death of Oralia Milcantos, Lupita's live-in companion, awakens in all three women a deeper understanding of the possibility for empowering love and affection among women.[78]

The milagrito of a woman's face that accompanies this section, her features barely defined and partially hidden in shadow, echoes the shape of Oralia's life with the Dosamantes family and the unseen potential of women that Oralia's dying makes visible. As maid, companion, and generational peer to Mamá Lupita, Oralia has served the Dosamantes women, as they all remember upon her death, with love, affection, and sisterhood. However, Oralia's death raises narrative questions. Since she is the character most closely linked to indigenous spiritualities, does her death suggest the passing of this way of life? Or reinscribe the invisibility of native women? Or indicate the end of an oppressive ideal of service? Why does she, rather than the Christian Mamá Lupita, who also experiences a brush with mortality, die? Oralia emerges from out of the shadows at the moment of her death, her face and spirit visible to all and their love for her also out in the open, but the belatedness of the recognition is inescapable.

Oralia Milcantos—whose surname means "a thousand songs" and is reminiscent of the centrality of song in Nahua culture—perhaps represents another disjunction in the articulation of Chicana subjectivity. Norma Alarcón notes the conflictive position of "the figure and referent of the Chicana today" as "the descendant of native women who are continuously transformed into mestizas, Mexicans, émigrés to Anglo-America, Chicanas, Latinas, Hispanics—there are as many names as there are namers."[79] Reclaiming indigeneity through the use of the word *Chicana* historicizes the intersections of gender, race, class, and nation, but it is not equal to nor can it substitute for *indigenous woman*. Although implicit in the novel's representation of Oralia, this understanding is undermined by the character's removal from the text by death.

In contrast to the novel's opening focus on marriage and heterosexual union, the final chapter focuses on a group of women cleaning out Mamá Lupita's house, which she has given to Soveida. The gathering of Soveida, Dolly, Mamá Lupita, and Chata suggests that active solidarity rather than biology constitutes family. The four women, however, are not enshrined as a new model family. Instead, they represent a network of nurturing and supportive relationships that includes Mae Lu, the white masseuse who is a cousin to Soveida's deceased husband; the owners and staff of El Farol, who constitute Soveida's "other family"; and Soveida's childhood friend Lizzie, who is now a lesbian feminist nun.[80] No longer constrained by what Alarcón identifies as "a cultural order that has required the masculine protection of women to ensure their 'decency,'" the women who gather together form a new kind of kinship, for here, as Alarcón suggests, "'family' may be a misnaming in lieu of a search for a more apt term for communitarian solidarity."[81]

Sexual Violence in the Construction of Self

While the impact of prevailing religious tradition comes under scrutiny in Soveida's journey of spiritual mestizaje, her narrative addresses an even more foundational discourse in the formation of the female subject in Western culture: the interrelated triad of sex, gender, and desire. This triad surely takes shape through religious discourse yet it is not solely an effect of religion but is instead generated by Western philosophies and ideologies and their discursive histories. Questioning the assumed immutability of the category of sex in contrast to the now presumed culturally constructed character of the category of gender, Judith Butler suggests:

> Gender ought not to be conceived merely as the cultural inscription of meaning on a pregiven sex (a juridical conception); gender must also designate the very apparatus of production whereby the sexes them- selves are established. As a result, gender is not to culture as sex is to nature; gender is also the discursive/cultural means by which "sexed nature" or "a natural sex" is produced and established as "prediscur- sive," prior to culture, a politically neutral surface *on which* culture acts. . . . At this juncture it is already clear that one way the internal stability and binary frame for sex is effectively secured is by casting the duality of sex in a prediscursive domain. This production of sex as the prediscursive ought to be understood as the effect of the apparatus of cultural construction designated by *gender*.[82]

Butler's interrogation suggests the impossibility of locating any original, essential, or foundational sex prior to the mechanisms of social regulation. Her analysis of how sex, gender, and desire are mutually constituted through discourse and furthered in strategic performance opens the possibility for seeing, imagining, and participating in critical transformations of these conceptions.[83] Chicana narratives enjoin this critical project in subjecting naturalized notions of gender and sexuality to scrutiny.

Within this framework, Butler echoes other feminist scholars in recog- nizing the paradox of an incest taboo that does not actually prevent in- cest, a taboo, as we see in this novel, that functions to dismiss or ignore incest—because it is taboo, it cannot be acknowledged—while at the same time eroticizing it. This gap between the stated aims of the law and its effects motivates Butler's feminist analysis. Drawing on Foucault's critique of the repressive hypothesis and Gayle Rubin's work on the genealogy of sex and power, Butler questions the assumption of a sexuality that exists prior to the law and suggests instead that the law produces both normative and transgressive sexualities.[84] Butler explains that her interest in sex and gender transformations, which the separation between prediscursive and discursive sex forecloses, and her examination of the law that produces and prohibits sexualities aim not to deny the materiality of bodies but instead to continually interrogate the relationship between discourse and the formation of bodies.[85]

In this instance Butler's discussion of the formation of sexuality serves to consider *Face of an Angel*'s treatment of this topic. Early in the novel, Soveida reveals that the Dosamantes family history is riddled with domestic violence, sexual abuse, and child molestation. Later, chapter 9, "The Boogeyman," begins by recalling the cautionary folktales about La Llorona, La Sebastiana, El Coco, and El Cucui in Chicano/a cultural and literary traditions. Soveida's brief and perfunctory review of these tales quickly gives way to revelations about the real bogeymen and bogeywomen in her and her cousin Mara's life: Soveida's father, Luardo, who sexually abused Mara; her grandfather Profe who beat his wife; her pedophile Tío Todosio; her breast-obsessed cousin Adrino; and a mother and grandmother who looked the other way. The chapter begins with precisely the kind of colorful and folkloric tales that Soveida cannot tell, since they cannot match the fear inspired by the real dangers that she and Mara have encountered as victims of Luardo's depredations. Paradoxically, the power of sexual prohibitions prevents the women of the Dosamantes family from even speaking about what they all appear to recognize, yet it does not prevent the sexual abuse. Soveida's growing awareness of these gaps in patriarchal social regulation of appropriate sexual desire emerges as critique. Her recollection of sexual abuse occurs, not surprisingly, with her entry into normative heterosexuality (coming of age, dating, marriage), but this fades in importance as her adult working life develops.

Even when it is discussed, *Face of an Angel* does not dwell on Luardo's depredations; indeed, Soveida does not provide any graphic detail and frequently refuses extended conversation with Mara about these topics. Is this refusal a cover-up? A way that the text manifests its unwillingness to confront some issues? A sign of its prioritizing ethnicity, race, or religion over gender and sexuality? A lapse in representing Soveida's consciousness? Her reluctance to talk with Mara about these experiences troubles the text, yet it is Soveida who shows readers this reluctance in the scenes she describes. *Face of an Angel* avoids sensationalism, including lurid details not, I suggest, in order to avoid confronting the issue, but instead to avoid further eroticization of the violation.[86] Instead, what unfolds in Soveida's narrative is an exploration of the social, political, and religious frameworks within which sexual violence occurs. The novel resists sensationalizing sexual violence by examining, as Butler does, its relationship to the varied discursive realms of the law. Significantly, Soveida's narrative connects the values, beliefs, and desires behind Luardo's sexual abuse of children with his self-perception, his sense of male entitlement, and his disregard for women generally and for Dolores in particular, and it links Mamá Lupita's and Dolores's inaction with their religious frameworks and socialization in subordination.

The issue of child molestation is never really solved in the sense of open confrontation and resolution. Soveida recalls her discovery of Luardo's abuse of Mara and the strained family conversations about Mara in which everyone seems to dance around the knowledge of it, yet readers are never provided with a scene of open revelation, confrontation, and catharsis among those involved. A younger Soveida repeats the behavior of Lupita and Dolores, for example, by refusing to hear Mara's story or avoiding the topic in conversation with her. However, in later years Soveida begins to understand that Luardo's abuse of Mara was not an aberration from his general behavior or from the dominant social norms. The gaps and limitations in the self-awareness of the Dosamentes women prevent any direct confrontation between Mara and Luardo, as well as any just resolution. This narrative irresolution reveals the importance of developing a critical consciousness, of engaging in spiritual mestizaje. It also refuses to locate a resolution solely within the private, domestic, or familial sphere, recognizing the interrelationship between that socially produced space and the discursive constructions and material realities of social relations, power, gender, and sexuality. Doris Sommer's observation that the reticence about full revelation in testimonio inhibits readers' identification with the protagonist and instead encourages an awareness of difference may illuminate

Face of an Angel's representation of sexual abuse in that the latter short-circuits readers' identification by withholding resolution on this issue, an action that also places a greater demand on readers to acknowledge multiple inequalities.

New Relations

In mapping its Chicana protagonist's journey of spiritual mestizaje, *Face of an Angel* reveals the web of discourses that contains its Chicano/a characters, and the difficult and critical path toward new embodied forms of consciousness that they repeatedly join, but Soveida's confrontation with the oppressions that limit her allow her to participate in creating a feminist spiritual praxis at novel's end. The novel remembers, and historicizes, the possibility and necessity for this transformation by referencing key twentieth-century movements for gender and race equality in its protagonist's life. Soveida's awareness of the Chicano Movement, gained through her marriage to Ivan Eloy, feeds her transformation when she recognizes his inability to see or accept women as anything other than subordinates despite his progressive politics. In another instance, feminist spirituality becomes a real option for her, in part through the knowledge that she gains from a childhood friend who believes in a female and feminist God. From its setting at the U.S.-Mexico border, *Face of an Angel* takes on a feminist transnational politics in its engagement with the conditions of work in the service industry, both domestic and commercial, that involves women and men on both sides of the border. The novel's spiritual mestizaje eschews romantic or essentialist notions of Chicano/a family, religious tradition, ethnic community, or feminist solidarity through spiritual mestizaje.[87] In its attention to the circumstances and histories (of privilege, race, dominant ideologies, national borders) attaching to each particular character's location and in its concluding portrayal of cross-border, non–biologically determined community of women, it highlights the mutability of dominating social structures. The novel's exploration of solidarity as well as difference among unique female characters links many kinds of struggle for social justice, which it firmly links to a new spiritual commitment, not one dedicated to the pieties of old, but one that can serve the future.

Memory, Witness, and Liberation in Demetria Martínez's *Mother Tongue*

In an interview published in 1999, Demetria Martínez observes that the convergence in the 1980s of testimonios by Latin American political prisoners and by women speaking out about sexual abuse influenced her conception of what became her novel *Mother Tongue* (1994).[88] In acknowledging how she drew inspiration for a novel from her response to these events and texts, Martínez underscores the dialogic nature of her discourse and lends support to a reading of her novel as a fictional testimonio. As a reporter, Martínez covered the movement in the 1980s to provide sanctuary for refugees from the war in El Salvador, but she does not write a narrative of her experience as a reporter covering this story—which would be her own testimony—nor a fiction set in El Salvador that aims to bring that period of Salvadoran history and experience more sharply into our consciousness, what Linda Craft has termed *testimonial fiction*. Instead, she creates a fictional testimonio: her protagonist, María, recounts her passage toward *concientización*. María's spiritual mestizaje occurs through her involvement with the Salvadoran solidarity movement, a journey that is both interior and social.

Mother Tongue, like *Face of an Angel*, is a narrative of spiritual becoming and social and political awakening. While its Chicana feminist spirituality is rooted in the specific imaginative, theoretical, and spiritual work of Chicana feminists, it shares in a general trend among the U.S. populace in the latter half of the twentieth century away from a traditional religiosity centered in a local branch of a religious denomination and toward more open-ended spiritual forms and practices. In his study of contemporary spirituality in the United States, Robert Wuthnow notes that a "spirituality of seeking" increased while confidence in organized religion declined over the late 1970s and through the 1980s. This seeking has created greater openness to multiple sources of spiritual connection and a stronger sense that one's relation to the divine is fluid rather than housed in one sacred space. Wuthnow attributes these changes to broader social shifts: "In settled times, people have been able to create a sacred habitat and to practice habitual forms of spirituality; in unsettled times, they have been forced to negotiate with themselves and with each other to find the sacred."[89] While *Face of an Angel* locates spiritual renewal in the feminist, ethnic, racial, and labor movements between the 1960s and the 1990s, *Mother Tongue* takes the turmoil of the U.S.-sponsored war against the people of El Salvador in the 1980s as the "unsettling" catalyst for change in the spiritual lives of María and José Luis.

The novel fluctuates between two key time frames: 1982, when María, the narrator and protagonist, and José Luis, a Salvadoran refugee, share a brief love affair; and 2002, when María—meditative, self-critical, questioning— writes the story of that time and her life since then, without José Luis, for her son, who is named after his father. A third time frame, when María and her son travel to El Salvador, forms the last section of the novel and most likely occurs in the late 1990s, since exhumations of mass graves there are on the agenda of human rights activists but have not occurred (the first was in 2000). In the first time frame, persuaded by her Aunt Soledad to help the local sanctuary movement, María meets, desires, and falls in love with José Luis, a recently arrived Salvadoran refugee who will be staying at Soledad's house. In the early 1980s a church-based movement developed in the United States to provide sanctuary to those fleeing government violence and repression in El Salvador. The Salvadoran government, long an oligarchy, sought to crush the growing popular demands for greater economic (land) and social equalities, the expansion of Christian base communities inspired by liberation theology, and guerrilla movements fighting for similar goals.[90] In *Mother Tongue*, José Luis, an activist and seminarian in El Salvador, flees his country after witnessing the brutal deaths of many of his friends and after his subjection to torture. A working-class Chicana raised by a single mother, whose death after a long illness leaves her orphaned at nineteen, María is in a different type of exile—alone, unemployed, unsure of her future, and afraid of her past. In the service of both helping José Luis and getting closer to him, María—formerly known as Mary until José in an act of solidarity returns her to her name in Spanish—also becomes involved in the solidarity movement, participating in protests, letter-writing campaigns, and educational events on the situation in El Salvador.

María indicates that her story is a form of testimony, pulled together from letters, a tape recording, newspaper clippings, journal entries, but most of all memories. She notes the problematics of "remembering" and "disremembering," the way that "for the sake of the story" she will have to make up what she doesn't recall, and sees "meaning where there may have been none."[91] Her comments create several effects. If memory is inherently social, María's difficulty in remembering measures her present distance from the communities of her past—both activist and religious. Her admission also frames her project as an interpretive work of storytelling that invites other interpretations of the narrative as readers consider the "evidence" she offers of her experiences. María's retrospection serves the construction of her contemporary subjectivity, a process that unfolds in the telling. Just as important, her memory counters prevailing historiographies that actually impede certain memories.[92] *Mother Tongue* remembers both the violence inflicted on El Salvador with U.S. government support and the gendered violence of patriarchy at a time when many sought to erase both from our collective memory—the first under the rubric of national reconciliation in El Salvador and the second through the forgetfulness that has characterized the backlash against feminism. The novel represents—in the characters of Soledad and María—what Saldívar-Hull terms a "bridge feminism" that "deconstructs geopolitical boundaries." The phrase *bridge feminism*, notes Saldívar-Hull, derives from the groundbreaking anthology *This Bridge Called My Back*, affirming not only the shared experience of oppression between people of color in the United States and in the third world but also the commitment to learn about and remember each other's struggles.[93] In section 5 of the novel, in the third time frame, María's adult son recalls a speech by the new archbishop of El Salvador, which he describes as "something about how there will be no peace until all of El Salvador's dead are named and honored, and all the killers brought to justice."[94] In this way *Mother Tongue* insists that memory must serve justice.

In line with Gayle Greene's observations that women writers generally engage in "more productive forms of memory" than mere nostalgia, María's memory in *Mother Tongue* aims for awareness, critical reconstruction, and continued self-transformation.[95] María's self-reflexive examination of her love affair with José Luis dismantles the ideology of romance and romantic love in which it presents itself. With hindsight, she recognizes in her attraction to José Luis a desire for adventure, a restless spiritual seeking, and an adherence to norms of romantic love, which allows her to examine, in the present, the motivations, desires, and gaps that led to her participation in the romantic plot. María reveals her willfulness and therefore her agency, albeit a naïve one, in creating the "story" of herself and José Luis: "Love would ripen in the light of time we spent together, like an arranged marriage. Except that I was doing the arranging. And calling it fate."[96] This confession marks one of many small turning points in María's narrative, moments that accumulate to alter her consciousness. In this instance, she experiences, as she writes, an awakening to the power of dominant paradigms and prevailing norms as well as her consent to them, an awareness essential to her ability to alter her life script.

The recognition of an earlier, misguided agency facilitates her ability to create a new story for herself. María makes this act of creation explicit in the conclusion of section 5 when she declares that she is "just beginning to discern the shape that was there all along, just beginning to become me," a statement that curiously combines creating anew—"becom[ing]"—with return or shedding: "there all along."[97] This evocation of a serpent-like renewal, her spiritual mestizaje, locates her on the road to an Anzaldúan new mestiza consciousness. In this process, she experiences a transformative spiritual and political awakening through her unflinching assessment of the workings of power and the historical resistance to it in the borderlands as these have influenced the national, social, and religious paradigms that inform her subjectivity and agency. Her new consciousness registers an appreciation for the discontinuities that mark the lives of the marginalized, since these are frequently the sites out of which new subjectivities and cultures are born.

Although the letter from José Luis to María that constitutes the epilogue indicates that María, José Luis, and their son are reunited, it does not reinscribe the romantic plot. Instead, José Luis's letter is signed in friendship. His prayer to be remembered occurs in the context of his ongoing work to aid refugees and war survivors and implies both a broader request for a spirituality that serves justice and a call to remember the war in El Salvador and its toll. María and José Luis are finally reunited, not in romantic love but in renewal of the work for justice, and she describes herself as finally having learned what Soledad told her years earlier: "the only way to take the war out of a man is to end the war, all wars."[98] *Mother Tongue* thereby critiques the romance of victimization as well as its own romantic plot line.[99]

The novel, therefore, explores not only political commitment, justice, love, and spirituality but also the nexus of these in the context of nation, gender, and religion.[100] María's remembrance of her involvement in support of Central American struggles for liberation is also her journey toward a fulfillment not defined by her relationship to a man—what, in retrospect, she describes as her life "asleep," without "a plot line." In that life, María says, "to love a man more than one's self was a socially acceptable way for a woman to be insane."[101] Both aspects of the novel's politics involve a renegotiation with religion and religious institutions, but it is different in each case. While José Luis wrestles with the calls of liberation theology and national liberation, María faces the oppressive conflation of religion, nation, and gender formation.[102] While María's voice drives the narrative, we are also privy to the journals of José Luis as the narrative constructs a tale of two people, each in flight, each on a path of spiritual seeking, who collide.[103] As she tells it, María's mestiza consciousness does not come from José Luis but from the recognition of her difference from José Luis and a critique of their respective gender and national formations. In exploring the contrasts between the meaning of nation and gender in José Luis's and María's lives, and between Guadalupe and the Mother of the Disappeared in María's life, *Mother Tongue* affirms a transnational and feminist practice of spiritual mestizaje against a politics of heroic national liberation.

Dead Women as Metaphors for Nation and Religion under Siege

The haunting moment of terror around which María's narrative revolves and which it seeks to explain is when José Luis, temporarily gripped by the memory of his brutally slain lover, Ana, attacks María, imagining that she is the soldier who has tortured and killed Ana. This violence has been foreshadowed by José Luis's journal declaration that "a bomb is ticking inside me" and, indeed, by the novel's structure of revealing, successively, ever more intimate acts of violence.[104] Yet, María's careful reconstruction of the past does not suggest that José Luis's violence against her was the natural and inevitable outcome of suppressed rage or frustration, nor solely attributable to something like post-traumatic stress disorder, although, as José Luis tells us, she does strongly encourage him to seek counseling. These may be partial explanations but they do not fully explain why José Luis attacks María and not someone else, nor why María lacks a similar propensity despite her own violent victimization. Nor does it explain the association María makes between José Luis's violence against her and the childhood experience of sexual molestation that she recalls in the moment of José Luis's attack.

One of José Luis's journal entries begins to suggest some of what leads to this particular act of violence. Wanting to but not confessing his overwhelming sense of vulnerability to María, he writes, "The problem is we're not seeing or hearing the same things."[105] We might be tempted to accept José Luis's voice here as the authority on María, that is, he sees and hears war and its aftereffects while María lives in a fantasy, but to do so would be to ignore María's voice and the possessive conflation between woman and nation that emerges in the narrative. José Luis has a hard time seeing María as an ally rather than as a well-meaning but naïve gringa whose body and sleeping pills help him to endure his exile and forget his pain, that is, a woman who is a refuge from the struggle, not part of the struggle.[106] María willingly accepts this role until her involvement in the solidarity movement deepens her consciousness so that when she sees what he sees—sees herself in his eyes—she is startled by the disparity between his view of her and her own view of herself as a Chicana.

Remembering how he looked at her in the wake of the news that several nuns had been murdered in El Salvador still pains her twenty years later. María does not excuse her own willful blindness but neither does she overlook José Luis's internalization of toxic values and beliefs. She describes his anger at her as a "dark light" that has forever "scorched his vision." Describing the same incident in his journal, José Luis regrets his anger but writes, "it is not her fault that her culture has made her who she is."[107] His condescension, lack of knowledge of the Chicano/a experience in the United States, and gendered objectification of her combine to disable him from seeing María, let alone seeing her as an ally, despite his previous hand to her as a friend. His blindness is matched by that of María, who creates romantic fantasies about herself and José Luis that obscure the real José Luis and his real dilemmas.

Blocked vision is a recurring phenomenon in this novel and represents a failure to understand the self or another, that is, the inability to surmount difference. What accounts for this blocked vision? Elizabeth Coonrod Martínez finds that the novel poses the necessity of recognizing both situations—that of Salvadorans and that of Chicana/os as minorities in the United States.[108] María and José Luis both openly confess the shortsightedness, selfishness, and lack of compassion they bring to their relationship; however, *Mother Tongue* does not suggest that their failings are exclusively personal, that is, unrelated to their interpellation by discourses of nation, race, religion, gender, sexuality, and ethnicity. What it does strongly suggest is that a concientización of that interpellation might make it possible to create new discourses, new paths. Soledad's voice plays a key role in this fictional testimonio, reminding María both in 1982 and at the moment of rereading twenty years later of the power of "social structure" and the possibilities for justice, love, and beauty in a life led with consciousness of its workings.

María's narrative accounts for her own blocked vision and traces her route toward understanding. For example, in the humorous scene of her inexplicable yet wild participation in a sale of undergarments in a store, madly grasping an iconic piece of lingerie, she indicates the pervasiveness of the gender and sexuality norms at work on her sense of what constitutes love, sexiness, or sexuality as well as her reinscription of these in performance. As Butler suggests, the "agency conditioned by those very regimes of discourse/power cannot be conflated with voluntarism or individualism, much less with consumerism, and in no way presupposes a choosing subject."[109] María's description of herself in this moment as being seized by an inexplicable desire speaks to her position in the Foucauldian power/knowledge grid. As he suggests, the "economic exploitation" of desire that arises in response to the sexual revolution is another example of how power, having produced knowledge of the body, reasserts itself to control the body. María's account of her experience in the store begins the work of making, as Foucault suggests, "unacceptable the effects of power."[110]

Her testimonio also offers a partial, subtle, and indirect account of José Luis's blocked vision. Stereotypical or clichéd understandings of each other convey the unwitting submission by each to the grids of power and knowledge that delimit their lives. María describes José Luis as a man who keeps his emotions bottled up, who deems it unmanly to cry, who fears emotional connection—in many ways, he is stereotypically masculine. But the counterpart to this masculinity is a vision of femininity in which women exist to assuage men or to represent the violated nation—woman as metaphor. The narrative repeatedly and disturbingly invokes women as victims—raped, brutally murdered, dismembered—forcing readers to ask: to what

purpose? In *Mother Tongue*, José Luis mentions the disappearance or murder of his seminary friends and the murder of Father Gustavo, but graphi-
cally describes the violations of women's bodies, including Father Gustavo's
sister and Ana, José Luis's deceased lover, while María, reading from the
daily newspaper, conveys the gory details of two nuns found murdered in
El Salvador.[111] Whether in private discourse or public media, the contrast
between the privacy accorded the male body in death versus the spectacle
of the female body in death is striking. If both nation and theology appropriate women's dead bodies in their cause, where does this leave actual
women? As a metaphor for nation, woman cannot be real, and thus, to the
extent that narratives of national liberation link woman and nation, they
also logically enact her erasure.

Writing about Central American literature of the pre- and postrevolutionary period, Ileana Rodríguez observes, "nation as rhetoric and
as fiction is feminized, and, insofar as it is an inapprehensible signifying
chain, nation (as woman) remains codified as body."[112] And she notes about
two Nicaraguan texts, "death of the state and death—murder, or disappearance—of woman occur simultaneously." In her interrogation of the equation between the woman's body and the nation in this literature, between
women's dead bodies and dead, dying, or embattled nations, Rodríguez
finds that the loss of heterosexual erotic love enacts a metonymic chain (nation, woman, heterosexual love) that is integral to the narrative valorization of (option for?) homosocial patriotic love.[113] Rodríguez's critique of
the degree to which these texts unwittingly perpetuate rhetorical violence
against women as they uphold nation is especially pertinent in examining
this novel's portrayal of the connections between Central American and
U.S. movements for change.

Mother Tongue wrestles with the problem of nationalism versus feminism not primarily as two different and allied struggles but as two movements that must be examined in relation to each other.[114] It resurrects the
metaphoric relationship between woman and nation in the context of
the U.S. war against El Salvador, where dead women's bodies signify the
death of the nation. It also recreates the metonymic chain that Rodríguez
identifies in the character of José Luis: the loss of his lover Ana signifies a
loss of nation and creates an inability to love that is healed by turning to
homosocial patriotic collectivities that act out of love for nation. José Luis's

testimonio, included in María's remembrance, describes his entry into the seminary as fulfilling an agreement with the now-slain Father Gustavo. His entry into the all-male seminary to continue the work of Father Gustavo follows the attack on his village and murder of Father Gustavo and his sister. José Luis's active engagement with a theology of liberation that includes support for efforts to achieve greater economic and social justice provides an opportunity for him to deepen his understanding of the inequalities impacting women, which is reflected in his agreement with María's stance on female ordination—an example of how the narrative presents not stereotypes but complex characters working their way through varied forms of containment.[115] However, in the United States, José Luis is plagued by doubt and guilt that he has abandoned the struggle:

> If there is courage to be found, maybe it is in the hearts of those who have headed for the mountains with guns of their own. The rebels feed the people, teach them to read and write. But they also teach them to defend what they have gained. That is the courage of choosing not to be a martyr. I thought I had made that choice, too, by coming here. . . . I am tormented, wondering if I did the right thing. Or if I should be in my country, fighting. With words. Or with guns.[116]

José Luis and María face complex dilemmas that may retrospectively appear simpler than they are. As this passage indicates, José Luis wrestles with the fear that he is a coward, that he has abandoned his nation in need, and that he is perceived as a martyr. He expresses these fears in language that contrasts the religious ("martyr") with the political ("my country, fighting"), a juxtaposition that also suggests gendered understandings of struggle (passive martyr and dead woman versus active fighter and heroic rebel). He resists being read as a martyr, passive victim, and woman. Undoubtedly this fear and anxiety are, in part, propelled by his work as someone who testifies to the atrocities in El Salvador, someone whose very body signifies victimization to the audiences he addresses. The complexity of his situation raises questions about the strategy of winning support in the United States for stopping the war in El Salvador based on a politics of sympathy and not solidarity. José Luis's journals suggest his struggles to understand some of these issues—and, as readers, we wonder whether a theology of liberation is sufficient for social transformation or whether the misapprehension or absence of a theology of liberation in the United States is the problem, that is, its confinement to a national context in El Salvador and not a transnational one across borders.

Although written to her son, María's testimonio is also an exercise in self-healing, to free herself from the pain of abandonment and violence so that she can speak openly of José Luis and give her son (who is named for his father) the father he never had, at least discursively. As she writes, María reveals that the lover whom she had willed herself to believe was dead may very well be alive. Her writing is also, therefore, preparation for the possibility of meeting José Luis again. In chronicling her movement from sympathy and passivity to a stance of compassion and action for the future, which she sees embodied in her son, she also fulfills of a *manda* or promise in gratitude for God's guidance. In return for the continued gift of life for her struggling newborn son, María had long ago promised God to tell José Luis, her son, the story of his arrival into this world, that is, she has sworn not to forget the past if they are given a present and a future. The act of making such a pledge and then carrying it out is itself an interesting aspect of María's spiritual understanding. She is not the passive martyr in this scenario whose sacrifice brings about redemption. Instead, she actively prays, promises, and fulfills that commitment, creating redemption. The past becomes present again in María's story, allowing a different outcome, when her son remembers that María once told him he has the angry streak of his father, a memory spoken aloud that enables him to confess his long-standing anger over his father's absence and to achieve some resolution. Knowing his past makes it possible for him to create a different future. But this passage also suggests that, as her son matures, María recognizes that there is a danger to him—of unacknowledged pain, of ideas for social change that are not rooted in understanding one's connection to others in the world—that must be averted with the truth, told compassionately and honestly, the promise fulfilled.

A Chicana Feminist Journey of Spiritual Becoming

In keeping with the metafictional strategies of this narrative, José Luis's struggle with the nexus of liberation theology and national liberation is not readily apparent but must be deciphered through an examination of the series of texts within the text. Similarly, but in reverse, María's efforts to remake the connections between religion, nation, gender formation, and sexuality span her past diaries and her present narrative. Between her earlier resistance to normative paradigms and her return to San Rafael Church lies a journey of spiritual mestizaje defined by a recognition of both the gifts and obstacles that she has inherited from her religious history as an individual and as a Chicana, and the development of a spiritual practice inclusive of the varied religious traditions that guide her life in the present. María arrives at an appreciation for an activist spiritual life in union with others—even across national boundaries—and an understanding of the possibility for constructing a feminist spirituality. Her return to San Rafael Church represents not a return to the fold but a renewed spiritual practice that now includes an appreciation for Catholic faith rather than unthinking loyalty to dogma.

From the beginning and throughout the journal entries from the 1982 period, María describes herself as a confused spiritual seeker: "I saw myself whispering his false name by the flame of my Guadalupe candle. . . . Before his arrival the chaos of my life had no axis about which to spin. Now I had a center. A center so far away from God that I asked forgiveness in advance."[117] She invokes both the Babylonian goddess of love and war and the mestiza and syncretic figure of Guadalupe, yet in her testimonio María is critical of her youthful, undirected search for a relevant spirituality. While she finds sacred inspiration in multiple traditions, María the author of this testimonio, rather than María the subject of the testimonio, retrospectively checks her selective citation of spiritual influences and her blindness against the example of spiritual mestizaje offered by her Aunt Soledad.

In the first time frame of the novel, María's longing for, alienation from, and appreciation of her cultural inheritances are apparent in her observations about San Rafael Church and its members and indicative of the histories and commitments she negotiates. She declares herself envious of the solid faith of the old women parishioners but only watches them from afar.[118] Her admiration of these women is, in part, an acknowledgment of her history as a Chicana in New Mexico, a descendant of Bernardina de Salas y Trujillo, the woman who had mixed "straw and mud to coat the church's outer walls" a century earlier. San Rafael Church represents both the Mexican settlement of New Mexico and a history of dispossession that continues to mark María's identity and that of the Chicano/a community;

she notes after overhearing the conversation of the old men who gather in the plaza near San Rafael: "They wondered aloud, as they did every year, whether the heat was not a sign from God, a punishment for having sold so much land to the gringos from back East." Dispossession is most evident in one of the central tropes of the novel: language. Through the letters of Soledad, we learn that María is reclaiming her mother tongue, Spanish, a project that José Luis helps her with and that represents the process of recovery and reappraisal in which María is engaged.[119] This attention to the marginalization of Chicano/as in the United States against the increasing tendency, spurred by globalization, of viewing U.S. populations as homogeneously complicit in their government's international policies underscores already existing fractures in the nation.

Spanish is a sign both of removal—the Spanish-speaking population displaced by the arrival of Anglos—and of invisibility since the Spanish-speaking are not really seen by those around them and for whom they work. María reflects that the tourists could not see José Luis, that he, along with the numerous other Spanish-speaking refugees who gardened and cleaned in the city, who lacked the resources to "reinvent themselves," "became empty mirrors. A ghostly rustle of Spanish spoken in restaurants above the spit of grease on a grill." Eventually she reclaims her name, changing from Mary to María, but the moment in which this happens is not a joyous rebirth; she desperately identifies herself, saying, "It's me, María," to ward off José Luis's fists as he lapses into a hallucination of the war in El Salvador.[120]

María's utterance releases a repressed memory of childhood sexual abuse, one that is linked in her mind to the televised images of the Vietnam War during her victimization, creating another association between the wars of the nation and violence against women. The memory of the war in Vietnam (ostensibly waged to protect national security interests against the supposed rising threat of communism) is coded into María's memory of the violation of her body, emphasizing her erasure by the discourses of the nation. She remembers this not only because she is once again subject to violence, but because in this moment of violence her body—like the women's dead bodies used in discourses of national liberation—is the body sacrificed by José Luis in his struggle with the effects of victimization. Her words become an assertion of self that her childhood abuser had somehow "canceled" out, she recalls. In the narrative present, "It's me, María" represents the memories, experiences, observations, and meditations that María weaves together to construct a contemporary self. It is, too, a statement of presence that is simultaneously a recognition of the knowledge stored in her body that she must synthesize into her spiritual and rational being. This process leads María toward a transnational perspective in her ongoing journey of spiritual mestizaje, evident in her more active involvement in movements for world peace, her son's interest in global environmental issues, and most tellingly in her adoption of devotion to the Mother of the Disappeared.

Recreating her relation to the sacred is also her rebirth into a new self. This difficult process calls her to critically assess and historicize her identity on the U.S.-Mexico border. In *Mother Tongue*, María moves from disconnection from her past to doubt of her past, which, as Greene suggests, distinguishes treatments of memory in feminist fiction: "Memory is our means of connecting past and present and constructing a self and versions of experience we can live with. To doubt it is to doubt ourselves, to lose it is to lose ourselves; yet doubt it we must, for it is treacherous."[121] For Greene, feminist fiction disallows "complacency about the past," and feminist metafiction concerned with memory, in particular, exposes the discursive construction of the normative values and beliefs that impact behavior.[122] *Mother Tongue*'s fragmentary quality, its questioning of memory as much as its recourse to memory, its inclusion of multiple witnesses and retrospective telling underscore the necessity for doubt and the engagement that doubt represents in María's journey and transformation. The novel adopts Anzaldúa's unceasing epistemic inquiry.

María's implicit critique of Catholicism emerges in the interstitial spaces between her memories and other texts and includes the learned association between sexuality and "wrongdoing" and the gender discrimination that prevents women from serving in the clergy. What she arrives at, in the end, is that women of faith have and might continue to make of Catholicism something useful in their lives, a renewed spirituality that departs from the doctrinal rigidity of an institutional church. Her testimonio presents various aspects of her spiritual dilemma, and the narrative charts her journey toward an awareness that can begin to resolve it.

Running throughout the narrative is a recognition of the continuity, rupture, creation, and recreation simultaneously at work in the formation of collectives and individuals. While retrospectively more aware of her spiritual formation, María's testimonio identifies her nascent consciousness in her contemplation of a photo from 1982 of her home altar, a collection of Christian and indigenous sacred objects:

> Santo Niño de Atocha, a Christ child on a throne who wears out his shoes as he wanders around each night doing good deeds; miniature Taos Pueblo incense burner; painting of Our Lady of Guadalupe from Nogales; African fertility doll, her coal-black head shaped like pita bread; mouthwash bottle filled with holy water Soledad had a priest bless; a film canister full of healing earth from the sanctuary at Chimayó. I liked it that José Luis and I made love in the presence of my santos. I knew they had blessed my love for him, however imperfect it was, however mad. They were not like the white God I'd had to kill, that women like me must kill if we are to have any hope of ever finding God. Nothing replaced Him for a long time. But looking back now I can see that the growing chaos inside blazed away dead growth, clearing a space, however violently, for God to be reborn.[123]

María apprehends herself as a raced, gendered, sexual, and spiritual subject in this retrospective evaluation more profoundly than she did previously. Earlier, she was critical of her appropriation of Eastern goddesses and religious texts as uncentered and naïve; here, she appraises her openness to the multiple spiritual traditions of the Americas as necessary to her ability to reconcile the body and the soul in her spiritual practice. She is stymied in this by a religious education that repressed her sexuality and so it is not surprising that María seeks to resolve the split between her spirituality and her sexuality.

Although José Luis tells us that María admires his religious commitment, María does not embrace his Catholicism, even if it is a liberation theology, because for her it has ceased to have meaning, signifying repression and submission in both her mother's and her own life. Instead, she seeks a spiritual practice and a faith in which she can fully participate. Soledad is a key figure in this narrative, for hers is the voice of experience—teacher, elder—in negotiating race, religion, gender, and nation, the voice that guides María from afar even after her death. Soledad provides a connection—through her engagement with Catholicism, popular religious practices, indigenous and alternative spiritualities, and activists of other faiths—to a spiritual mestizaje that María slowly appreciates and through which she becomes more deeply aware of the complex spiritual history and multiple religious traditions that are her inheritance as a Chicana subject. María learns, in part, that this is a life work.

Yet Soledad's presence in the narrative is also an absence: in 1982 she writes from afar, and when María writes her testimonio she has already passed. To the degree that she is present in the narrative, Soledad is a mobile figure, capable of adopting a variety of protective coverings that might be necessary for survival or justice. She resembles Chela Sandoval's subject with a differential consciousness, but is also capable of transformation through a conscious and critical appraisal of what she has inherited akin to Gloria Anzaldúa's shape-shifting new mestiza.[124] Soledad can adhere to a religious gender norm—marriage within the church—without internalizing toxic aspects of the norm. This is a repetition with difference that knows, acknowledges, and alters the norm, à la Butler, and the maintenance of space for resistance, à la James C. Scott's "hidden transcript."[125] This mobility, however, is not entirely a choice; it is, to a large degree, made necessary by the discourses and materialities that maintain asymmetries of gender, race, class, and sexuality.

As Martínez explains, she views María's process as the acquisition of a political consciousness of local and global inequalities wedded to a spiritually driven struggle for justice, a vision that can draw María and José Luis together in alliance:

> What happens in the novel is that María comes to understand more intimately the nature of power and structural evil. She sees that evil is not just a series of individual acts by people with good intentions, but that it is integral to the systems in which we live, whether you call that system patriarchy, imperialism, etc. I think the object, as you say, wasn't to compare or to ask the question who has suffered the most, but to think about the political roots of all pain. When we can understand the roots of our own pain, first, we realize we're not alone, and the healing begins. We forgive ourselves. And second, we can build coalitions with other people we thought were really different, whose pain we previously could not understand.[126]

Martínez reiterates a view expressed by Cherríe Moraga and echoed by Lourdes Torres and others that the recognition of one's particular oppression has the potential to open one to solidarity with those suffering other forms of oppression.[127] Justice can only be created through recognition of local and global circumstances, suggesting that what constitutes justice must be negotiated by those in search of it.[128] In remembering and reconstructing a spirituality that serves justice, *Mother Tongue* redefines the meaning of suffering. Rather than simply accepting suffering as that into which we are born, which we must endure until heavenly redemption, María's story presents suffering as the route by which she recognizes and embraces solidarity with others in struggle.

Transnational Spiritual Mestizaje: From Guadalupe to the Mother of the Disappeared

Despite her love and admiration for both Soledad and José Luis, María does not adopt liberation theology as a route for returning to Catholicism. Why not? She appears to adopt its views of compassion and solidarity as faith in action, God's commitment to the poor, and "critical reflection on praxis,"[129] yet attributes many of her steps in transformation to other experiences and encounters, including her relationship to her son, the "medicine" of storytelling, the counsel of mestiza Soledad, the small acts of justice and mercy that characterize the life of her new lover, and finally, her encounter with the Mother of the Disappeared. That the figures of Our Lady of Guadalupe and the Mother of the Disappeared bookend this narrative suggests a circularity and return, though clearly with a difference.[130] The images indicate the centrality of sacred female figures in María's spirituality. However, these two sacred figures at opposite ends of the narrative suggest a shift. Does María move from veneration of one brown-skinned, female figure of the divine to another? Despite distancing herself from Catholicism when she meets José Luis in 1982, her devotion to Guadalupe continues, and images of Guadalupe appear throughout her home. At a time in her life when María feels able to explore her sexuality outside of the strictures of the church—to know lust, desire, sex, and orgasm through experience—she repeatedly invokes Guadalupe as her spiritual guide and companion. In this she is not alone. In a nonfiction work, Chicana author Sandra Cisneros also hails Guadalupe as a companion in her discovery of her sexual self:

When I look at *la Virgen de Guadalupe* now, she is not the Lupe of my childhood, no longer the one in my grandparents' house in Tepeyac, nor is she the one of the Roman Catholic Church, the one I bolted the door against in my teens and twenties. Like every woman who matters to me, I have had to search for her in the rubble of history. And I have found her. She is Guadalupe the sex goddess, a goddess who makes me feel good about my sexual power, my sexual energy, who reminds me that I must, as Clarissa Pinkola Estés so aptly put it, "[speak] from the vulva . . . speak the most basic, honest truth," and write from my *panocha*.[131]

María's testimonio conveys both reverence for and intimacy with Guadalupe and with every one of the santos on her altar. The presence of Guadalupe in her life suggests that the sacred is mobile, with her, a way of being in the world with love.

Various studies of Guadalupe agree on the significance of her presence as an Indian, that is, of race and ethnicity to the newly converted or converting indigenous population as well as the criollo and mestizo elites of New Spain.[132] To the extent that gender has entered into analyses of historical accounts of Guadalupe or doctrinal debates on her significance, it has been limited to largely uncritical readings of her primacy as Holy Mother. Jeanette Rodríguez updates these analyses of Guadalupe's meaning in women's lives, while Chicana literature and art have reframed the significance of Guadalupe as either an indigenous goddess or an Indian woman (versus Indian mother) whose image foregrounds gender oppression.[133]

Guadalupe has traditionally been viewed as both the mother of the church and the mother of the nation; the two discourses have been intertwined since the earliest accounts of her appearance. Both Jacques Lafaye and D. A. Brading note that Miguel Sánchez's famous seventeenth-century work on Guadalupe is inspired by the view that Guadalupe's image is that of the Woman of the Apocalypse who appeared to St. John the Evangelist, representing both Mary, the mother of God, and the church.[134] In Sánchez's view, according to Brading, Guadalupe established the Americas for the church and the Mexican nation:

Only the Mexican Church owed its existence to the direct intervention of the Mother of God. In effect, the discovery of the New World marked a new stage not merely in the institutional life of the Catholic Church, but also in its spiritual development, since the apparition of the Guadalupe image signified that the peoples of Mexico, not to say America, had been chosen for her protection. It was in recognition of that unique distinction that it later became common to inscribe copies of the image with an epigraph taken from Psalm 147, "Non fecit taliter omni natione," "It was not done thus to all nations."[135]

Although Sánchez referred to the Mexico City of New Spain in the seventeenth century, the association between Guadalupe and what would become the Mexican nation was set. She adorned the banners of those fighting for independence from Spanish rule in 1810, and a century later her image accompanied the movement for land led by Emiliano Zapata.[136]

While these facts about Guadalupe's presence in social and political struggles are often cited, it is equally important to consider the specific implications of these conflations. In the immediate postrevolutionary period, according to Marjorie Becker, Catholic elites and the church promoted a spirituality that encouraged submission:

> It was a symbolic system largely based on gender that called for a self-denial that the priests referred to as purity. That is, Catholic elites had developed a symbolic system that depended on an understanding and acceptance both of women's actual abnegation and of that abnegation as a metaphor designed to restrain the potential nonconformity of Indians, peasants, workers, all subordinate groups.[137]

Religious services where the poor were clearly separated from the rich, pastoral documents that counseled the submission of women to men, and church praise for the entrepreneurial success of *hacendados* contributed to maintaining an economic and political system that favored big landowners over workers and men over women.[138] Becker suggests that within this religious system Guadalupe figured prominently as the mother of the poor, and there was much encouragement for devotion to her as a balm that was personal and intimate:

> Consciously or not, priests offered their blessing to the widespread tendency to cradle her image in the hand and to confide to her an array of grievances and longings. They even tolerated the tendency of poor

Ario women to imagine the stamped images of the Virgin on paper as the incarnation—rather than the representation—of the Virgin. They loosened the tendency to appropriate Mary, to use her in personal ways for personal problems.[139]

Peasants and indigenous people accepted this encouragement from the Church and elites as they also welcomed efforts by Lázaro Cárdenas and his government to empower campesinos. Becker notes that "secular missionaries," or officials and employees of the Mexican government in Michoacán in this period, promoted equality, education, modern health practices, and land rights. The anti-religious or anti-clerical views that held sway in the Cárdenas administration yielded somewhat, in this case, to the views of the campesinos and indigenous populations of Michoacán, who drew from the discourses of both Catholic elites and secular missionaries in fashioning a government that would live up to the ideals of the Mexican Revolution and respect what she describes as "the campesinos' view that invisible realities, even possibilities, deserved meticulous care."[140] As Becker observes, the revolutionary movement's welcoming of women into the public sphere as "helpmeets of revolutionary men" was not unlike the traditional role assigned them in a church-dominated society: women remained subordinate to men even under liberal rule.[141] The return of a public Catholicism, therefore, represented the ability of male peasants and campesinos to craft an order more favorable for them:

> From a short-term, local perspective, the peasants had collaborated
> with Cárdenas to resolve festering problems. The culture of purity
> and redemption would no longer be the same. While the church doors
> swung open again, and while La Purísima's message of modesty and
> public powerlessness was still considered potent for women, the combi-
> nation of a land redistribution and a secular framework provided men
> with alternatives. No longer did they need to view God as celestial ar-
> chitect, drafting elaborate plans for landowners' homes and scribbling
> cramped afterthoughts to house the poor.[142]

Becker's analysis illuminates the intersections of religious, national, class, ethnic, and gender discourses in the making and remaking of Guadalupan devotion. While Becker does not equate this with doctrinal change she does suggest the significance that discourses in the popular renewal of faith had on effecting local change.[143] Although focused on one region, Becker's work provides insight on the gendering of religion and spirituality in the national project as well as the deep-seated faith in Guadalupe.

As one of the holy figures that blesses her "imperfect" love against the judgment of an imagined white, male God, Guadalupe is an intimate presence to María in a difficult time, not unlike Guadalupe the intimate friend and confidante imagined in other Chicano/a fiction. She is also the indigenous goddess of the Americas to whom María turns at a moment in life when race and ethnicity figure prominently in her identity. It may be that Guadalupe also represents a more abstract mother figure for María at this stage of life. Yet the historical meanings illuminated by Brading, Lafaye, Becker, and others that attach to Guadalupe may also be the reason that María's adoption of a devotion to the Mother of the Disappeared seems to replace or eclipse her devotion to Guadalupe. María's confrontation with the ways that discourses of gender and nation have colluded to erase women might be kept in mind when considering her early devotion to Guadalupe and late devotion to the Mother of the Disappeared, especially since Guadalupe is a symbol of church and nation. Néstor García Canclini's observation that there is typically little room for critical discussion of objects or practices that constitute a national cultural patrimony would suggest that what appears to be María's turn from Guadalupe to the Mother of the Disappeared indicates a shift from what has perhaps become an overdetermined figure to one representative of contemporary concerns and needs.[144] María does not overtly express this, yet while she describes Guadalupe as a part of her devotion in 1982 she makes no mention of any continuing devotion in the period thereafter where she defines herself spiritually as a Quaker and politically as a peace activist.

The incorporation of the Mother of the Disappeared into her pantheon, however, brings María back to San Rafael Church, and this new incarnation of a brown-skinned holy woman represents a renewal, with difference, of the promise and protection of Guadalupe. When María prays to the Mother of the Disappeared, she invokes her protection for Chicanas, joining those in El Salvador who have done likewise. The Mother of the Disappeared now appears as a sacred figure representing those struggling for justice across national boundaries, in contrast to the historically nationalist apprehension of Guadalupe; the Mother of the Disappeared becomes, for María, a symbol of transnational feminist struggle and of a socially relevant church. The Mother of the Disappeared is also more closely tied in the public imagination with actual "children," and this may appeal to the mature María, now herself a mother. Since María's testimonio treats the latter not with a conservative traditional perspective of motherhood as women's service, sacred vocation, and biological imperative but instead as a connection to being in the world and a commitment to its future, her new devotion would be fitting.[145] María's return to San Rafael Church, in this reading, renews her relation to the sacred in a way that codifies her rejection of both normative gender and sexuality and the ethnic and national oppressions that continue to operate in her life. The Mother of the Disappeared is revered by those in struggle, both women and men who have suffered through nationalist wars, and represents their demands for justice. The author of *Mother Tongue*, Demetria Martínez, discussing her poetry and fiction, describes just this kind of renewal when she states: "Part of the journey is stripping away who we imagine God to be and allowing new images of God to emerge to speak to the times."[146]

María's renewed spirituality allows her to fully recognize in her Aunt Soledad a model of spiritual practice that is also grounded in the struggle, historic and contemporary, to eliminate inequalities. The novel's portrayal of Soledad draws from the experiences of Chicana feminist and liberation theology movements of the 1970s and 1980s in shaping new spiritual praxis. For Chicana feminists within the Catholic Church, this meant lobbying for greater inclusion of women in all aspects of church life.[147] Other Latino/a movements within the church lobbied for greater ethnic sensitivity, as is evident in the proposals advanced in 1972 by the first national encuentro for Spanish-speaking leaders of the church in the United States, which included:

> that basic Christian communities become a priority; that women be ordained as deacons; that non-territorial parishes be established for the Spanish-speaking; that mature married men be considered as possible candidates for the priesthood; that the training of all candidates for the priesthood in all the dioceses of the United States should include formation in spoken Spanish and Hispanic culture.[148]

These proposals suggest that the church was out of touch with its Latino/a members and prompt us to consider how this context might be present in the novel as a backdrop for María's alienation from San Rafael Church. The 1972 encuentro voiced support for the practice of liberation theology by calling for "base communities," which are gatherings, according to Leonardo Boff and Clodovis Boff, where adherents "read the Bible and compare it with the oppression and longing for liberation in their own lives."[149] While this movement created an opportunity for women to participate in formulating theology, argues María Pilar Aquino, it remained an androcentric movement focused primarily on political and economic tensions in the public sphere rather than violence in the private sphere with little, if any, attention to the politics of gender and sexuality.[150] While María expresses sympathy for José Luis's liberation theology, she does not appear to join in the movement, though she remains active in social justice issues, until much later in life upon her return from El Salvador. In contrast, Aunt Soledad opts to work within this system and finds many like-minded believers within the church with whom she can work.[151] Soledad provides an alternative model of politically engaged womanhood for María, as well as valuable resources and counsel. In a letter to María she recalls her long-standing involvement in political issues and her deeply rooted faith. An immigrant, Soledad's dedication to a borderless world eventually leads her to participation in the sanctuary and solidarity movements, indicating how the socially and historically significant concerns of Chicanas in relation to the border take on an international character in the context of global politics.

Soledad marries and divorces four times in her life. None of these facts of her life diminish her spirituality, the calm faith that allowed her, as María says, the "energy to try and change the world."[152] Soledad is perhaps the fictional counterpart of the feminist activists within the Catholic Church in the 1980s that are the subject of Mary Fainsod Katzenstein's work—a movement that grew and manifested in a variety of voluntary associations and small organizations that advocated female ordination, altered the rules governing women religious, and participated in Central American solidarity work and gay rights activism. For feminists in the Catholic Church, women's issues were part of social justice work. However, as Katzenstein observes, the church hierarchy sought to silence these dissenters, especially those pressing for female ordination.[153] María's memories of Soledad and the inclusion of Soledad's voice in the form of her letters to María serve to incorporate the story of this intra-religious movement into the witness of the borderlands experience, creating a polyphonic counter-memory to the official stance of the church.

Just as the novel's narrative voices suggest multiple churches, so too does its attention to the sites of resistance. Of necessity, the sanctuary movement operates underground, skirting official spaces. Consequently, Soledad's home, María's home—in the shadow of San Rafael Church—and places such as Sandoval's barbershop become focal points for much of the movement's sheltering, organizing, and lobbying efforts in opposition to a government acting in complicity with the Salvadoran regime. As Scott notes, intimates in experience and struggle require space away from the dominant gaze in order to organize opposition, what he terms the "hidden transcript." In *Mother Tongue*, ordinary neighborhood locations become these sites. However, as Scott suggests, these are not "merely the social space left empty by domination" but are "won, cleared, built, and defended."[154] Soledad's many security instructions, including "assume the phone is tapped until proved otherwise," represent vigilance in maintaining room for oppositional politics.[155]

Scott outlines the "public transcript of domination" as consisting of the following: "a domain of material appropriation (for example, of labor, grain, taxes), a domain of public mastery and subordination (for example, rituals of hierarchy, deference, speech, punishment, and humiliation), and, finally, a domain of ideological justification for inequalities (for example, the public religious and political world view of the dominant elite)."[156]

Soledad's instructions to María echo this description of domination as she schools her niece in the art of outward deference—what to tell the immigration authorities, how to dress José Luis in a "Yale sweatshirt" and a "Harvard T-shirt"—and privately counsels her on the injustice of the U.S. government's position in El Salvador.[157] It is not surprising then that María's estrangement from the church coincides with her initiation into resistance. Sanctuary and solidarity activists, feminist activists, and adherents of liberation theology in the United States, despite enormous vitality, were not the official voices of the church. However, in Latin America, liberation theologians have been significant voices for change and were, as the novel portrays, influential in movements for social change. In Chile, for example, the liberation theology movement was key in forming a committee to monitor human rights under Pinochet that later became the official church Vicariate of Solidarity (which prevented the junta from dismantling it).[158]

Mother Tongue does not assert an equivalence between María's suffering and that of José Luis—María recognizes the disparity in their suffering—but poses the necessity for them to work in concert to achieve liberation and explores the conditions for and terms of such an alliance. Similar to *Face of an Angel*, *Mother Tongue* expresses a strong ethos of understanding oneself in relation to both others and the world that requires Buddhist mindfulness. Indeed, taking strength from Eastern spiritualities, María reminds herself to stay present at various points in the narrative. Thich Nhat Hanh describes mindfulness as a *practice* of presence to oneself and to others that can move through varying degrees to make transformation possible.[159] We might read María's narrative as a Buddhist search for awareness and full presence—as a Chicana, a sexual and spiritual being, and an activist. Although María no longer sees one Buddhist saying as the sum of all wisdom, through her journey of spiritual mestizaje she has incorporated some of its teachings into her new mestiza consciousness. The novel honors the routes by which women have engaged in social change in their particular locations by focusing on María's renewed commitment to a just spiritual praxis, which can be achieved by negotiating the points at which gender, sexuality, race, and class intersect in struggles for justice. The novel's pairing of the Salvadoran struggle against brutal repression and a Chicana struggle against violation and imposed silence becomes the occasion for a consideration of the path toward a feminist, transnational, new mestiza consciousness and spirituality.

Arrivals: Definitive and Provisional

Face of an Angel and *Mother Tongue* represent the struggles of working-class women who are also simultaneously raced and gendered subjects in an inhospitable imagined nation. In contrast to testimonial fiction that bears witness to a historical struggle by fictionalizing it or the testimonial novel, these works present the process of coming to consciousness in fictional form, with characters that represent individual spiritual mestizajes.[160] Through memory, these novels uncover the intimate relationship between the public and personal and the political and spiritual.[161] One way they perform this work is through an interrogation of the discursive constructions and material realities of women's bodies, especially Chicana bodies, often against the background of a history of misrepresentation—as metaphor, as ever-available sexual object, and so on. These novels cross borders to address the struggles of other women and workers; *Face of an Angel* depicts the resistance of El Farol's restaurant staff and the Mexican women who perform domestic labor, and *Mother Tongue* represents the victims of U.S.-backed violence in El Salvador.

In these novels, protagonists embrace their historically situated difference as a way toward solidarity with wisdom.[162] In their journeys, Soveida and María are called upon to create a new spiritual praxis that reflects their commitment to justice. Both find that this leads them to greater appreciation for figures of female divinity and to informed reinterpretations of existing religious texts and icons. In this way, they become conscious and active participants in shaping faith and worship. Acts like these, resignifying and recoding signs to empower, argues Chela Sandoval, form a key component of a "methodology of the oppressed."[163] The new and more just spiritualities imagined in these novels appear as transcultural phenomena that emerge from intense journeys of spiritual mestizaje.[164] In critically reenvisioning Christian, indigenous, and Eastern spiritual beliefs and practices, these novels bring the richness of historical spiritualities into the present.[165] Like Anzaldúa, these characters traverse the Coatlicue state to more effectively build forms of community and agency not wedded to exploitative paradigms.

The creative remembering of communal religious histories and practices represented in these novels appears central in the effort to resist oppressive aspects of the modern state.[166] Critical memory becomes, in the narratives of Soveida and María, the act of creating something new out of the past.[167] Each of these novels, in its imagined memory, is engaged in this negotiation, creating the present as well as the future in a way that constitutes an intervention against the limitations of nationalism and patriarchal doctrines as well as the asymmetries of gender, sexuality, race, and class.

3   *Sacred Fronteras*

> At a certain point we come to realize that not only men are
> worthwhile. Yes, we, too, count for something.[1]

These words, spoken by an unnamed woman in a rural village
of Mexico and featured in the documentary *Flowers for Guadalupe/Flores
para Guadalupe,* describe the emergence of a community different from
the one that had existed before, and this reconfiguration is one repeatedly
enacted in Chicana literary and cinematic texts of the 1990s. The woman
speaks as part of a group that has come together to hear the latest news
from the Zapatista movement in Chiapas, Mexico, and her words indicate
a growing consciousness of gender and sexuality in communal movements
for social change. In what may at first glance appear ironic, this deepening
awareness of the need of communities of women to address gender inequality and sexual oppression occurs through rather than outside of their spiritual practices.

In the three texts that are the focus of this chapter, Norma Cantú's
Canícula (1995) and the documentary films *Flowers for Guadalupe/Flores
para Guadalupe* (1995) by Judith Gleason with the Colectivo Feminista de
Xalapa and Elisa Mereghetti and *Señorita Extraviada* (2001) by Lourdes
Portillo, the spiritual and political are wedded in transnational visions of
justice. These texts focus overwhelmingly on the popular religiosity of
women's spiritual practices. What is significant about these practices in the
latter half of the twentieth century? Why the need to represent them? Do
they serve merely to identify the ethnicity of characters or actors? Or are
they rhetorical foils deployed by Chicana writers and filmmakers in the service of another agenda? In narrating and visualizing women's spirituality,
these texts tell a complex story about the intersection of race, ethnicity,
nation, gender, sexuality, and religion in the formation of transnational
subjects. The spiritual mestizaje that they represent, bound up with the remembrance of the material and personal histories of women at the border,

is also an assertion of collective presence against the collusion of ideological and material forces that render them invisible and expendable. Each text makes use of a series of formal innovations that advances the project of speaking across borders, at times echoing Anzaldúa's strategy of autohisteoría while at other moments adopting the pattern of the Latin American testimonio. *Canícula*, *Flowers*, and *Señorita Extraviada* make known, and even accept, the gaps and fissures that inevitably come with community, yet they also recognize transnational feminist spiritual communities and envision new ones.

The multiple and sometimes contradictory voices recorded in *Flowers* attest to its goal of departing from traditional ethnography's tendency to present authoritative knowledge about the exotic Other at a safe distance. Instead, *Flowers* creates a dialogue by juxtaposing various women testifying to the presence of Guadalupe in their lives. It is their voices that guide the film rather than that of an invisible and authoritative narrator. The film centers on the annual and massive march and pilgrimage of thousands of women to Tepeyac in Mexico City, the site of Guadalupe's appearance. The film primarily covers the contingent of women from Xalapa as they prepare for and participate in the pilgrimage, but it also includes a women's relay race to Tepeyac, scenes of local village festivals for Our Lady, and a ceremony honoring Guadalupe in Brooklyn, New York, organized by Xalapans residing there. These spiritual movements cross multiple borders and the women who participate in them testify, in this film, to the empowering presence of female divinity in their lives.

Señorita Extraviada explores the disappearances and murders of over three hundred young women, at the time the film was made, on the border between the United States and Mexico in Ciudad Juárez, Mexico. At this writing, the number of women who had been killed or disappeared in Juárez exceeded five hundred, with no resolution to this crisis on the horizon. The film seamlessly melds together documentary, lament, and call to action by adopting the requiem as its framework. The requiem remembers and honors the dead in speaking, in singing, in chanting, and in communion, elements that Portillo adapts to the visual technology of the film. Loved ones, primarily mothers and sisters, remember the murdered and disappeared young women in narrative (testimony), photographs (which become banners for justice), and ritual (painting crosses throughout the

city). The film remembers the women themselves, their individual uniqueness, within the material and social world of the border in a post-NAFTA
era of globalization. Its focus on the basic moral and ethical demands of the
families and women activists and the spiritual element of their struggle for
justice, most evident in the ubiquitous black crosses on pink backgrounds
painted on posts throughout the city, suggests not only the significance of
the spiritual in these lives but the attempt to create new and more just spiritual communities.

Canícula names itself a fictional autobioethnography, indicating the
mix of personal and collective moments, histories, and experiences that it
constructs to represent the life of a brown girl in a Chicano/a community
on the border between the United States and Mexico in the latter half of
the twentieth century. It is an innovative novel in its combined use of the
linguistic and visual to create the narrative of Azucena/Nena's transformation from girl to woman, a story that is also a collective one of transnational
community. *Canícula*'s attention to the polyphony of the border and the
construction of visual archives about Chicano/as yields a variation on the
testimonio—echoing Mary Louise Pratt's description of testimonio as
autoethnography—through which the narrator recreates Chicano/a community across borders and against misreadings of it.[2] *Canícula*'s eighty-six
brief—most are only one to two pages in length—and evocative chapters
describe a circle of lives bound together in spiritual communion despite, or
perhaps because of, both discrimination and misfortune over the span of
several decades. It is not a story about the power of faith, but rather a medi-
tation on it. *Canícula*'s narrative of remembrance makes visible the agency
of frontera subjects in the creation of transnational spiritual communities
of healing as it offers a contemporary alternative reading of the region in
contrast to an ever-increasing rhetoric and image of the border as a site of
irremediable danger, violence, and lawlessness.[3]

Canícula participates in what literature scholar Genaro Padilla has identified as a "retrospective narrative habit" of Mexican American autobiography, that is, the narrative creation of an individual life within a community. The crafting of an "imagined cultural community of the past," argues
Padilla, anchors identities under attack in a specific history as it manifests
the "desire for historical presence" under current conditions of continued
marginalization. Padilla recognizes the oppositional quality of such narra-

tives, reading the seeming quiet of women's autobiographies in particular as participating in a combined movement of assertion and resistance.[4]

While Padilla suggests that late-twentieth-century Chicano/a autobiographers situate themselves within "a social space of multiple identities" yet "speak another (contradictory?) desire for a unitary and collective cultural economy imagined in the past, or on the other side of the border,"[5] *Canícula* imagines a transnational collective past and collective present wherein subtle differences unfold. The contrapuntal juxtaposition of photographic and linguistic elements destabilizes a purely ethnographic reading and metafictionally invites varied reader interpretations. The multiple recollections, told from the present, often mark the distance between what was known then and what is known now.

As was also true of the novels discussed in chapter 2, these narratives focus on the representation of activities and sites traditionally marked as "women's spheres," including the home and neighborhood and the care and maintenance of families. However, in contrast to the texts discussed in the previous chapter, each of these narratives situates the domestic sphere in relation to a public sphere, that is, the border, the nation, the city, the church, the maquila, and in relation to a public discourse, such as those surrounding education, politics, socialization, employment, immigration, globalization. Therefore, in each of these texts the family and domestic life function within a system of multiple spheres and discourses. We might read these, as Nancy Fraser suggests, as competing publics, in recognition of the masculinist and bourgeois idealization of the liberal public sphere that excludes many from its civil society.[6] While this reading does not suggest an idealized view of the domestic sphere, following Fraser, neither does it idealize the liberal public sphere where social and economic inequalities delimit who can speak, or the sphere of state and citizenship in which participation may be limited to a vote that may or may not be counted, or the economic sphere where the lack of effective union organization leaves most people to face corporate power as individuals. As Keta Miranda notes, "Binarisms of public and private . . . reify male authority and female dependence, while closing off the interconnections of work, family, and the state."[7] Instead, each of these texts suggests an understanding of the domestic and familial space as another kind of public space and not merely as an invisible, empty,

or abject space where the unremunerated work of social reproduction continues mechanically.[8]

For many of the women in *Flowers*, the work of social reproduction in the domestic sphere necessitates a struggle with the state over improvements in infrastructure, education, and access to land. In *Señorita Extraviada*, the homegrown activism of mothers and sisters and fathers of the disappeared propels the movement for justice which calls upon the media, government, and society to act to end the violence. For the characters in *Canícula*, the spiritual is deeply social and communal, encompassing both faith and practices that ensure the spiritual and physical well-being of family members and community.

Both the films and the fictional autobioethnography represent women in the process of performing community by sharing work, stories, struggle, knowledge, photos, play, and prayer. The physical nature of many of these activities is striking as these narratives foreground women's bodies in action. *Canícula* deftly evokes bodily sensations, locating memory in sensation, transforming formerly invisible women on the border into flesh and blood. The text highlights women's specialized knowledge of the body in the curandera tradition of preparing home remedies to cure ailments. The vitality of women's spiritual communities becomes evident in the many expressions of it in *Flowers for Guadalupe*, especially the long pilgrimage and marathon to Mexico City. For the women involved in them these activities represent both sacrifice and commitment because they challenge and renew the body, indicating an awareness of physical being—as women, Indian, working class, peasant, mestiza, dark-skinned—that interacts with spiritual being. Finally, the requiem of *Señorita Extraviada* represents a private sorrow made public, a lament not only for the dead and disappeared young women but also for the daily violence inflicted on women in the borderlands.

Scenes of communal participation in institutional religious life, popular religiosity, and extra-institutional spiritual practices, beliefs, and traditions that are particular to the borderlands strongly suggest the power of the spiritual for Chicano/a and Mexicano/a racial and ethnic communities. They coincide with Stephen C. Holler's observation that "Hispanic/Latino popular religion always has some kind of connection to the Church, whether it be weak or strong. And it always retains an important relationship to its own particular ethnic origin."[9] Yet these scenes also suggest that the connection with religious institutions is one of negotiation coupled with the practice of spiritual imagination among border subjects, echoing Gloria Anzaldúa's theorization of spiritual mestizaje as the ongoing soul work by which we are transformed and through which we transform the world, creating new cultures, values, homes.[10] Guadalupan ceremonies in Mexico and the United States in *Flowers* feature indigenous and mestizo elements that suggest the agency of indigenous and mestizo diasporic communities in creatively changing and maintaining religious and cultural continuity.[11] Holler's observation, which is echoed by other religious studies scholars, that "popular religion is the cultural resistance of a dominated people to keep alive its own collective memory and identity"[12] becomes apparent in the veneration of the indigenous Guadalupe in *Flowers*, the saints and sacred sites represented in *Canícula*, and the religious iconography in *Señorita Extraviada* as well as the latter film's adoption of the requiem as a framework for remembrance.[13]

Several women in *Flowers* express their relationship to Guadalupe as an ally in the struggle for social justice and their religious belief as something that finds expression in their actions for improved conditions for mestizo and indigenous communities. In this they coincide with liberation theologians who seek to distance themselves from power by "resolutely casting [their] lot with the oppressed and the exploited in the struggle for a more just society."[14] *Flowers* demonstrates the enduring influence of liberation theology in the Americas despite institutional shifts away from this perspective. In addressing the specifics of women's oppression within political and social structures, the women in *Flowers* align themselves with the 1979 declaration of Latin American bishops at Puebla de los Angeles, Mexico, who urged the church to be involved in social and political issues when they said, "Our social conduct is part and parcel of our following of Christ."[15] However, for the women of *Señorita Extraviada*, that activist church is absent. Religious belief provides succor to the families of the women killed or disappeared, who, like the women depicted in *Flowers*, are motivated by their faith to fight for justice. The enormous gap between their efforts and their effect, especially since they receive little if any support from entities and organizations that could make a difference, is chilling. *Señorita*, therefore, documents both the tremendous and systematic violence directed against women and the struggle to build a meaningful spiritual community in the face of that violence.[16]

To a greater degree than in the novels of the previous chapter, these texts also attempt to understand existence in terms that other discourses do not provide. *Canícula*'s exploration of a transnational subjectivity, *Flowers*'s examination of working-class and immigrant women's subjectivity, and *Señorita Extraviada*'s focus on women colonia dwellers and maquila workers all centrally frame women's relation to the sacred and divine as a key aspect of their identities, but not necessarily one separate from other aspects of their identities. That spiritual community and understanding are not experienced equally should not surprise any more than the ability of spiritual women to remake relationships or build new understandings to fit their needs.

In recognizing an alternative form of knowledge in women's communal and individual religious practices, these narratives contest the paternalism toward third world women that, as Chandra Talpade Mohanty notes, views them as backward, traditional, unaware, ignorant, and unchanging.[17] *Canícula*, *Flowers*, and *Señorita Extraviada* instead consider how spiritual practice emerges from dialogue in specific historic moments, how competing and conflicting discourses shape subjectivities, and how neoliberal policies affect transnational subjects in the everyday.

Memory, Gender, and the Sacred *en la Frontera*

The opening pages of Norma Elia Cantú's *Canícula: Snapshots of a Girlhood en la Frontera* present an interesting and important series of texts: a photographic tableau in which items of personal, religious, and national significance are layered over each other; lines from a Mexican children's game; quotes from Susan Sontag and Gloria Anzaldúa on photography and the borderlands, respectively; a dedication to "family on both sides of the border"; a table of contents that defies linearity; and a map of the region where *Canícula* is set that emphasizes (in bold print) the presence of the frontera as a geographic and social entity rather than the dividing line between two countries. These varied texts ground readers in the central concern of this fictional autobioethnography: la frontera is a unique social space beholden to two separate nations and yet of neither. *Canícula*

10. Book cover of *Canícula: Snapshots of a Girlhood en la Frontera*
by Norma Elia Cantú (University of New Mexico Press).

explores the photographic, folkloric, narrative, and religious performances
through which frontera space and community are created, revealing the
interrelationship between individual and collective memory. A text that
challenges hegemonic views of the region, it gently addresses tensions of
gender and sexuality on the frontera.

Canícula's transnationalism requires a textual confrontation with the
rhetorical and discursive strategies that structure nation and the literary
and historical hierarchies that are its resources. As Jana Evans Braziel and
Anita Mannur state, transnationalism is "the flow of people, ideas, goods,
and capital across national territories in a way that undermines nationality
and nationalism as discrete categories of identification, economic organization, and political constitution."[18] *Canícula* effects a subversion of nation
on multiple levels as it participates in the "border writing" that José David
Saldívar identifies as "a continuous encounter between two or more reference codes."[19] Its incorporation of actual photographs to represent fictional
characters, its reliance on the trope of memory, and its narration of performance and ritual create a multilayered critique of la frontera. The choice to
emphasize the Spanish *frontera*, which is synonymous with boundary, mar-

11. Map of the frontera by University of New Mexico Press in *Canícula: Snapshots of a Girlhood en la Frontera*, by Norma Elia Cantú.

gin, and new field all at once, over the English word *border* is not primarily a linguistic reflection of the sociopolitical divide but a different understanding of the region that this text proposes. In this analysis I suggest that *Canícula* enacts spiritual mestizaje as a central component of its alternative understanding of the region as frontera.

In examining the multiple crossings, the differential economies that structure the border, and the ongoing construction of the border against which it labors, *Canícula* disrupts both the border binary, as Mary Pat Brady observes, and the autobiographical form, as Timothy Dow Adams, Debra Castillo, and María Socorro Tabuenca Córdoba observe.[20] In a discussion elsewhere of the pairing of photos and prose in this text, I suggested that the language frequently reveals what the photo cannot; both forms of representation are essential to this telling.[21] That reading emerged from a sense of the insufficiency of the photo as well as its role in disciplinary systems (the photo identification cards, for example, necessary for crossing the border, which also reinscribe it) and history making that *Canícula* disputes. However, while *Canícula* exerts disruptive power, it also traces a feminist transnation that values the bodies of brown girls and spiritual communities of women. Its pairing of two mediums to create a third, unique text echoes the frontera invoked in the title and opening pages. The inclusion of the photographs and their interaction with the prose demands a fuller accounting if we are to understand *Canícula*'s subversion.[22]

Twenty-three photographs appear in *Canícula*. Two of these are small passport-sized images attached to immigration documents, five are formal portraits (childhood, communion, school, military, wedding), and the remaining photos are snapshots of individuals, family members, friends, and gatherings. The text, as the narrator, Azucena/Nena, tells us in the prologue, is a carefully constructed selection of images, stories, and memories drawn from a larger store: Nena and her mother sit down to examine family photographs; their shared memories, along with those of Nena's five sisters and father, become the text that we read. In declaring that Nena's story is "one" with those of others on the frontera, *Canícula* situates individual memory within a larger group.[23] These gestures establish the framework for this work of remembrance as a collective one, emphasizing Nena's social location as a sister and daughter in a fronterizo Chicana/o family, which enables her to reconstruct the past but also indicates this fiction's debt to and adaptation of testimonio.

Individual memory is always indebted to a collective framework. In creating a "complete picture," or narrative, individual memory dialogues with collective memory (manifest in language and conventions), taking from it and contributing to it in a process that makes individual identity within a collective or social framework possible.[24] As a locus of language and conventions, narrative and its creation become a site for the interplay between these two poles. Neither is static, reflecting shifts in both social milieus and individuals. Nena's metaphor for this process—"drawing it out as carefully as when she ripped a seam for her mother, slowly and patiently so the cloth could be re-sewn without trace of the original seam"—conveys her participation in the renewal of collective memory as it emphasizes the work and lives of women, around which this narrative revolves, and suggests the healing, figured as patient sewing, that the narrative performs. The entry of the histories and memories of previously marginalized groups into the mainstream frequently occasions both reexamination and debate, creating an inescapable presence at the moment in which they become controversial.[25] The past, of which Nena writes, is therefore not wholly in the past, confounding readings of remembering as mere nostalgia, ethnographic record of loss, or photographic death.

Photograph as Evidence, Aura, and Object

Roland Barthes declares in *Camera Lucida* that the effect of the photograph upon him is "to attest that what I see has indeed existed."[26] Furthermore, he states, a photo is "not a memory, an imagination, a reconstitution . . . but reality in a past state: at once the past and the real,"[27] drawing out the evidentiary quality of a photo and suggesting its attraction to viewers who, upon seeing it, might imagine themselves in its history (he comments on how viewing a series of photographs leads him to consider his own presence or absence from the scene). It is important to note that "what I see has indeed existed" is not equivalent to "what I see is *all* that existed," nor will "what I see has indeed existed" necessarily be the same as "what *you* see has indeed existed." While Barthes limits his observation to a broad statement—the photograph confirms that something has existed or, better, "what I see" has existed—his observations of particular photographs are subjective readings that contribute to his development of the theory of *studium* and *punctum* in interpreting photographs.[28] The Barthian analytic for reading photographs will necessarily yield different readings of the same image or object for punctums are as individual as people.

The photograph's social function or its role as a disciplinary technology also merits discussion. That the photograph is proof of something makes it a material object, and as Elizabeth Edwards and Janice Hart note, Barthes's meticulous descriptions of the physical state of photos he discusses in *Camera Lucida*—their wear, discoloration, tears, and so on—emphasize both that they are objects and that they are used to perform narratives.[29] Among these narratives, according to Suren Lalvani, is the classification of bourgeois and deviant bodies. In the latter task, the photograph's material and evidentiary qualities are made to produce knowledge about bodies (and power over them, while simultaneously subjugating other knowledge about bodies).[30] While Cantú owes much to Barthes's text, cites it, even patterns *Canícula* after it by describing her text as a series of ruminations about photos, ultimately, *Canícula* tends toward reading the photo as material object in a way that calls into question the Barthian analytic as it explores history and politics on the border.

In its incorporation of photographs, *Canícula* must confront two things: first, the ways that Chicano/a and Mexicano/a bodies have been disciplined, read, and interpreted through visual technologies; and second, the fact that it is unlikely that Cantú and many of her readers share the same studium. But perhaps these two things are actually one. After all, the image that the former generates indeed enters the realm of studium in the interpretation of new images. However, the studium, as Barthes defines it, encompasses broader cultural knowledge, and while for Barthes the studium is universal, *Canícula* recognizes that it cannot be.[31] Part of its narrative is directed toward creating a studium of the frontera for readers, creating knowledge about the borderlands, thereby making the photographs that are a part of the narrative intelligible. By situating the visual images within its narrative of the frontera, *Canícula* emphasizes the role of visual technologies in the construction of subjectivities and spaces. It also indicates that the photograph is a piece of the story and the narrative another piece; neither is the whole of the story, an assertion furthered by moments when *Canícula* offers a verbal description of a photograph that diverges from the visual image, and by its effort to provide story and context for a visual image in a way that might make a punctum possible.[32] Nena's narration of her visual experience of some photos does not have the effect, as in Barthes, of making other visual interpretations invisible or peripheral. It cannot. Instead, *Canícula* simultaneously cedes to readers the possibility for constructing their own meanings and assumes the authority to see, read, and interpret photographic evidence of life on the frontera against any ostensibly universal or disembodied eye or I—which is also always historically situated.

Nena's remembrance of her brother Tino carries a particular charge because he dies in war. His departure from their frontera community can only be felt by readers if they first have some knowledge of Tino's relationships and person. Nena approaches the task carefully, showing a young Tino as she tells of his eventual death, recounting his illness and then her father's grief over his later death, describing their shared cross-border journeys as children of the frontera. Only then does the photo of Tino the soldier appear. Only then can this young, vital, forward-looking face wound readers as they wonder, along with Nena, what life he might have had if he had not been killed in war.[33] The imagined life and death of the character Tino precede the photo of a young Chicano soldier who represents him. When readers finally see it, they already know Tino as a familiar character, and their being allowed to see it is also a request to join in mourning his death. The photo makes a distant memory a current one, the past alchemically brought to life in the present, and especially relevant as Chicano soldiers continue to die in the wars of the United States.

Each of the photographs in *Canícula* brings people from the past—including Nena's siblings, grandmother, parents, and even her younger self—to life again in a way that coincides with Barthes's interest in the magic and mystery of the photograph.[34] As Nancy Shawcross explains, Barthes recognized that "photography's potential is to engage the spectator, *a living soul*, in an image that coequally exists *as* a living soul or entity" because the image does, in fact, share "with the subject in phenomenal synchrony, a direct relationship to physical reality. The light that emanates from the subject is the same light that creates the latent image on the photographic plate."[35] This aspect of the photo's materiality, she continues, gives it the possibility of turning the viewer into an artist or witness: the viewer sees an object, the artist engages an image that contains something of which we too are composed.[36] *Canícula* follows *Camera Lucida*, a text that represents Barthes's previously articulated desire for creating a text in which reader and writer are collaborators,[37] in engaging the photograph as testament, magic, and material object in a way that includes readers in the construction of meaning. However, it offers to readers and interpreters the knowledge, information, detail, and history in which to ground their readings.

The "real" aspect of *Canícula*'s photographs contributes to its creation of an imagined community in both theoretical and literal senses. The formal portraits represent key moments in the life of its fictional narrator and her family, while the snapshots flesh out the daily creation of community in the actions of its characters. In this text, faith, prayer, healing, and religious community form so much of the fabric of life in the frontera that it is impossible to separate community from religion, so closely identified is one with the other. In a series of interrelated vignettes, Nena remembers the frontera community and her own awakening to womanhood in that site, uncovering the varied discourses and materialities that shape it and her. Although largely set in Laredo and Nuevo Laredo, the stories also crisscross southern Texas valley towns and beaches as well as northern Mexico towns and cities.

The imagined community here is not the nuclear family but rather frontera inhabitants, including neighbors, extended families, and co-workers. While some photos, especially in "Cowgirl" and "The Wedding," emphasize a normative heterosexuality, several photos, like the one of Bueli with the girls, picture women primarily in the domestic sphere and in relationship to each other as caretakers, guides, mentors, and friends. Many of *Canícula*'s vignettes involve observations of domestic scenes and women's lives and relationships in this sphere, as well as Nena's reflections on friendships and other relationships. Halbwachs notes that "a recollection of a picture or of an event is a state of consciousness of some complexity" that includes both elements that can be intelligible to anyone in the group and an individual and unique coherence of elements.[38] Nena's discussions of the photos included in the text, as well as her descriptions of other, absent photos, repeatedly reveal this interplay between collective and individual memory. Her remembrance recreates the social space in which Nena is "schooled" in being a fronteriza, a daughter, a sister, a racialized subject, and a spiritual subject.[39]

The contrast between the profane and sacred worlds of life on the frontera becomes immediately evident in the first few pages and resonates throughout the narrative. The first chapter, "Las Piscas," describes the dusty, sweaty, and difficult work of cotton picking. Nena describes to readers a photo of her smiling family picking cotton, but she tells readers what it hides from view: the "acrid smell of the pesticide" that nauseates, the "glassy fibers" that get under the skin, the insects that leave welts and "even pus-filled ampulas," and the "aching feet and backs."[40] Language reveals what the photo cannot: the imprint of labor on the body. Nena has so carefully described the photo without ever showing it in this case that readers are left with the impression that they have actually seen it. But the photo she refers to cannot convey the information that she has, suggesting that this may be an instance when the photo is of a piece with the action of the foreman in keeping written track of the amount of cotton picked by the narrator, part of a system of surveillance in the fields that commands obedience, even smiles. Nena contrasts the photo to her own bodily memory, the remembered odors, pains, discomfort; the narrative of her bodily experience contradicts the text of the photo that, nonetheless, sets this remembrance into motion.

The tone of the second chapter, "May," turns in another direction. This chapter includes a photo of four smiling children and a stern-looking grandmother dressed in their Sunday best: they are about to participate in the May feast day celebrations for Mary. The feast day is described as pleasurable, in positive terms—the balmy day, the delicate and beautiful native flowers, pretty dresses, singing in Spanish, and the nearness of relatives—that associate the practice of faith with fulfillment and accord the participants in this ritual the power of shaping their practice with their gifts.[41] The ordinariness of the photo and narrative belie the memory's spiritual significance. As the "experience of faith" or a "way of life," the spirituality of Nena's family is evident in the everyday. Theologian Anita De Luna suggests that the spirituality of Latinos "is pervasive and absorbing in every dimension, every circumstance of life," which is one reason that religious icons and practices proliferate in the daily lives of the spiritual.[42] The scene echoes De Luna's description of Latino/a popular religiosity with its detail of the elements of dress, decoration, and performance in this ritual.

At other moments, religion overwhelms. In the church, Nena joins in the ceremony but is once again overcome by a strong odor: "the smell of incense so strong I want to faint."[43] Instead, she counts the lines on her wrist and daydreams of going to Monterrey. As in the cotton fields, Nena fears she might yield to overpowering smells, yet in both cases she continues, forging a body and a self that stand within both systems—work and church—yet retain a critical distance from each. After overcoming her lightheadedness, Nena does not return to prayer, but to her own daydreams and meditations, reveries that extend into the night, long after the church service has ended, as she counts the stars in the night sky.[44] The relationship to the natural world that marks this narrative of spirituality—the flowers, the spring season, the stars—faintly echoes the pre-Cortesian imagery and ritual which Latino theologians have identified as an aspect of mestizo/a spirituality.[45] The photo captures the group dressed for one special occasion—a tall Nena with her flounced skirt and her cousin Lalo are looking at something off-camera rather than into the camera—but the narrative situates the image in a beautiful, yearly spring ritual that honors Mary, making the photo more fully comprehensible. Together, photo and narrative attest to a mestizo/a spiritual tradition through which the extended family defines itself but which the young Nena also senses as potentially overwhelming. Her spiritual mestizaje becomes evident in these moments of tension that may represent the conflict between home and institutional religiosity or a subtle renegotiation of religious training that the child Nena experiences but only the adult Nena, in recollecting the story, recognizes and remembers.

Not only or primarily a source of tension, in *Canícula* the church is also a bridge between the nationalities, languages, and social relations that characterize frontera existence. San Luis Rey Church in the United States and Santo Niño de Atocha Church in Mexico are equally prominent in the narrative as sites of worship for Nena and her family, representative of her personal formation within Catholicism and her family's collective history as members of a faith community. She also describes ceremonies at Mother Cabrini Church in the United States and Sagrado Corazón Church in Monterrey, indicating multiple locations for the faith communities in which her family participates. In emphasizing the cross-border character of this community, *Canícula* furthers the creation of the frontera as a unique social space, one that comes into being through participation in shared religious traditions that defy borders.

Religious and sacred sites, including regional shrines, home altars, and alcoves, frequently provide the opportunity to counterbalance the negative effects of life on la frontera. Nena's family visits the shrine for the Virgen de San Juan in the Valley in gratitude when they are spared from flood and sickness; the statue of St. Joseph at Mercy Hospital provides solace, hope, and help at the birth of Nena's baby sister Esperanza; the image of Nuestra Señora del Perpetuo Socorro comforts during her brother Tino's illness.[46]

In recollecting these sites and ceremonies, Nena maps the institutions and relations of her frontera community of working-class Chicano/as and Mexicano/as despite border restrictions and in contrast to contemporary hegemonic narratives that cast these groups as interlopers rather than natives.[47] Published in 1995, after at least a decade of U.S. government efforts to militarize the border region, *Canícula*'s fictional remembrances contrast sharply with the demonization of border communities propelled by racialist and nationalist discourse. As Joseph Nevins notes, in the late 1980s and early 1990s in the United States, anti-immigrant sentiment was on the rise, as were media coverage of violence at the border and demands for stricter border controls. Since then xenophobia has continued to flourish, often leading to violence against immigrants. Two major efforts to increase policing of the boundary were implemented in the 1990s: Operation Blockade/Hold the Line in El Paso in 1993 and Operation Gatekeeper in 1994.[48] In this context, Nena's narrative intervenes against the construction of a hegemonic collective memory that would erase the frontera in favor of the border. While her effort appears remote in the current climate, *Canícula*'s insertion of a frontera collective memory into the broader imagined community of the United States is not.

Canícula foregrounds the significance of ritual, ceremony, and popular religious practice on the frontera as part of its quiet subversion. Diana Taylor's observation on the displacement of ritual and practice by writing during the conquest illuminates the significance of *Canícula*'s tactic:

> Nonverbal practices—such as dance, ritual, cooking, to name a few—that long served to preserve a sense of communal identity and memory, were not considered valid forms of knowledge. Many kinds of performance, deemed idolatrous by religious and civil authorities, were prohibited altogether. Claims manifested through performance, whether the tying of robes to signify marriage or performed land claims, ceased to carry legal weight. Those who had dedicated their lives to mastering cultural practices, such as carving masks or playing music, were not considered "experts," a designation reserved for book-learned scholars. While the Church substituted its own performatic practices, the neophytes could no longer lay claims to expertise or tradition to legitimate their authority. The rift, I submit, does not lie between the written and

spoken word, but between the *archive* of supposedly enduring materials (i.e., texts, documents, buildings, bones) and the so-called ephemeral *repertoire* of embodied practice/knowledge (i.e., spoken language, dance, sports, ritual).[49]

Applying Taylor's distinction between the archive and the repertoire to this text amplifies the resistance in *Canícula*'s strategy of incorporating photographs, folklore, recipes, descriptions of performances and rituals, and narrative into one text, a text that accepts each medium as equally authoritative. Indeed, Cantú's text offers these up as alternative archives of la frontera.

Nena's elaborate descriptions of the special garments, candies, candles, jewelry, foods, flowers, and other items that accompany religious ceremony suggest specialized knowledge of creating sacred ritual and signal the value placed on beauty and communal participation in spiritual ceremony. These religious items also serve as "objects of memory" in the narrative, sometimes prompting Nena's reconstruction of events and emotions.[50] To outsiders, their use signals participation in a community.[51] Yet, they can also embody an aesthetic and mark a class position: Nena's modest items indicate her family's socioeconomic standing.[52] In some ways, religion structures the narrative, while in other ways, it circulates throughout the narrative and engages other discourses—such as that of class, race, ethnicity, gender, and nation—to elucidate girlhood on the frontera.

Both the process of remembering girlhood and the remembrances themselves are marked by Nena's desire to retrace her female lineage, to recuperate the community of women who loved, nurtured, and educated her. Nena's narrative forces readers to see women who are typically rendered invisible by virtue of their race, gender, and place in the domestic sphere despite their multiple roles as farm workers, midwives, mothers, wives, caretakers, cooks, curanderas, beauticians. Many of these women join together in a Catholic Church community, yet the Church never eclipses their bonds to each other. For example, in "Comadres," three women offer support for personal decisions in each other's lives that run counter to Catholic teachings, including marriage outside of the Church and reproductive choices.[53] In "Doña Carmen" Nena describes the way that the ritual of the Christmas posada hosted by this generous woman brings the group together: "we all helped with the preparativos, although we usually did anyway, even when it was some other neighbor who was the madrina."[54] Even the children have a say in shaping the event when English Christmas carols are included in the festivities at their insistence. When the Christmas ceremonies come to an end on February 2 with the Levantar al Niño, both God and Doña Carmen are honored: "Mami always told us to offer prayers of thanksgiving, and as I followed the others at the conclusion of the Acostar and of the Levantar al Niño when we each came up and kissed Baby Jesus, I thanked Doña Carmen."[55] In this scene Nena is schooled by her mother in spiritual community, instruction she takes to heart in honoring the manifestations of grace in her life with prayer and thanks. The church and family are revealed here as competing publics, their relationships intermeshed yet separate, and the practice of religion in this narrative indicates the degree to which popular religion expresses itself in both supposedly private and public spheres.[56] These passages also suggest that, as Yolanda Broyles-González observes, "*mujeres* (women) are the chief transmitters of spiritual practices in the home, and to the seven generations, while also often serving as the chief mediators between the home and external religious institutions and sites."[57]

In "Bueli," Nena points out the calendar from San Luis Rey Church hanging on the living room wall. In the photo that accompanies this chapter, the reader can see the calendar on the wall behind the three granddaughters crowded around grandmother Bueli. Does the calendar, positioned behind and above the women, reinforce the overarching social authority of the Catholic Church over the lives of these women? Not quite. The visual image of the photo coupled with the narrative is more complex. In "Bueli," Nena tells us, "Espy's two-year-old face looms huge in the foreground," the visual equivalent of her own narrative effort to bring the stories of women's lives to the fore in a "picture" that also includes the institution of the Church.[58] Adams notes that this is one of the instances in the text where the photo does not correspond to the narrative description of it, for while the narrative mentions Tino, he is not visible in the photo.[59] Yet he is present to Nena in her memory of this and other events. The contrast does not delegitimize either the photo or her prose description, but instead suggests that both must be considered.

The text accords importance to women's voices and to women's specialized knowledge and practices, particularly the curandera tradition of healing and women's leadership in ensuring community survival. Nena's remembrances of her grandmother Bueli are especially important in this regard. On the night of her grandmother's death, Nena experiences a vision of and message from Bueli to care for her infant sister. When Nena rises to check on the infant, she encounters her mother in grief over Bueli's death: "We both cry, hug. When I tell her what Bueli said, Mami instructs, 'Pray so her spirit can be at peace.' And I do."[60] Although the passage might suggest the imposition of normative gender behavior—the injunction to care for children—it also reveals the power of the spirit that binds these women together in caring for each other, a power that is partially enacted through prayer, as well as alternative ways of seeing and the transmission of Bueli's knowledge to another generation.

One instance of Nena's successful apprehension of Bueli's instruction appears in the chapter titled "Halloween," where Nena misses school when her foot is burned by a falling pan of hot grease:

> I miss school for two days. When I go back, my foot and ankle wrapped in gauze and cotton bandages attract attention. I'm embarrassed. When my social studies teacher, Mrs. Kazen, the wife of a future senator, concerned, asks, I tell her the truth.
> "Did you go to the hospital? Did a doctor examine the burn?"
> "No," I answer, knowing it's the wrong answer, but not wanting to lie.
> She shakes her head, so I know not to tell her how every three hours, day and night for three days, Mami, remembering Bueli's remedios, has been putting herb poultices on the burn and cleaning it thoroughly. She's punctured the water-filled ámpula with a maguey thorn and tells me there won't even be a scar. And there isn't.[61]

This passage epitomizes the quiet subversion of *Canícula*. Here, the ritual performed is a healing one. Its procedures, materials, and practitioners—its theory—are not only clear to Nena as a child, though she doesn't share them with the dismissive teacher, but remembered by the adult Nena, who chronicles the knowledge of frontera inhabitants about how to avoid scarring.[62] Mrs. Kazen represents both the immediate and future power of the state, which quickly dismisses those who do not adhere to its cultural codes. Nena's secret is the secret of female healers and home remedies whose power—both medicinal and spiritual—will keep her from literal and figurative scarring in the context of the political dynamics of the borderlands.[63]

Despite the fact that she knows that "yes" is the "right answer," that is, that a performance of adherence to cultural norms is required, she does not supply it. Her quiet "no" and her remembrance of her mother carrying out Bueli's prescription for treatment are honored by her even as a child, and in that childhood action, remembered by the adult Nena, we see the kind of quiet insistence on a spirituality informed by multiple sources that characterizes this text. The frequency of death and serious illness throughout *Canícula* suggests the precariousness of life on the border as well as the sense of responsibility for the well-being of a community that drives Nena's text.

In the two chapters that follow "Halloween," "Camposanto" and "Huesario," Nena recalls her grandmother Bueli's Day of the Dead ceremony as she joins in preparing the paper flowers that the women in her family will take to the resting places of their departed loved ones. Her injury precludes her joining in the visit to the *camposanto*, but her narrative remembers her ancestors nonetheless. In these practices, Nena reveals spiritual practices that blend Catholic and Mesoamerican spiritual symbols.[64]

Canícula does not present prayer and religious ceremony as a magical solution to social ills. Despite Nena's daily prayers for her brother in Vietnam, Tino is killed in the war. Her father's intense grief over this loss leads to religious doubt, just as Doña Carmen's loss of a child to illness also results in shaken faith. These moments of skepticism reinforce the power of faith by highlighting the pain of a fracture in the community created, in part, through religious belief. Carmen's and Papi's losses suggest the complexity of social relations and realities that challenge relation to the sacred. However, Nena's sympathy for the immediacy of Carmen's and Papi's emotions conveys a compassion and identification born of her own spiritual strength.

On the other hand, too close an identification with the church signals something gone awry. Epifania provides a good example of someone whose extremely pious activities suggest overcompensation, for Nena tells us that Epifania "not only attended daily mass in the morning and daily rosary in the evening but also helped with two masses on Sunday and yet was known as the biggest gossip in the neighborhood."[65] In "Nun's Habit," Nena's recollection of having nearly fainted yet another time in church leads to the revelation that parents steered their children away from the convent or the priesthood—vocations deemed boring by the young Nena—and even went so far as to send children away to reconsider such inclinations.[66] But the narrative also suggests that this parental concern is linked to the view of a nun as someone "living without children, not married," and therefore is an indication of the strength of normative heterosexuality. Indeed, the pairing of boys and girls for photos and the concern for the family's unmarried female relative strongly suggest that heteronormativity is a part of girlhood on the frontera.

In *Canícula* we have an alternative story of the borderlands and a healing memory of frontera spirituality that is also a story of cultural change and transformation. What Nena wants is not the past—an impossibility, as Barthes notes, that the photograph itself makes evident—but a richer, more layered story of frontera communities and of Chicana girlhood through which we might better understand the present.

Walking Community: Flowers for Guadalupe/Flores para Guadalupe

The most prominent figure in the pantheon of Chicana foremothers who has been reinvented and reclaimed by feminists is Our Lady of Guadalupe. Countless artists and writers working in varied mediums have recreated La Lupe,[67] confirming Gloria Anzaldúa's assertion that Guadalupe "is the central deity connecting us to our Indian ancestry . . . the single most potent religious, political and cultural image of the Chicano/*mexicano*," because she symbolizes hope, faith, ethnic identity, and tolerance for ambiguity.[68] These contemporary renderings of Guadalupe have also redefined her significance in Chicana lives by interrogating or subverting the gender and sexuality norms traditionally associated with Guadalupe and imagining new spiritual formations around devotion to Guadalupe.

In Mexico, particularly among Mexican women, Guadalupe has long been a central figure in mestizo/a national identity, the Catholic religion—especially popular religious worship—and gender formation. Therapists Rosa Maria Gil and Carmen Inoa Vazquez observe that the power of the tradition of devotion to the Virgin Mary is a key factor in promoting a psychology of Marianismo among Latinas that, to their detriment, valorizes subservience and self-abnegation.[69] Historically, the adoption of Guadalupe as the patroness of the new Mexican nation, Jacques Lafaye notes, was preceded by the widespread identification of her miraculous American presence in the previous century with the causes and people of New Spain.[70] Lafaye observes that, in the tumultuous period of the late eighteenth century, the efforts of the Spanish Crown to restrict the independence and authority of religious orders in New Spain led to the expulsion of some orders and the closure of others. The resulting interruption of clerical ministry to the populace at large, Lafaye suggests, redoubled the centrality of parish life as well as the devotion to the most widely known and revered figure of Mexican Catholicism, Guadalupe, presumably in contrast to the clergy's more learned and orthodox views of Catholicism.[71] The association between Guadalupe worship and popular religiosity, and between Guadalupe and indigenous figures of divinity, are strong elements in the religious history of Mexico and have frequently been regarded with suspicion by church authorities.[72] As the central figure of Mexican and Chicano/a Catholicism, a symbol of both the Indian and mestizo Mexican nations, the most well-known and revered figure of female divinity in Mexican and Chicano/a cultures, and the empress of the Americas—by papal decree—Guadalupe has been invoked to justify submission and obedience, revolution, social justice, and, as Chicanas have demonstrated, feminist liberation.[73]

It is not surprising then that such an important figure and her many devotees would become the central subjects of documentary film. *Flowers for Guadalupe* (1995) chronicles both the presence of Guadalupe in the daily lives of Mexicanas and Chicanas and the evolving understandings of Guadalupe in these same lives. The film follows the progress of cross-country and local pilgrimages as well as ceremonies in honor of Guadalupe in Mexico and in the United States. Alternating between a series of interviews and footage of masses, marches, home altars, and ritual preparations in honor of Guadalupe, the film offers testimony to her presence in everyday life. *Flowers*'s distributor and partial funder, the Filmakers Library, describes it as a documentary wherein "twenty-three women speak out, in traditional testimonio format."[74] This reference to the Latin American genre of testimonio is apt in that the film mediates the voices of Mexican women, in much the same way that the as-told-to editor of a traditional testimonio mediates, and because both the individual interviews and collective perspective of the film offer stories of hardship, journey, and concientización.[75] However,

Flowers also alters the testimonio form by including stories of revelation, linking spiritual, political, and social in a portrayal of spiritual mestizaje. This is a significant shift that stakes a claim for knowledge and transformation through spiritual and body as well as rational awareness.

As we know, the camera is not a neutral observer, but socially situated.[76] Ethnography in particular has been understood as a discourse of domination where power rests with the interpreting community and knowledge is achieved through distance and control.[77] While ethnography that serves these interests is indefensible, my analysis works from the premises that, although a filmmaker may hold greater power than that of his or her subjects, it need not be employed in the service of domination; and that viewers are not simply consumers of what the film offers but arbiters of it, able to appreciate cinematic excess or recognize the paradox and ambivalence embodied in the creation and viewing of ethnography. How the filmmakers of *Flowers for Guadalupe* frame and address their subjects—the use of particular camera angles and cinematic techniques, as well as their selection of scenes and narration—work to diminish viewer distance from and omnipotence over the film's subjects.

In its focus on pilgrimage, *Flowers for Guadalupe* documents a spiritual practice that predates the Spanish conquest and that continues to flourish and evolve in the Americas.[78] The narrator explicitly asserts that both pilgrimages and marathons or relay runs in honor of Guadalupe have origins in pre-Columbian religious rituals involving homage (in the form of bringing flowers) to Tonantzin, advancing a feminist perspective on mestiza/o spirituality and the blending of diverse religious traditions. Aligning themselves with this long tradition, the narrators and participants assert their agency in creating religious ritual and knowledge.

The film documents four ritual performances of devotion to Guadalupe. The first is revealed through footage of women of all ages, in traditional and contemporary dress, marching through the Mexican countryside despite rain, sun and heat, and washed-out roads. We soon learn that these women, from the pueblo of Amealco, are participants in a pilgrimage from the state of Querétaro to Tepeyac. In the Querétaro women-only pilgrimage to visit Our Lady of Guadalupe, which began only thirty-six years ago in this form, the women of Amealco, on whom the film focuses, walk approximately 150 miles in eight days to meet up with women marching from other areas just outside of Mexico City. The various marching groups form a contingent of thirty thousand and proceed into Mexico City and to Tepeyac together. The second ritual performance the film includes is that of a group of women who together make a pilgrimage to Tepeyac and then return to their hometown via a relay race. The runners, who began training in late summer, cover the more than two hundred miles from Mexico City to their hometown cathedral in thirty-four hours, arriving late on December 11 just before, the narrator tells us, the local priest "coldly closes the door." The third ritual performance is a local town celebration in which Guadalupe's statue is removed from the church, re-dressed in new robes created just for the occasion, and returned to the church in a procession that winds through the town. The next morning, regional groups performing indigenous dances continue the ceremony in honor of Guadalupe on her feast day. Finally, the fourth ritual performance is a procession, including dancers and mariachis, through the streets of Brooklyn, New York, to commemorate Guadalupe's appearance in the Americas.

Throughout, the documentary captures individual and collective moments of communion with Guadalupe, the decoration of domestic home altars. As the artist and art historian Amalia Mesa-Bains suggests, the spiritual in contemporary Hispanic art is "an expression of cultural memory" whose forms and content emerge from "blends of pre-Hispanic, Yoruba and colonial religion and spirituality expressed in a popular arts tradition" and whose existence is an "affirmation of an ancient worldview."[79] Mesa-Bains's discussion of contemporary Chicana art practices presents a relevant frame for reading the art that women in *Flowers* create, as well as the film's transnational feminism. The film echoes Chicana revisions of Our Lady in focusing on Tonantzin/Guadalupe and in framing women marching and running in honor of Guadalupe to reveal the power and beauty of Mexicana brown bodies in motion. The aesthetic and spiritual traditions portrayed in *Flowers for Guadalupe* (and encapsulated in its very title) provide a view of an ongoing process of performative transculturation in the Americas (rather than the third world origin of first world cultural production). The emphasis in *Flowers* is on living practice rather than lengthy background, history, or footage of traditional worship. This choice prioritizes the daily creation of spiritual community in the actions of the women interviewed. For example, in María Luisa Cordova's story of her involve-

12. All-woman pilgrimage from Querétaro to Tepeyac. Still photo from
Flowers for Guadalupe by Judith Gleason, the Colectivo Feminista de Xalapa,
and Elisa Mereghetti.

ment in Guadalupe celebrations, the request to provide a new dress for the
church's statue of Guadalupe becomes a communal activity requiring the
assistance of her family—in financial contributions and physical labor—
that culminates in activities involving the whole community, including a
neighborhood vigil with music and refreshments followed by a morning
procession to the church.

Unfolding in an interactive format and style, *Flowers* makes extensive
use of interviews combined with footage of women experiencing emotional
communion with Guadalupe to convey spiritual revelation.[80] Although the
film posits the exploration of an ongoing tradition of Guadalupe worship,
the narrator, with one exception, refrains from explaining the significance
of this worship in individual or collective lives, allowing the participants in
public and private devotion to speak for themselves. *Flowers* thereby shifts
the authority from the author or filmmaker to the women participants as
witnesses to their own activities and states of being, which is an aspect of
the interactive mode of documentary. This mode is registered in the credits
for the film, which are shared between director Judith Gleason and col-

13. Women in training for relay run pilgrimage to Tepeyac. Still photo from *Flowers for Guadalupe* by Judith Gleason, the Colectivo Feminista de Xalapa, and Elisa Mereghetti.

laborators Elisa Mereghetti and the Colectivo Feminista de Xalapa.[81] According to the documentary film critic Bill Nichols, "the exotic, local, sacramental, and complex are frequent sources of excess," as are the "random and inexplicable," yet *Flowers* avoids representing Mexican women, spiritual beliefs, and ritual practices as merely excess and therefore subordinate to other women, to rational thought, or to civic or secular activities.[82] Neither is its focus on religious orthodoxies, but on popular practice.

In the film, several women describe Guadalupe's presence in their lives through sacred visions and little miracles. For example, Doña Irene Martínez relates a memorable dream vision of Guadalupe appearing on every side of every leaf of a nopal plant, and in response to her dream she creates a simpler version of the Guadalupe nopal. Carmela Barranco explains how, in the midst of her prayers to Guadalupe on behalf of her sick daughter, her very lifelike home statue, made by skilled craftspeople, shone bright and her home filled with the scent of roses, and her daughter was healed. Maria Victoria Fidencia Juárez de Arevalo describes a wind and a light that came to her during a communal rosary, which she felt as Guadalupe's presence and to whom she appealed, an experience that healed her of the symptoms of diabetes that she had been experiencing up to that point. These testimonies convey both myriad forms of communion with the divine and the strong sense of Guadalupe as a healing presence in women's lives. The pauses of the speakers and the presence of the camera recording their testimony, the small moments of quiet reflection that emerge in the interaction between camera and speaker, are repeated later in the film when participants in a community organizing group discuss their status as women and their thoughts on the need for social change, a move that does not subordinate one form of action to the other.

A range of Guadalupan experiences emerges in interviews with activist women who are fashioning new relationships to Guadalupe and new interpretations of her image. Mirna García Chaparro, a coordinator of the march and pilgrimage from Amealco, for example, explains that since many husbands objected to their wives' participation in managing this event it is now organized by younger, single women, leaving little room for objections. Gloria Vilis Rico, an organizer of the relay run, describes the event as a combination of a pilgrimage in gratitude to Guadalupe for divine intercession and the active maintenance of the health and self-preservation of women. Guadalupe Abdo, coordinator of the Christian "Promise" program for women, involving thirteen communities in the region of Los Tuxtlas, has adopted Guadalupe, the holy mother-to-be, as a symbol for the rural women she serves who are giving birth to new selves after having been condemned to silence for centuries.

Flowers also presents women who are critical of a religious emphasis on individual experience (to the exclusion of social action), traditional Marianismo, the promotion of silence about sexuality or domestic violence, and the class-biased dismissal of popular religiosity. Early in the film, Margarita Zires, a university professor, explains how her interest in studying the progressive aspects of Guadalupe worship and her discovery of the existence of "many Guadalupes" that together define a heterogeneous Mexico forced her to confront her own class and race biases against the popular worship of Guadalupe. Maria del Montserrat Diaz, a founder of the thirteen-year-old Feminist Collective of Xalapa, observes that, while devotion to Guadalupe provides opportunity for critical self-reflection and "tranquility" in managing daily problems, an exclusive focus on interiority "does not take into account how difficult it is for women in the current conditions," nor does it encourage women to seek social solutions for social problems. Diaz expresses particular concern about the pressing problem of "violence haunting the family, violating the supposed security of domestic life." Another response to this separation comes from Eduarda "Lala" Campos, a colonia activist of modest means, who asserts that "politics without religion limps, like a wobbly table," and explains that, for women in the Union of Settlers, "of the Virgin we ask, of the government we demand."

Some of Eduarda Campos's peers also speak in this film as do a number of women gathered for a meeting to hear more about the uprising in Chiapas. Both groups of women link their spiritual and social consciences. "In this life our hope is the salvation of this country," states Campos, emphasizing a view of religion that directs its adherents not merely to passively await a better afterlife but to work to make this life better. One woman in the Los Tuxtlas group gathered to discuss Chiapas notes that they are deeply affected by low salaries and a lack of food and other resources. She continues, "I used to say, 'I am worth nothing. A man is a man. A woman counts for nothing,' but now I see that what value men have can be mine also."

If *Flowers* were to leave these critical observations in the voices of educated, middle- or upper-class women such as Zires and Diaz, it would reinforce the biases against women's popular devotion to Guadalupe that other aspects of the film seek to undercut. Instead, the film presents women from diverse class backgrounds who share a consciousness about the need to end social injustice. *Flowers* presents all of the women in the same way, facing forward with the interviewee speaking to the camera and the filmmaker absent. Nichols observes that this format generally undercuts the interactive mode by erasing signs of mediation and placing the filmmaker in the position of power, authority, and knowledge. However, he continues, the filmmaker's absence also, paradoxically, removes the filmmaker from the historical present, in this case the ongoing transcultural process, making her a non-authority.[83] This is a curious tension in *Flowers* that, ultimately, serves the film's transnational feminist aims. The authority of the speaking women is also reinforced by the large number of interviews, a series of testimonies, and by the silences that viewers are privy to: the camera continues to roll when a woman pauses to consider or experience, or simply stops, making the viewer very aware of the mediation of the filmmaking process, turning these pauses into moments when silence signifies attentiveness.[84]

Cognizant of how the documentary interview is implicated in the maintenance of hierarchy, control, power, and knowledge, the makers of *Flowers for Guadalupe* carefully negotiate use of the interview technique.[85] The film moves between interviews of women testifying to their spiritual lives and women in action (marching, preparing altars, running relay races), indicating that the interview is a departure from what it seeks to represent, an artificial site created for communication. Meanwhile, the audiovisual and narrative focus remains on each woman's voice, presence, and particular language and the transculturative elements of her Guadalupe devotion.[86] The filmmakers also include scenes of women who refuse the camera's gaze, who laugh at being filmed (on the march), who hold roses up in front of their faces to avoid being seen (at the cathedral), or who look down or away from the camera that is filming them (in the colonia). In these ways, *Flowers* interrupts readings of the citation and performance of religious ritual or the internalization of religious discourse as merely assimilative or acculturative processes that reproduce religious hierarchies of power and hegemonic religious ideologies. In its management of documentary techniques, *Flowers* accords both its subjects and its viewers a critical agency.

In the three interviews I have already briefly described, women assert not simply their allegiance to a divine figure, but their interaction, exchange, and dialogue with Guadalupe. In subtle ways, the women indicate their participation in the creation of moments of grace—in crafting an altar in response to a dream, in acquiring a skilled and lifelike image that facilitates healing, in having joined with others to pray rather than remaining isolated and fearful. Each interview also reveals an awareness of the distance between ideal and actual, underscoring a sense of the intangible in Guadalupe's presence. The film further validates the testimony of these women by turning to the *retablo* tradition in Mexico, combining visual images of numerous retablos offered in thanks to Guadalupe for her intercessions with an explanation of this widespread and long-standing practice. In this cinematic gesture, the weight of collective practice works to de-exoticize the testimonies of divine intervention.

As the narrator of the film states in introducing the segment on immigrant Mexican women in Brooklyn, "the Virgin of Guadalupe has always accompanied her people across the frontier." This portion begins to explore the complex relationship between religious discourse and national, Latino/a, and transnational identities in the United States. The three women interviewed in Brooklyn, Guillermina Cuacuamoxtla Torrealba, Guadalupe Chávez, and Consuelo de Pasos, indicate that they are from the states of Puebla and Oaxaca in Mexico, where the film and we as viewers have already been, but now reside in the United States. The film reveals a community formed by successive migrations, earlier immigrants becoming networks of support and employment for relatives, friends, and acquaintances from their home regions, thereby creating the phenomenon of region-to-region migration, which is the pattern in immigrant communities across the nation.[87]

Brading observes, "As Mexicans now settle in the United States, so they take their devotion with them, thus extending the range of the Virgin's realm."[88] Brading's observation about this extension of Guadalupe's influence indicates its scale, which he understands through the lens of his extensive work on the historical record of Guadalupe worship bridging differing national, racial, and religious interests. The historical pattern he identifies continues in the transnational crossings of Guadalupe in *Flowers* and in the Mother of the Disappeared in *Mother Tongue*. Scholarly explorations of the significance of religion in immigrant life have noted that a transnational religious practice develops as a result of migration—which is not generally initiated by religious institutions but emerges from the experience of immigrants forging new spiritual and material connections or, at other times, from the actions of religious institutions in creating formal ties between communities in different parts of the world.[89] The activities of the Mexican community in Brooklyn appear to bear out the observation that the religion of immigrants is not unchanging in their new environments, and voluntary religious association may take on greater importance for an immigrant community.[90]

The mass media frequently represent immigration to the United States as an action driven by the desire to enjoy both the wealth of material life in the United States and its democracy. These interpretations are founded on a long-standing mythos of immigrant desire at odds with patterns of U.S.–Latin American relations and consequent migrations. They also remain wedded to a conception of the ideal, individualist immigrant that U.S. narratives have enshrined, and stand in contrast to the evidence both historically and contemporaneously that what immigrants, including Mexican immigrants, seek is the ability to thrive in community with others.[91]

The inclusion of interviews with women in the twenty-year-old Mexican immigrant neighborhood of Williamsburg in Brooklyn and footage of their Guadalupan ceremonies creates a chronicle of transnational spiritual mestizaje wherein women bring a critical awareness of their new location to play in shaping an inherited spiritual practice. They embrace and perform transnational subjectivities through this practice and invert what Arturo J. Aldama identifies as one effect of the border, that is, the enforcement of "a discourse of inferiorization on Mexicans and other Latinos, especially those whose class position, ethnicity, and skin color emerges from the *campesina/o* and urban proletariat groups."[92] Aldama suggests that the "border" of "racialist and gendered obstacles—material and discursive" follows Mexicans and Latino/as wherever they travel in the United States.[93] To protect themselves, *Flowers for Guadalupe* suggests, Mexican women create spiritual communion at the nexus of different cultures and nationalities.

The visual images of this Brooklyn community—scenes of processions, dances, and masses in honor of Guadalupe that feature many young faces—and the discourse of citizenship in the interview with Guadalupe Chávez, suggest that this is not simply an immigrant Mexican community, but also a native Latino/a community. All three women pointedly indicate that they have worked, lived, raised families, and built communities in New York for many years (Torrealba for twenty years, Chávez for twenty-five, and de Pasos for over thirty years). The film's emphasis on these facts conveys both a sense of their difference in the United States and their acquired rights as long-time residents, naturalized citizens, and contributors. Chávez explicitly argues that, in contrast to the discrimination and hardship they face in the United States, they are a community that deserves the citizenship and rights that measures such as Proposition 187 (1994) in California would deny. In 2010 anti-Latino/a immigrant movements went even further in delimiting Latino/a civil rights by approving the racial profiling measure SB1070 in Arizona and launching legislative efforts on similar measures in a variety of states. *Flowers for Guadalupe* and the women whose testimonios it incorporates contest both the rhetoric and the practices that allow for commercial transnational crossings but outlaw human transnational crossings. Joseph Nevins observes:

Thus, in the case of the United States, although the unauthorized immigrant is very much part of a transnational society of which the country is a part—that is, of a network of social relations that go and emanate from beyond U.S. territory, that impact upon Americans, and that Americans help to produce and reproduce—the dominant view is to regard the "illegal alien" as someone whose supposed criminal activity (in violating immigration laws) is independent of the actions of people and institutions in the United States.[94]

Visually, the film conveys the impact of police and state authority on Latino/a lives by focusing the camera on police cars and police officers at the margins of their procession, a ritual performance that claims the geographic space of Brooklyn for the social and spiritual community of Mexicans, Latino/as, and Chicano/as. Chávez insists that the "remembrance of Mexico's Tepeyac" is "how we carry Mexico, who we are with us, wherever we are," implicitly denying the erasure of difference and self that old theories of Americanization and new English-only movements demand. The maintenance of this difference, as Chávez and others articulate it, is not an essentialist stance but instead presents itself as an engagement with cultural memory. Jeanette Rodríguez suggests:

> Cultural memory continues to exist because it feeds a basic need for identity, salvation, hope, and resistance to annihilation. The cultural memory of the Guadalupe event exists because there is a need for it. The story speaks of the restoration of human dignity in a voice once silenced and now restored. It speaks of the restoration of a lost language and a way of perceiving the divine. It speaks of accessing lost symbols and transforming them in a new time.[95]

Rodríguez's observations suggest some reasons that continued devotion to Guadalupe might be important for this immigrant group. The transnational consciousness of the women in Brooklyn emerges in their discussions of the political and social issues they encounter and their religious community life. Connected to both here and there, the women fashion lives from both, resisting the social and economic pressures to become assimilated individuals.

In this context, consider again the introduction to this segment of the film. While the narrator comments on religion crossing borders as we are visually transported by airplane to Brooklyn, viewers are already grounded in an understanding of Guadalupe worship as one that precedes the current U.S.-Mexico border, as one that arises out of multiple border crossings. The Brooklyn community is no longer an anomaly but part of an ongoing process of hemispheric contact and exchange. The United States is not separate from but a part of the Americas.

As the film moves toward the key spiritual event—the convergence of pilgrims at Tepeyac and December 12 celebrations elsewhere—the documentary's lone male interviewee speaks. Seminarian Ariel Martínez of the Order of Oblates Mary Immaculate explains that popular religiosity may be an obstacle to "authentic faith" and that "one of [the] challenges within the church is precisely the purification of this religiosity." As we hear these words, we witness the massive march of female pilgrims as they progress toward Tepeyac, praying as they walk, and relay team members running through dark streets. Martínez suggests that it is a focus on constructing an inner temple and not a material temple that will "make the world more egalitarian." As he speaks, the film shifts to colonia scenes with women carrying pails of water on their heads, walking on unpaved roads past rickety dwellings constructed of metal sheeting. In the series of interviews that follows his, we hear and see women for whom Guadalupe is an ally in the struggle for social justice: members of the Union of Settlers, Tenants and Petitioners for Housing in Veracruz and a community of women in Los Tuxtlas also organizing for better living conditions.

The interview with Ariel Martínez raises a challenge to viewers. The fact that he is the only male interviewed suggests that his words merit scrutiny. Perhaps the film is simply making apparent the point made by Leonardo Boff that "a theologian is a social agent, operating from a particular place in society [and whose relationships with other agents] can be competitive, cooperative, or conflicting."[96] Martínez's apparent dismissal of the types of religious devotion practiced by Indian and mestiza women calls attention to intersections of race and gender that may impinge on his views, that is, perhaps his unwillingness to accept their actions or speech as theological or even liturgical expressions has something to do with the fact that Indian and mestiza women, though perhaps recognized as catalysts, or in the case of official Guadalupe narrative, scribes, have not historically been official interpreters of her significance. Martínez's dismissal accentuates his view of the illegitimacy of women's voices and spiritual practices in these arenas. His perspective contrasts with those of the many women whose faith and spiritual practices populate the film.

Flowers for Guadalupe explores the heterogeneity of religious expression among Mexican women and the varied meanings they ascribe to their faith, illuminating feminist aspects of women's participation in religion. But it is not exempt from moments of the imperialist ethnographic gaze that perpetuates the trope of the exotic Other.[97] Opening images of the pilgrimage from Amealco to Tepeyac, for example, focus on the colorful dresses, swishing skirts, and seas of straw hats worn by the indigenous women. The camera's focus on color, costumes, and flowers in the events outside the cathedral, coupled with the narrator's comments on the "authenticity" of the dance steps rather than their religious significance also suggests traditional ethnography. However, the film does include women in a wide variety of Western dress and uses techniques such as filming the women marching from the ground level, emphasizing their stature. Ultimately, the mediation of *Flowers* does not displace the authority of the women who are its subject in favor of its own.[98]

Hansen, Needham, and Nichols argue that creating an alternative to ethnography's involvement in discourses of power would necessitate "dialogue, heteroglossia, political reflexivity, and the subversion of ethnocentrism."[99] *Flowers for Guadalupe* clearly aspires to this alternative model on many levels; the collaborative creation of this documentary and the many and differing voices it incorporates give a strong sense of its political position. It appears to be guided by a growing trend in documentary, according to David MacDougall, toward "polythesis: an understanding that comes out of the interplay of voices rather than merely their co-presentation."[100] Consider, for example, what emerges in the interplay between the voices of Ariel Martínez and Eduarda Campos (a conversation about the role of religion in social change), or between the voices of Doña Irene Martínez and Margarita Zires (a conversation about spirituality in women's lives). *Flowers for Guadalupe* deepens our understanding of Mexicana and Chicana religious expression, revealing feminist aspects of Guadalupe worship and feminist reinterpretations of Guadalupe and forms of devotion. Invoking Guadalupe as her guide, Eduarda "Lala" Campos closes with an observation that echoes many of the voices of the Mexican women in this film:

"We believe that she wants for us a better life, a dignified life . . . liberated from all this hunger, this misery."[101]

The Death of Spiritual Community?
Señorita Extraviada's Frontera

Señorita Extraviada (2001), Lourdes Portillo's documentary about the disappearances and murders of hundreds of young women at the U.S.-Mexico border, presents a startling contrast to the affirmation and hope of *Flowers*. Only six years after *Flowers* but thousands of miles away and seven years after the implementation of the North American Free Trade Agreement (NAFTA), *Señorita Extraviada* presents a haunting portrait of life on la frontera, a geographic and social space that cuts across national borders. *Señorita*'s frontera is where communities fragment and die. Here, the words of Eduarda Campos echo without answer, the demands of the film's subjects for justice, equality, and dignity remain unfulfilled.

The gap between the hopefulness of *Flowers for Guadalupe* and the requiem of *Señorita Extraviada* startles. *Señorita*'s work is to track the rapid reconfigurations of frontera space that engender violence against women. Social space is not static. If *Canícula* emerges out of the desire to remember an ethnic, racial, and gendered spiritual community differently and *Flowers* presents a continued struggle, also spiritual, to constitute that community, then *Señorita Extraviada* exposes the viciousness of economies bearing down on women and movements for social justice.

The theologian Gustavo Gutiérrez says that given its influence:

> The Latin American Church must make the prophetic *denunciation* of every dehumanizing situation, which is contrary to fellowship, justice, and liberty. At the same time it must criticize every sacralization of oppressive structures to which the Church itself might have contributed. Its denunciation must be public, for its position in Latin American society is public.[102]

In *Señorita Extraviada*, we see not the church's public denunciation of violence but instead the emergence of spiritually inspired mobilizations demanding an end to the murderous violence against women in Juárez organized not by religious or civic leaders but by ordinary men and women.

As film scholar Rosa Linda Fregoso has observed, the film explores multiple causes for the murders and disappearances of women:

> Lourdes draws attention to a confluence of intersecting and overlapping forces including but not limited to broader structural processes of economic globalizations and the neoliberal policies of the patriarchal state, as well as more localized virulent forms of patriarchal domination. Ultimately, Lourdes turns her critical gaze onto the patriarchal state, a feature that some audience members have criticized for de-emphasizing the role of global capitalism.[103]

The multiple sources for the violence against women in Juárez lead Fregoso to describe the murders and disappearances of women as femicide. Despite the dire situation in which they find themselves, women in Juárez resist the paralysis of fear. The film, according to Fregoso, documents their radicalization and participates in their activism for justice. She notes that one of the registers through which the film unfolds is religiosity, and the film's religiosity, like the women activists themselves, "gives voice to a new consciousness."[104] These important aspects of the work that the film does on the subject of religion are tempered, however, by its sense of the spiritual vacuum that the women, and the film, face. My work seeks to further examine the film's representation of and participation in spiritual mestizaje, to consider why its examination of femicide in Juárez prompts both a critique of religion and an assertion of spirituality, and how its spiritual frame is of a piece with its activist project.

Señorita Extraviada introduces viewers to the industrial city of Ciudad Juárez and its various work and living areas, particularly the colonias, which are populated by a seemingly continuous internal migration of people from other parts of Mexico to the frontera in search of work. However, the work is not an end in itself, but instead reflects the desire for life, health, family, and community, human needs that are visible throughout the film, implicating the national and international policies and practices that prevent the realization of these desires.[105] At one point, the filmmaker states that young women migrate to Juárez in search of economic independence; however, one young woman she interviews, who expresses a desire to work in the maquilas, tells her that she wants the job so that she can help her family. The young woman's response suggests her sense of responsibility for contributing to her family's well-being, and such a response coming from such a young woman indicates the precarious economic position of the family, as well as their lack of options. Yet the patriarchal ideology of the family also fuels official inaction on the murders and disappearances. *Señorita Extraviada*, therefore, reveals competing discourses on family and community in the context of globalization: one that sanctions violence against women and one that authorizes their communal efforts to end this violence. The family members who are organizing against this violence, whom the filmmaker recognizes as the only trusted and reliable sources, act out of love and become the leading characters in the struggle to redefine family and community to include engagement with the religiously inspired ideals of justice, equality, and love. A film in search of justice, *Señorita Extraviada* enacts spiritual mestizaje, critically questioning the material, ideological, and religious foundations of both the violence against women and the inaction of the authorities, as it strives to create a new spiritual community that will join the struggle.

From the beginning, *Señorita Extraviada* appears to question traditional religiosities. A wide-angle shot of Mount Cristo Rey, a weathered volcanic mountain at the borders of New Mexico, Texas, and Mexico, appears as the film opens. Actually situated in New Mexico, the mountain and the monument are visible from both El Paso and Ciudad Juárez; they overlook the desert areas where women's bodies have been discovered. The Cristo Rey monument is more than forty feet high, a white statue of Jesus Christ against the cross, but this is a robed Jesus with arms outstretched in welcome, his palms free of nails. This detail is not visible on-screen, where the white statue appears as a tiny figure on the right summit; viewers unfamiliar with it might miss it entirely. Pictured as something far in the distance, almost indecipherable, the Cristo Rey monument overlooks the areas where the murdered women's bodies are left.[106] The film's focus here might be read as either a cruel irony or an attempt to find some spiritual solace. This reading proposes to read it as a call to spiritual mestizaje.

The camera zooms in on family members and activists painting utility posts with images of black crosses on pink squares, an image that has become a symbol of protest over the unsolved murders and a remembrance of loved ones lost. There is little other religious iconography present in the film, and for this reason, the few instances of it are especially significant.

The principal suspect arrested for the murders, Sharif, wears a large silver cross around his neck in one interview, where he sits casually at a conference table with unidentified Mexican men, presumably investigators, his arrogant demeanor evident. Because Sharif becomes a central figure in the investigation, repeatedly linked to different gangs of men arrested for the murders and to the cult-like character of many of the slayings, he features prominently in the film. In contrast to this image of a cross-bearing alleged perpetrator of violence against women, the film offers fleeting glimpses of altars to Guadalupe in two of the victims' homes, those of Maria de Jesus Talamantes Rodríguez and of Sagrario Gonzalez. Talamantes Rodríguez, who was raped and assaulted in police detention and filed charges against the police, provides testimony in the film of police involvement in the murders of young women. Gonzalez disappeared in 1998, and her family helped to found Voices without Echo to fight for justice. In the home of Talamantes Rodríguez, the camera pans the humble dwelling, briefly revealing a prominent image of Guadalupe on one wall. In the home of Sagrario Gonzalez, the camera reveals two altars, one beneath a large photo of Sagrario and the other beneath a large reproduction of Guadalupe on the opposite wall. Gonzalez's mother describes her as a kind, well-loved daughter who taught catechism and belonged to the church choir. The film later shows Sagrario's sister painting a black cross on a pink square in Juárez, followed by a march of the mothers of the disappeared through the streets of Juárez. The statuary and metal cross in settings associated with the femicide contrast with painted crosses on ordinary streets and home altars to Guadalupe in the homes of women activists, visually suggesting the feminist spiritual mestizaje necessary for effecting change.

Señorita Extraviada focuses on the dispossessed. The homes where the mothers and sisters of the disappeared are interviewed are humble, often with little adornment and few furnishings and of rudimentary construction. The colonias where they live resemble the conditions that the women in *Flowers for Guadalupe* are struggling to change; they lack paved roads, water, and sewer service. The principal sources of employment, the maquilas, pay only $4–$5 a day, prompting children to join their parents in work at a young age. In making the harshness of life in the colonias of Juárez evident, the film suggests that there is another violence daily imposed on its many dwellers, who are deprived of some of the basic necessities of life.

While there have been numerous U.S. films about repression, disappearances, and violence in Latin America, these, as Chilean playwright Ariel Dorfman observes, have generally focused on prominent individuals. Dorfman wonders, commenting on films about the disappearances and murders of Chileans following the coup that toppled Salvador Allende in 1973, whether people in the United States can have compassion for the many poor and silenced people who suffered the same fates as the prominent individuals depicted in the films, but whose lives and misfortunes are never represented.[107] In documenting the massive femicide in Juárez, Portillo turns her lens on those most frequently overlooked: dark-skinned and poor women. But how should one contest the pervasive fetishization of women's bodies? Or an economy that views women's bodies as replaceable machine parts?[108] Or a society that devalues women's bodies, choices, lives? How does one inspire compassion and action? How does one make audiences feel that this is not just a Mexican national problem or an economic problem, positions which provide viewers with a comfortable distance? Portillo adopts the structure of the requiem and the spiritual understanding it embodies to demand compassion, empathy, and action from viewers.

Portillo's spirituality and her own journey of spiritual mestizaje are not unimportant in her filmmaking career. Fregoso links Portillo's filmmaking to "practices of the heart," which include her sense of herself as someone who is a medium for the just aspirations of the oppressed.[109] This self-identity becomes apparent in one interview; when asked why she makes documentaries like *Señorita Extraviada*, Portillo responds: "I think my mother taught me this. My mother was someone who really believed in justice. I want to leave this for the future generations, so there's an example of people standing up for justice."[110] Her identities as both a mother and a Mexicana/Chicana are significant, she says, in the evolution of her spirituality, which has not been constrained by middle-class prejudices against indigenous spirituality. She attributes her ability to make *Señorita Extraviada* to the protection of the murdered women: "the spirits of all the women are looking out for me. The girls are protecting me."[111] This spiritual fortification and commitment to justice made it possible for Portillo to create what she describes as a film that examines an evil that "has been allowed to thrive."[112]

Portillo's identity as a mother has been significant from the beginning of her filmmaking career. For example, in making her first documentary, on the mothers of the Plaza de Mayo in Argentina, Portillo describes herself as bonding with the women as fellow mothers rather than as fellow Latin Americans or fellow feminists. In that project, motherhood provided a lens for Portillo to examine the struggle of Argentine women for justice.[113] The film she and Susana Blaustein Muñoz co-directed, *Las Madres: The Mothers of Plaza de Mayo* (1985), opens up feminism to include the battles of women on behalf of their disappeared children against political repression—acts that redefine gender norms. National borders, the predominant paradigms of feminism, or narrowly defined Chicana/Latina identities have never circumscribed Portillo's interests; instead, she practices transnational feminism as a filmmaker attentive to the histories and struggles of women in the Americas. She describes her own spiritual and ethnic transformation while making the film *La Ofrenda: The Days of the Dead* (1988):

> Now I feel like I can say safely that I'm a Chicana and I feel very good about saying that I'm a Chicana. But I can also say that I'm a Mexican, and I also feel very good about that—but not necessarily in a conflictual way, you know. And it came about by making *La Ofrenda*. I don't come from the type of class that would celebrate the Day of the Dead. . . . I come from like a lower-middle class family in Mexico, and traditionally the middle classes in Mexico reject anything to do with indigenous culture. But in becoming a Chicana, I incorporated all the things that had enriched me—like indigenous culture—and also accepted the fact that that's a very Chicano way of viewing my world. So *La Ofrenda* was instrumental in making me feel comfortable about my triple identity.[114]

Portillo identifies the bias against popular religiosity that is voiced by Ariel Martínez in *Flowers* as a class and race bias, a view that echoes the interview with Margarita Zires in *Flowers*. Her comment on becoming Chicana echoes Anzaldúa's conception of the new and transformative mestiza consciousness, in which the spiritual is central. Portillo's sense of filmmaking as engaging in an ongoing process of inclusion, dialogue, and change also partakes of this view.[115] However, her "strong roots in Mexican Catholicism" are also evident.[116]

Portillo's adoption of the requiem for telling the story of the murdered and disappeared women creates a spiritual framework for a narrative that the film hopes will move viewers to demand justice. The film recognizes spirituality as an agent of social change, yet it also works to uncover the significance of spirituality in the crisis of Juárez. The two courageous women who openly challenge the government's complicity and inaction in these murders—Maria de Jesus Talamantes Rodríguez and the sister of Sagrario Gonzalez—both keep prominent altars to Guadalupe in their homes. The film links the visual scenes of the altars with the women's testimonies of their activism, creating an association that renders both as spiritual acts. The demand for justice, therefore, takes the shape of an active prayer that pervades the funeral mass for Maria Isabel Nava, disappeared in 2000. Nava's parents denounce the callous disregard for their daughter's life shown by Suly Ponce, a special prosecutor, who refused to investigate her disappearance and whose office they believe spread false information about the case to the media. Their insistence on the return of their daughter's remains and a proper Christian burial, their insistence, that is, on the funeral ritual to consecrate her body to another world, becomes a highly political act in the context of the blatant disregard for the lives and bodies of young Mexican women. The mass brings together families of the disappeared, and the camera shows their automobiles, to be driven in the funeral procession to the cemetery, covered with slogans of protest and demands for justice. The funeral cortege reaffirms the honor, dignity, and grace of the body and person of Maria Isabel Nava as it voices a political protest over governmental inaction to solve the murders and restore justice. In this instance, families join respect for the sacred with respect for women. We see a more subtle spiritual protest later when, following her account of her horrific detainment, torture, and rape, the camera focuses on Maria de Jesus Talamantes Rodríguez as she bows her head in silence. It is a sacramental film moment, the silence and gesture conveying the need for a spiritual response as well as a political one.[117]

Yet these protests are small in size—the march and funeral cortege appear to involve a few hundred people—and the murders continue. In this context, it is telling that the film does not include any footage of leading public figures, community organizations, or institutions, including religious ones, calling for justice. The frustration and anger of the families of the murdered and disappeared further suggest that their efforts are repeatedly blocked. The black crosses on pink squares, like the roadside crosses

14. Interior of home of Maria de Jesus Talamantes Rodríguez, with prominent image of Our Lady of Guadalupe. Still photo from *Señorita Extraviada* by Lourdes Portillo.

and flowers that they take after, become ubiquitous, a new non-institutional religious ritual that insists on remembering that a woman was murdered and that justice has not been served. In this sense, the film as requiem also reflects mourning over the horrific state of inaction and silence surrounding these murders, mourning over the actions and values that allow for such atrocities, and mourning for the loss of justice, equality, and freedom—losses in which viewers are also implicated.

The requiem structures the film but does not tell viewers what to think. *Señorita Extraviada*, like *Flowers for Guadalupe*, works to subvert the ethnographic economies of documentary that endow the filmmaker and viewer with knowledge and control. In this case, the notes of the requiem circulate throughout the documentary. Not confined to a single scene set in a church or cemetery, the requiem calls viewers to participate in mourning, eliminating distance and control. Portillo is the narrator of the film, but rather than a strictly authoritative or explanatory narrator, she provides a running commentary of her search for answers, inserting her questions, doubts, and intuitions about the veracity of what she hears into the film and at times recounting her witness of events while in Juárez, all of which destabilize her control and viewer desire for control.[118]

The documentary's appropriation of another genre—detective fiction—furthers this destabilization. As in her earlier film, *The Devil Never Sleeps* (1994), Portillo frames this film as a quest to solve a mystery, to get answers. Writing about detective fiction, Ralph Rodriguez observes that texts in this genre "typically end with the mystery solved and a conclusion reached."[119] In both films, however, viewers are denied the formulaic solution to the mystery. Obviously this is in part because neither film is genre fiction; nonetheless the filmmaker's adaptation of this genre in *Señorita Extraviada* matters. The film portrays Portillo's decision to travel to Juárez to investigate the murders, and offers various theories about who is responsible for the killings. In detective fiction this process of eliminating suspects leads to a solution, and as we know, that is not where *Señorita Extraviada* eventually arrives. Instead, viewers are confronted with the complexity of the situation for the inhabitants of Juárez and of the difficulty of achieving justice or making social change. The failure of the genre here mimics larger failures.

Portillo's choice in framing the story in this way may also suggest how she conceives of the role of the imagined viewer. As an investigator whose search opens the door to an assessment of discourses, histories, and financial and political economies at the border, the filmmaker becomes a spiritual activist detective:

> I ask myself why are poor young women so close to the U.S. left so forsaken? I feel that for me to stand by and witness these crimes without acting, I am being degraded morally, so I decided to act and focus my work in telling their harrowing tale. . . . The labor of making this film is my offering to the hundreds of young women who have been sacrificed along the U.S.-Mexican border. . . . My sincere hope is that the film and its power can indeed effect some changes in the consciousness of the viewers."[120]

This invitation to activism accompanies screenings and information about the film at its own website.

The narratives of family members whose daughters and sisters have been disappeared or murdered provide the lens through which both personal photographs and media photos are interpreted. A striking feature of the film is its visual tracking of sandals, sneakers, work boots, clogs, oxfords, and other footwear. Shoes signify. For those who blame the women for their own deaths—the film includes footage of both the governor of Chihuahua and the assistant attorney general making these assertions—manner of dress functions as evidence of the women's own culpability. In one shot, we see a newspaper story on the murders that features an image of bloodied feet in white sandals in the desert, a visual accusation against the victims. Is the image contrived or real? It is a photo that carries an accusation *and* sensationalizes a woman's murder—two sides of the same perspective on gender. It is worth noting that *Señorita Extraviada*'s footage of the personal effects of the murdered women recovered from the desert shows primarily sneakers, work boots, and oxfords, which raises questions about why that particular photo is featured on the front page of the newspaper.

Judith Galarza of the Latin American Federation of Families of the Disappeared suggests that murder victims are selected on the basis of photographs, since women in the maquilas often purchase pictures of themselves from photographers who frequent the work sites on payday. Galarza tells us that they are coached to assume the poses of models for these photos and speculates that these photos become a way of targeting specific women. Although it runs the risk of reinforcing codes of normative gender and sexuality that deny women control over their own bodies, Galarza's explanation is necessary to combating the slurs and myths about the murdered women with the facts about a common practice for acquiring portrait pictures.

The film goes even further in discrediting a reading of the photos that would blame the victim by showing how ordinary the supposed "model pose" is in the photos of Sagrario Gonzalez, disappeared in 1998, as her family describes her kindness, mild manner, and activities as a catechism instructor. Viewers cannot help but notice that Gonzalez wears a nice sundress and plain black shoes of the type useful for daily wear, highlighting the selective publicity of photos that revictimize the murdered women. Galarza's comments and the media attention to footwear indicate interpretations of images that are dependent on the social location of the seer. The film offers and questions photographic evidence, allowing interpretations to emerge from those for whom the photographs were meant that counter the discourse of blaming the victims. The action of Sagrario Gonzalez's family in creating an altar for her using the supposedly incriminating photo transforms the meaning of the photograph itself. In altars of remembrance to the slain, these photographs take on new meanings: ritual remembrance shifts viewer appreciation of the photos from material revictimization and archival evidence of loss to spiritual presence.

The film itself becomes a ritual of remembrance, the funereal score and haunting choral performance of the requiem sonically involve viewers in the film's lamentation in ways that the visual alone cannot. In calling upon viewers to remember these women, the film asks us to join in community

15. Interior of home of family of Sagrario Gonzalez with altar for Sagrario. Still photo from *Señorita Extraviada* by Lourdes Portillo.

with their families to combat femicide.[121] There is an implicit appeal to viewers in the film's attention to the faces, names, and facts of the murdered and disappeared women: claim them.

American and Mexican writers, journalists, and filmmakers have participated in sensationalizing and ultimately dismissing the femicide in Juárez.[122] Yet *Señorita Extraviada* consciously resists the widespread practice of turning the murdered women into spectacles for public consumption. At the first public screening of a portion of the documentary, which I attended in 2000 at the annual conference of the American Studies Association, when the film was still in progress, Portillo addressed this problem and how it ran counter to her aim in creating the film. Fregoso, who was also present on the panel, contrasted the sensationalism of lurid descriptions and spectacular photos with the feminist ethos of Portillo's project. Indeed, Portillo has accompanied the film on many showings since its debut, always including information on how to get involved in the movement for justice for the murdered and disappeared women in her post-screening comments.

Another approach to touching the public conscience about the violent disregard for the lives of women and the poor in Latin America is the work of the performance artist Coco Fusco. In "Better Yet When Dead" (1997), Fusco addresses women's lack of control over their own bodies as well as the spectacularization of their deaths by displaying herself in a coffin. In her piece "Votos (Vows)" (1999–2000), she explores the "powerlessness, of failed agency, and drained will" through a performance of self-abnegation modeled on the female mystics of the Middle Ages in which she wraps herself in rope, writes phrases on the wall, and invites the audience to write phrases on the wall and to cut her hair. She says, "The idea of being mistaken for dead evoked the condition in which many women actually live."[123] Fusco's performances often jolt audiences into recognition of damaging practices and ideologies. She is one of several artists working in Latin America whose art critically addresses the dehumanizing conditions created by globalization, though her work does not focus exclusively on an economic critique. However, a critique of globalization and its economic devastation that create both the desperation and the humiliation of the needy manifests in the work of the Mexican arts group SEMEFO and artists Teresa Margolles and Santiago Sierra. The work of these artists involves the display of human corpses and body parts as well as living Mexican workers in various poses questioning, Fusco suggests, the culture of violence engendered by an economic system in which the bodies of Mexican poor people are disposable and degraded. Fusco does not regard her own work or that of these Mexican artists as participating in the Mexican tradition of the Day of the Dead; these are not remembrances or celebrations of particular individuals but critiques of suffering. And while they all are informed by "a history of the Catholic relic," their focus is on fragmentation not communion.[124] Invoking or remaking religious forms does not always or necessarily signify the regeneration of spiritual community; in this case, they are implicated in social disintegration.

As Fusco's work demonstrates, there are multiple strategies for contesting the sensationalizing of the murdered women, and a number of artists and writers have engaged in challenging the insidiousness of this discourse in reproducing violence. *Señorita Extraviada*'s approach makes a demand on the viewer's sense of justice and compassion by engaging the requiem, enacting a ceremony of mourning for the women whose life stories—not just their death stories—unfold throughout the ceremony. In its attention to the testimonies of mothers, sisters, and fathers who seek an end to the killings, *Señorita* attacks the silence imposed on women workers in the maquilas,[125] on the working-class families seeking justice, on the dispossessed and marginalized young women who cannot afford to trust anyone in Juárez, and on all women who struggle under prevailing oppressive gender norms. The violence continues. Ginger Thompson, reporting for the

New York Times, reveals that "serial-style killings" have occurred in Toluca, Veracruz, and Tuxtla Gutiérrez.[126] Susan Ferriss, reporting for the *Austin American-Statesman*, notes that since 2001, over 1,180 "women, students, mothers, shop and factory workers" have been violently killed in Guatemala in an eerie repeat of the murders in Juárez.[127] The combination of spiritual and political responses to these atrocities also continues on both sides of the border. As the Chicana author Demetria Martínez notes, the practice of altars of remembrance is on the rise in New Mexico, fueled by the growing population of Mexican immigrants who can no longer build community in Mexico, and these altars include remembrances of the slain women of Juárez.[128]

Creating Spiritual Community

Canícula, *Flowers for Guadalupe*, and *Señorita Extraviada* all consider communities of faith organized by women en la frontera, revealing the ways that race, gender, class, nation, and sexuality intersect with religion at differing historical moments. However, these narratives go beyond this; they also show women engaged in questioning these intersections, gaining awareness of their participation in or difference from normative categories, and creating new spiritual communities that can serve women's needs. While the first two narratives explicitly assert transnational formations, the latter implies a transnational community in its focus on the global connections to the maquila industry in Juárez and in its use of the requiem. These narratives explore the frontera as a subaltern site that is continually reconfigured in the interactions between its inhabitants, historical realities, and the economic and ideological forces of globalization.

The critical remembrance of community that marks *Canícula*, the performance of alternative community in religious devotion that we see in *Flowers*, and the creation of new spiritual and activist communities in *Señorita Extraviada* constitute what Chela Sandoval terms a "revolutionary ideological tactic" through which "subordinated group[s] claim their *differences* from those in power and call for a social transformation that will accommodate and legitimate those differences. . . . The hope is to produce a new culture beyond the domination/subordination power axis."[129] In valuing and representing difference, each text asserts the production and existence of multiple forms of knowledge in contrast to existing structures of domination. These texts do not ignore the immediacy of multiple forms of subordination nor the differences among women. However, in reconstructing and reframing women's lives and activities in resistance, they assert a feminist oppositional and spiritual agency.

These representations of spiritual resistance to ethnic, gender, racial, and class discrimination suggest that the creative and critical remembering of communal religious histories and practices is central to the effort to combat oppressive aspects of the modern state. To remember, to speak, to write, to march, to chant, to run, to paint, and to create—in spiritual union with others—are all efforts to combat the erasure of the transnational female subject.

4 *Border Secrets*

How will we choose to describe our past, now, at this moment, as an enunciation in the present?[1]

Will history, its memory, its desire, free us, navigate us through passion where the unthought, the unspoken, shuffle through unidentifiable spaces, moving us out of Oedipus, from the colonial imaginary into identities where power relations that police, whether from above or below, are disrupted by a decolonial imaginary?[2]

Kathleen Alcalá's three novels *Spirits of the Ordinary* (1998), *The Flower in the Skull* (1999), and *Treasures in Heaven* (2000) explore the religious and political conflicts of the borderlands through the lives of three families whose fates repeatedly intertwine: the Catholic Quintanilla Navarro family, the Crypto Jewish Caraval/Carabajál family, and the Opata family of Chiri/Hummingbird.[3] The events in this trilogy occur over the span of approximately a hundred years, from the late nineteenth century to the late twentieth century, and encompass major historical events, such as the aftermath of the U.S. Civil War, the Mexican government's war against Indians in the northern states, Mexico's positivist social reform movements, and the creation of railroads and the concomitant industrialization of the borderlands.[4]

Spirits of the Ordinary tells the story of the troubled marriage of Estela Quintanilla Navarro and Zacarías Carabajál de la Cueva y Vargas in nineteenth-century Saltillo, Mexico, amid the long-standing persecution of Jews and Indians in the Americas. The family is Catholic, except for Zacarías, who is initially indifferent to religion, but later develops an affinity with the Crypto Judaism of his parents and ancestors. They raise a son, two daughters, and androgynous, supernaturally gifted, twins, whose lives cause consternation and wonder. A sixth child, an infant when this novel's main events occur, is raised by Estela alone in the second novel in the trilogy. The marriage of Estela and Zacarías dissolves over his yen for prospecting gold, and Zacarías, now free to wander Mexico's northern terrain, discovers the ancient dwelling of Casas Grandes and another, sacred calling as a healer and spiritual leader. As more and more native peoples arrive at Casas Grandes to hear Zacarías tell the stories of his Crypto Jewish family and their mystical Jewish beliefs, a spiritual renaissance unfolds that attracts the attention of the Mexican government. While native peoples are drawn to Zacarías's teachings, recognizing points of convergence with their own beliefs, the state's response is to crush any gathering of native peoples that has the potential to unite Indians in defense of their own rights. Since the Mexican military misunderstands Zacarías as a ringleader of Indian rebellion at Casas Grandes, the reign of repression that is loosed in response has immediate and direct consequences for the native peoples involved and for Zacarías's family back in Saltillo. This event reverberates throughout the trilogy as the point of contact between the three families who are its subjects, a cataclysm that sets into motion events that affect them all for generations.

The second book in the trilogy, *Treasures in Heaven*, follows the now-separated Estela Carabajál Quintanilla as she journeys to Mexico City and becomes involved in the positivist social reform movements of the late nineteenth century. Hired by the mysterious and wealthy reformer La Señorita, Estela becomes the director of a school for poor women and children as well as a collaborator in the publication of a feminist magazine. She is discreetly assisted in her social reform work and in the care of her infant son, Noé, by Julio and Mariana Caraval, her estranged husband's parents, who are forced to flee Saltillo by an angry anti-Semitic mob seeking vengeance on the family of the insurrectionary Jew Zacarías. In the capital, neither Estela's faith nor her work for poor women require secrecy in an era that would seemingly suggest otherwise, but her participation in a feminist movement to create greater equality for women and the operation of that movement remain underground, even in an era trumpeting social change. The affinity between the necessarily cautious Mariana and Julio, who as students of the Kabbalah[5] belong to a religious minority with a long history of clandestine survival, and Estela the social reformist is described by Mariana in the terms of her faith as a sharing in *"tikkun olam—the repair* of the world."[6] This understanding of shared beliefs and practices among adherents of different faiths, in contrast to state or institutional animosities, is an element of the spiritual mestizaje that the novels portray. At the societal level, the interactions among characters with different faiths and the encounters between competing belief systems that these create afford multiple opportunities for the active reshaping of religious or spiritual practice and faith. This trilogy explores these processes through specific historical moments in which these types of exchanges are heightened.

The Flower in the Skull further amplifies the intertwined histories of these families in its exploration of the lives of three generations of Opata women and their encounters with the religious, ethnic, and economic repression of the Mexican state and the discrimination and violence directed against Indian women in the U.S. Southwest. In this last installment in the trilogy, Concha, Rosa, and Shelly each tell their stories. Concha's parents were among those who joined in the spiritual renaissance at Casas Grandes in which Zacarías Carabajál played an important part (depicted in *Spirits of the Ordinary*). Her narrative recalls the loss of the family's ranchería in northern Mexico, followed by their displacement and her abandonment and exile in Tucson, Arizona, where she works as a housekeeper. Told from the viewpoint of Concha's daughter Rosa, the second section recounts Rosa's life as the daughter of a live-in domestic worker, growing up between the worlds of her mother and her mother's employer. Rosa eventually meets and marries Gabriel, the eldest son of Estela and Zacarías (mostly absent from the trilogy until now as the child away at school in the United States), who is a Protestant minister in the Southwest. The narrative of Rosa's daughter, that is, Shelly's mother, is absent from the novel, a gap in the story; paralleling this is Shelly's mother's marginal presence in her life. The third and final section is Shelly's testimony. An editorial assistant at a publishing company that specializes in coffee-table books about Indians and the Southwest, Shelly takes advantage of a work assignment to escape the daily sexual harassment of her supposedly progressive boss and in the process discovers her own family story. The great-great-granddaughter of Opatería who were at Casas Grandes (Concha's parents), and the great-granddaughter of Estela and Zacarías Carabajál (whose son Gabriel marries Concha's daughter Rosa), Shelly begins, in her narrative, to untangle the web of suppressions that her indigenous and Jewish ancestors faced, as well as the secrets by which they survived; she researches antique photos, some of which turn out be photos of her own family.

Spirits of the Ordinary and *Treasures in Heaven* are works of historical fiction; in the former, events are focalized through distinct characters and each chapter generally adheres to the perspective of a single character. In the latter, readers are informed by the narrator at the start of the novel that the story that will unfold is Estela's, yet the narrator chooses a more distant, omniscient stance from which to recount the events of Estela's life in Mexico City during the Porfiriato. There is, for each novel, a correspondence between form and content. For example, the multiple perspectives of *Spirits of the Ordinary* convey a strong sense of the still-heterogeneous population of northern Mexico in this period and the competing interests at play. Similarly, the omniscient narrator of *Treasures in Heaven* fits the novel's exploration of the positivist period, with its faith in central planning and universalism. *The Flower in the Skull* also matches form with content, melding historical fiction and fictional testimonio as it presents the first-person testimonios of three generations of Opata women in very different historical settings. This novel focuses on presenting a more pluralist history of the borderlands, told from the perspective of the marginalized, through which we see that inequalities continue into the present. The form it takes, the fictional testimonio, stages an intervention against these inequities, particularly violence against indigenous women, calling the reader to an awareness that might be the basis for action.

Imagining a Borderlands History

These texts take up history differently than the novels and films discussed in previous chapters. A representative but individual imagined recollection of personal or communal experiences characterizes *Face of an Angel* and *Canícula*. The remembrance of a pivotal and particular historical event and movement—the Salvadoran war and the U.S. solidarity campaign—from the perspective of those involved unfolds in *Mother Tongue*. The documentaries about women's spiritual communities and women's spiritually informed movements for equality, independence, and social justice focus on the formation of collectives. In these three novels, Alcalá imaginatively represents diverse social groups and individuals in conversation over several historical periods, revealing multiple and interwoven religions, ethnic and class groups, and political factions in the nineteenth- and twentieth-century borderlands. As with the other works discussed, this trilogy places importance on collective memory, cross-cultural encounter, and la frontera as a transnational space as it also participates in the project of exploring the nexus among spirituality, gender, sexuality, and race. Each novel in this trilogy presents itself (either in whole or in part) as the testimony of those in the borderlands, whether by the focalization of events through a variety of characters with differing perspectives or by the mediation of an omniscient narrator and scribe or by first-person testimonies, yet only *Flower in the Skull* takes the form of the fictional testimonio. The trilogy lays claim to the whole history of the region and its peoples; the many individual stories exist not in isolation from each other—as they would in traditional histories—but in interaction with each other. In imagining the complexity of the borderlands, this work situates itself among a growing body of literature that represents the interconnections among peoples in the Americas and examines, as one reviewer notes, the region's "deeply spiritual realm."[7]

In its exploration of the spirituality of the Americas, these novels participate in that "dialectic of difference" that critic Ramón Saldívar has identified in Chicano/a literature:

> This narrative strategy for demystifying the relations between minority cultures and the dominant culture is the process I term "the dialectics of difference" of Chicano literature. . . . For Chicano narrative, *history* is the subtext that we must recover because history itself is the subject of its discourse. History cannot be conceived as the mere "background" or "context" for this literature; rather, history turns out to be the decisive determinant of the form and content of the literature.[8]

We can see that decisive influence in these works not only in the critical recuperation of forgotten or marginalized histories but also in the narrative emphasis on voice, orality, and experience over the archive and in the patterns of testimonio that these fictions adopt. Paul Ricoeur reminds us of the significance of voice in history:

> Yet we must not forget that everything starts, not from the archives, but from testimony, and that, whatever may be our lack of confidence in principle in such testimony, we have nothing better than testimony,

in the final analysis, to assure ourselves that something did happen in
the past, which someone attests having witnessed in person, and that
the principal, and at times our only, recourse, when we lack other types
of documentation, remains the confrontation among testimonies.[9]

Alcalá drew extensively from archives in creating the characters and stories that make up these three novels—her research has been noted by several reviewers and by the author herself and is evident in the verisimilitude
of her fictional events—yet it was family stories that led her on the creative
journey that became *Spirits of the Ordinary, Treasures in Heaven,* and *The
Flower in the Skull.* Alcalá notes her initial skepticism toward family stories about Jewish and Indian ancestors: "We had these stories, but I never
believed them; people would claim anything to deny their Indian blood."[10]
She carries this critical examination of the racial ideologies embedded in
history into the novels, creating characters who question and reflect upon
both the archive and oral tales, juxtaposing competing accounts. Saldívar
observes that history is not merely real events but the ideological understandings embodied in textualizations of those events. Alcalá's critical recuperation of marginalized histories not only makes previously occluded
events more well known, she also explores *how* they have been known, a
revelation that presents the possibility for them to signify differently. Her
historical fictions answer Hayden White's lament that history becomes a
discipline at the expense of sublimity.[11] Each novel makes use of emplot-
ment, myth, and story—just as history does—to make history's discur-
sivity visible and to interrogate the relations and conceptions embedded in
it.[12] Robert Scholes terms this type of fiction the "new historical novel," a
form that reveals history as discourse in order to examine the why of historical change. The why is critical to the examination of domination and
exploitation, opening the door to future change.[13] The historian James F.
Brooks even suggests that some borderlands fiction, including Alcalá's, better captures both the transitional societies of the region and their "potential
for beauty and horror" than the work of "conventional historians."[14] For
Alcalá, the history that is of concern in these Chicano/a novels is not
limited to events north of the border but instead, following the historian
Emma Pérez, moves past either a nationalist or integrationist project and
toward a third space of feminist critique.[15]

In the character of Gloria Quinque, who is a product of and participant in progressive social movements in the Yucatán to improve the lives of
working people and women, *Treasures in Heaven* introduces its readers to
the little-known history of the feminist movement in Mexico in the early
twentieth century. In the acknowledgments to this novel, author Kathleen
Alcalá states: "I would especially like to thank Anna Macías, the author of
Against All Odds: The Feminist Movement in Mexico to 1940, Greenwood
Press, 1982, for her personal kindness and for writing her book. It was the
inspiration for *Treasures in Heaven*." The novel also draws on Macías's study
for historical accuracy. For example, the character Gloria Quinque, who
La Señorita recruits to edit (the fictional) women's magazine *La Linterna*,
is described in the novel as having studied at the school for girls founded
by Rita Cetina Gutiérrez, who, as Macías observes, was a well-known poet
and feminist activist in Mexico in the latter half of the nineteenth century. Cetina Gutiérrez was a regular contributor to *La Mujer Mexicana*,
a real-life feminist magazine that published until 1908, and a leader of La
Siempreviva, a feminist organization in the Yucatán that opened the first
school for girls in 1870, and this brief mention of her in *Treasures in Heaven*
grounds the historical imagination of this novel in the oft-forgotten feminist movement of Mexico at the turn of the century.

In the novel, Estela participates in this movement through her efforts to
provide health care and education to poor women and children in Mexico
City, supervised by La Señorita. The concern for women's health issues
that emerged under early-twentieth-century Latin American regimes most
likely owes less to the influence of feminism than it does to the popularity
of eugenics.[16] *Treasures in Heaven* seems conscious of this in contrasting the
aims and motivations of the positivist Mexican government with those of
the middle-class feminist reformers and the working women whose opportunities they sought to improve, as, for example, when La Señorita observes
how male patrons benefit from the regular medical review of prostitutes
ordered by the government for the health of women. The impact of the
1884 Civil Code, which reduced the rights of women; the lack of education available to women; the poor working conditions to which women,
especially those migrating to the cities, were increasingly subjected; and
the widely accepted sexual double standard were the issues that propelled
the Mexican middle-class feminist movement at the end of the nineteenth

century and the beginning of the twentieth.[17] These are also the issues that animate La Señorita's activism and advocacy on behalf of women in *Treasures in Heaven* and that come to define Estela and her life's work. As a historical fiction, the novel remains faithful to the era even in its ending: Estela returns to Saltillo, and La Señorita dies, showing the difficulty that this early feminist movement faced in building continuity of leadership. As Macías notes, gender norms, limitations on women's careers, powerful counterpressure from the government and church, burn-out, and the understandable yet unfortunate difficulties of effecting alliances with other liberals and radicals affected the early feminist leadership and the prospects for long-term leadership continuity.[18]

The stories that unfold in each of these texts, though imagined, are deeply grounded in the historical movements and conflicts in the borderlands. The writer's careful historical research comes to fruition in these novels, which are, significantly, not nationalist histories in any way but instead decolonial ones, in line with the work of Emma Pérez, for whom the feminist movement of Mexico is equally important. As the chapter's epigraphs suggest, Pérez theorizes the decolonial as the intellectual work necessary to move, through space and time, from the colonial to postcolonial possibility. In contrast to other readings of the postcolonial as contemporaneous with independence and nationalism, Pérez reserves the postcolonial for the future—"a hopeful utopian project"—and instead designates as decolonial the challenge of dismantling colonialism intellectually and materially following independence, that is, in the present.[19] Her historical study of feminist movements in the borderlands not only includes the story of the feminist movement in the Yucatán in the early twentieth century but also suggests that we read it as the origin of Chicana feminism in the United States. Pérez's decolonial history willingly, and necessarily, crosses borders just as *Treasures in Heaven*, *Spirits of the Ordinary*, and *The Flower in the Skull* locate characters not only in the United States and Mexico but also in the movement between the two nations.[20] The novel incorporates the story of the Mexican feminist movement in its transnational vision of solidarity among women of the borderlands and in its critique of normative gender and sexuality, which are perpetuated by received religious traditions but must instead be subjected to critical reevaluation in the process of spiritual mestizaje. Alcalá's novels share in Pérez's decolonial project, creating stories that make lesser-known histories more prominent, but more importantly, weaving these histories together in a narrative that defies borders.[21]

Together, these novels imagine a borderlands populated and contested by interconnected, multiply defined characters who must negotiate that multiplicity within the violent context of that place "wherever two or more cultures edge each other."[22] This trilogy focuses on the historical contest between divergent religious traditions and communities and explores the religious diversity of the borderlands. The spiritual seeking that characterizes Zacarías in *Spirits of the Ordinary* is echoed in the actions and awareness of Shelly in *Flower in the Skull* as she encounters the story of her Opata great-grandmother and in the vocation that Estela undertakes in *Treasures in Heaven* of providing education and relief to the poor women of the street and their children in Mexico City. For each of these characters, the achievement of a sense of self and a purpose in life that is at once spiritual, personal, social, and political occurs only through their willingness to "live in the crossroads," as described in one of Gloria Anzaldúa's poems.[23] The trilogy's attention to Catholicism; indigenous cosmologies, including those of the Tarahumara, Opata, and Tohono O'odom; and Jewish mysticism, or Kabbalah, conveys the religious pluralism of the borderlands while the books imagine the historical significance of religion and spirituality in the borderlands. Although only one of them properly fits the category of fictional testimonio as I have defined it, Alcalá's novels represent social transformations occurring through processes of spiritual mestizaje, suggesting that this critical spirituality is at the heart of the borderlands, both in its past and in its future.

Spiritualities of the Americas

In *Spirits of the Ordinary*, we meet Corey, a cross-dressing photographer who pursues her art throughout the Southwest. The guiding principle of her photographic method, "to conceal in order to reveal," also functions as the motto governing her life and the lives of most of the novel's other characters: "By concealing all but the essential line of a subject, be it the shadow of a nopal, a person, or a jug of water, Corey forced the eye to fill in the detail, brought the viewer into play as a willing or unwilling collaborator with the photographer in order to reveal to the eye what it was seeing."[24] Corey is disabused of her belief that "if she acted like a lady, she would be treated like one" by her mentor Mason Freewater, who helps her devise a costume for passing as a man. By performing another gender, Corey gains entry into the communities, homes, and societies of the Southwest and accumulates an archive of images of people of the borderlands (some of which later appear in *The Flower in the Skull*). The narrative suggests that her art and her mission share in a spiritual quest not unlike that of other characters in the novel when it describes her artistic sensibility as follows: "Corey had a burning vision that grabbed the viewer and said, in a cold, clear voice, 'This is holy.'"[25] This sense of the sacred in the everyday is one that the photographer works to capture and create, cognizant of both its presence (capture) and the necessity of her labor in making it visible (create). Her secular approach resonates with the more overtly spiritual practices of other characters.

Mariana Carabajál, too, shares this vision (though not the art of photography): "Mariana saw in every wing beat, every iridescent color in a feather, the meaning of the world."[26] It is possible to read in this parallel between Corey's and Mariana's visions a parallel in forms of devotion in which the creation of art and the contemplation of nature are both roads toward recognition of the divine. This correspondence of purpose is in keeping with the narrative's ethic of a pluralist approach to religion in the borderlands. While the mute Mariana pursues a more isolated, solitary contemplation that can only be shared with her husband, Julio, or son Zacarías in a limited way, Corey hopes to convey her vision to others through her photography. The juxtaposition between Mariana's private pursuit of understanding God and Corey's hope to publicly "convert" others rather than suggesting the efficacy or superiority of one or the other approach—private versus public, religious versus secular—appears instead, in the wake of the destruction rained down upon both Mariana's space of contemplation and Corey's work, to shift our attention from modes of perceiving the sacred to the contentious issues of who determines the sacred, what constitutes the sacred, and what room exists in the Americas for multiple views of the sacred.

In its comparison of the historic necessity for secrecy to ensure survival and its emphasis on the ineffable divine in both indigenous and Jewish worldviews, *Spirits of the Ordinary* initiates a consideration of the spiritual inheritance of the Americas. Following his teaching of the Kabbalah, his understanding of the four worlds of creation, and the importance of sa-

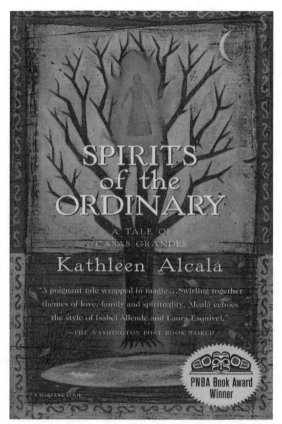

16. Book cover of *Spirits of the Ordinary* by Kathleen Alcalá, cover illustration © 1997 by Nicholas Wilton, reproduced by permission of Houghton Mifflin Harcourt Publishing Company.

cred texts and teachings in Judaism, Zacarías tells the indigenous audience gathered at Casas Grandes for a spiritual revival: "But I don't know what any of those laws mean in this land. They are very old, and from very far away. Now, we wait for the Messiah in secret, we say our prayers in secret, for the authorities would persecute us if they knew."[27] One of his Tarahumara listeners, Jesusita, responds to Zacarías's story by comparing it to the Tarahumaran creation story of four worlds and adds: "Of course, . . . everything is changing, now that you, our vecinos, our neighbors, are here. But we still have our sacred places, the caves and lakes where the creator spirit lives. These things, too, are secret. We must also pray in secret. But these things, the caves, the mountains, the sacred lakes, will never change."[28]

A correspondence between Kabbalah beliefs and Tarahumara creation stories emerges in this contact: first, each views divine creation as multilayered, with its own world existing in closer proximity to the Creating Spirit than other levels and yet distinctly separate from God; and, second, the pantheism of the Tarahumara (as expressed by Jesusita) and the infinite God of the Kabbalah both represent a very powerful Creating Spirit that exists beyond either the material or conceptual forms it takes in our world.[29] Both Zacarías and Jesusita wonder about how their spiritual beliefs and practices have undergone or will undergo change—in language that conveys the importance of cross-cultural encounter in shaping or transforming religion. The exchange between Zacarías and Jesusita is significant for the gender balance that it imagines: this is a religious dialogue between a man and a woman in which each "represents" a worldview. In these novels women, too, can speak authoritatively about religion. This dialogue does not suggest— nor does the novel in general—that these religions are the same. The language of both Jesusita's and Zacarías's statements, instead, rather pointedly insists on their difference—"we" and "you" mark the separation—as well as their respect for each other's difference. Through this exchange, where both Zacarías and Jesusita wonder about the interrelationships between place, people, and belief, readers may glimpse the transformations of belief or practice that critical evaluation of dislocation and cross-cultural contact engendered in the historical past and might again engender in the future.

In all three books, the borderlands and the Americas emerge as the meeting ground for varied religious traditions, a place where adherents of diverse beliefs meet and are altered by that contact. In *Spirits of the Ordinary*, Zacarías tells stories from both the Old Testament (learned at home) and the New Testament (learned at Catholic school); in *Treasures in Heaven*, Noé takes lessons on Kabbalah from his grandfather Julio while remaining, with his mother, Estela, a practicing Catholic, and at the same time, Estela's work among the poor brings her into contact with people of multiple faiths. In *The Flower in the Skull*, the hybrid spirituality of the Opatería— evident in the reference to Opata gatherings each evening to hear "stories of the place where we lived, of sacred mountains and rivers, of the miracles of Saint Francis"—appears to recede in favor of Christianity in one generation but resurfaces, like the protective Opata spirit of La Corúa (Great Snake), in later generations.[30] This movement through multiple belief systems, or the acceptance of more than one religious view of the world, appears in the novels as a critical component not only of individuals' and groups' ability to survive (war, displacement, exile) but also of an individual character's ability to participate in bringing about greater social justice. Survival here does not mean merely the material continuation of physical bodies but the distinctive spiritual and cultural vitality that, for example, the Tarahumaras express and understand through their sacred stories and their relationship to the land, or that is displayed in the observation of Shabbat through which Zacarías and his parents honor the sacred. In narratological terms, we repeatedly witness the operations of religion where focalization is the narrative parallel to the expression of a religious view of the world, and events and acts in the novels are narrative parallels to actions shaping the world.[31]

The encounter at Casas Grandes puts varied spiritual traditions into conversation, creating the opportunity for exchange and spiritual renewal. These cross-cultural encounters among different peoples and worldviews— in a search for common ground that narrative events confirm is life altering for every participant—are temporarily, but not definitively, crushed. What emerges at Casas Grandes is, following Alfred Arteaga, a hybridized discourse "that composes itself by selecting from competing discourses" and stands in contrast to the nationalist monologue of the Mexican government.[32] In the wake of his exchange with Jesusita, Zacarías's worldview has shifted, evident in the new way in which he sees his surroundings:

> Zacarías was filled with a great sweetness, a great calm. It had been in front of him all the time. It did not matter if he ever made a fortune. Zacarías had found it here, in this city of the ancients. The gold was in the brown skin of the people, the stone, the quality of light upon the cliff face. He would return home and ask Estela for her forgiveness; he would make peace with his father.
>
> Zacarías looked at his hands. They were the same broken hands as always, the nails ragged and black. He looked at his tattered clothes, his scraped boots. All the same. Touching his face, Zacarías felt the same angular features, the same care-worn brow, yet he knew he was not the same man. He felt that the glow came from within him, that the magic of the cliffs had entered into his body, his very bones, and radiated outward from his hands and face. Zacarías stumbled back to Las Casas, nearly blinded by a light whose source he could not name.[33]

Zacarías experiences himself, his surroundings, and the divine in completely new ways. His state mirrors that of a mystical experience with the peacefulness, transcendence, sense of self-worth, and ineffable that it creates.[34] His awareness of the "light" may be an interesting combination of belief systems; his sense of a "glow" emanating from within, inspired by the sacred experience and presence at the cliffs, suggests Christian mysticism where the experience is of union with God, as well as Jesusita's indigenous teachings on the deities of the natural world. However, he does not name the glow or light "God" and perhaps this lack of theism hints at a new understanding of the divine. The light might also remain unnamed as a marker of the distance between him and a transcendent deity, suggestive of Jewish mysticism where the aspiration is to remove the barriers between the subject and God, but where achieving union with God would be highly unusual.[35] It is Jesusita's explanation of her beliefs that prompts Zacarías to shift his gaze up from the ground and from the depths of the mine shafts that he habitually surveys to the light on the mountainside into which Casas Grandes is chiseled. This movement leads to Zacarías's transformation into a spiritual healer, and he becomes a much sought-after curandero among the native peoples. Some strands of Kabbalah, particularly in earlier periods, also practiced magic arts—a feature of Julio's mysticism that Zacarías unconsciously imbibes—and at Casas Grandes this merges in Zacarías with a tradition of curanderismo in the Americas, making him a prophet and a healer unique to the Americas.[36]

In *Spirits of the Ordinary*, the native peoples who gather at Casas Grandes also experience transformation. With their spirits and persons renewed, with their unity restored, and perhaps with a new sense of allies in struggle that contact with Zacarías provides, the indigenous people who gathered at Casas Grandes, though dispersed by the Mexican army, return to the jobs and towns of northern Mexico with a new confidence:

> Still, something had changed. The mining foreman found that a
> worker might meet his gaze instead of keeping his eyes cast downwards;
> the maids washed the clothes and sang to the babies but often, the mis-
> tress of the house might not recognize the melody or even the language
> of the song. The people who had been at Casas Grandes and returned
> carried about them the air of a shared secret, a renewal of resolve—in

what, no one could say for sure. Perhaps they felt that they had has-
tened the coming of the fourth world.[37]

The memory of the freedom to engage in the rituals, dances, and prayers
of their traditions at Casas Grandes, an ancient indigenous settlement of
northwestern Mexico, and to join in those of others—numerous native
groups are described as gathering together in what seems like a northern
Mexican counterpart to the late-nineteenth-century pan-Indian Ghost
Dance gatherings in the United States, which were also perceived as a
threat to the state and economy—fortifies the Indian people of northern
Mexico, who survive the army attack to continue.[38] While the passage
emphasizes a "renewal of resolve," it also, in equal measure, notes the continuation of solidarity gained at Casas Grandes in the actions, songs, and
languages of those who had been a part of the spiritual revival. Their songs
and languages, unknown to their employers, become a disguised form of
communication, allowing the indigenous people to exercise their beliefs
and culture hidden in plain view.

As a social site for the autonomy of and free communication among Indians as well as a spiritual center, Casas Grandes represents a victory for
the disenfranchised and marginalized, who rebuilt the settlement.[39] While
residents of Casas Grandes lose this rebuilt settlement to the fierce brutality
and overwhelming power of the Mexican army, they spirit Zacarías away,
preserving the opportunity for another Casas Grandes in the future and
for the secret practice of their spirituality in the present. This flexibility in
the face of power echoes throughout the trilogy when, for example, Shelly
in *The Flower in the Skull* realizes that she is among the Opata people she
has long sought, people who took on the trappings of the society around
them yet continued their ancient ceremonies,[40] or when Estela undertakes
elaborate precautions to protect the publication of *La Linterna*, which represents another social site of resistance that is as dangerous to the authorities as Casas Grandes.[41] Alcalá's novels imagine not only the stories of the
vanquished and victimization but also the stories of tactical retreat and re-
grouping in the face of the power arrayed against them.

But memory is not simply of "what was," something that occurred in
the past, at some other time, but includes "what happened," an act or acts
that, perhaps, contributed to the creation of a sacred event and most cer-

tainly brought about a change in those who participated. The quality of the memory here is active, present. The omniscient narrator's language suggests that this understanding of the performance of ritual ceremonies at Casas Grandes by indigenous peoples shares much with Kabbalah's emphasis on restoration of the world through good works and prayer. This confluence further accentuates the novels' investment in exploring meeting points between diverse religious traditions in the Americas as they transform readers' comprehension of the gathering at Casas Grandes from a static historical event, "what was," to a narrative event, that is, a change from one state to another, or "what happened."

This narrative suggestion appears to draw from both indigenous understandings of the reciprocity between humans and the natural world and from the teachings of Kabbalah. The latter also emphasizes the performance of restorative acts and the interrelations between humans and the divine world. Laenen describes it in the following way: "Not only concrete human action, but also the thoughts, imagination, intentions or inner contemplations of humans exercise an influence on the dynamic processes of the world of the sefiroth and thus also on the quantity, nature and quality of the divine light which descends to the earth."[42] The significance of the Zoharic perspective resides in its understanding of a reciprocal relationship between God and humans, as David R. Blumenthal notes: "God's relationship with the world is patterned on the model of a continuous flow of energy. God generates the energy, but it is man who must act like a prism, focusing and returning the energy to God. This energy, then, is renewed and returned to man, who once again focuses and returns it to God, and so on." Blumenthal further notes that this Zoharic understanding is both orthodox and heretical at once, orthodox in that it supposes partnership with God, as in rabbinic Judaism, and heretical in that it removes omnipotence from God.[43] This is perhaps another reason that Kabbalah becomes part of the imagined world in these novels: its history and existence as an authoritative yet explicitly evolving spiritual tradition that remains apart from mainstream Jewish faith. *Spirits of the Ordinary* imagines the role of religion in historical events in the borderlands and suggests to readers that these events might be remembered not only for what they were but also for what they gave rise to: continued processes of spiritual mestizaje.

The varied religious traditions of the Americas have long been a signifi-

cant component of Chicano/a narratives.[44] Chicano/a fiction of the 1960s
and 1970s frequently took issue with religious ideologies and institutions as
it addressed questions of identity, collective history, citizenship, civil rights,
class, race, and gender.[45] Works such as John Rechy's *City of Night* (1963),
Raymond Barrio's *The Plum Plum Pickers* (1969), Tomás Rivera's *. . . y no se
lo tragó la tierra* (1971), José Antonio Villarreal's *Pocho* (1959), Oscar Zeta
Acosta's *The Revolt of the Cockroach People* (1973), and Estela Portillo Trambley's *Rain of Scorpions and Other Stories* (1975) critiqued religious beliefs
that enforced passivity, subservience, and repression, or critiqued religious
institutions that were seen as lending support to governmental or economic
interests bent on suppressing Chicano/a communities. In *Pocho*, a Mexican
American religious inheritance forms part of the past that the subject seeking inclusion in the mainstream must leave behind. In very different ways,
Trambley's and Acosta's work as well as that of Rudolfo Anaya in *Bless Me,
Ultima* (1972) figure indigenous spiritualities as a component of Chicano/a
religiosity and identity. Anaya's work goes furthest in grounding its understanding of this spirituality in local history and a context of curanderismo
whereas in Trambley and Acosta a more amorphous indigenous spirituality
predominates, unconsciously registering a gap between its historical antecedents and contemporary attraction.

Spirits of the Ordinary, *Treasures in Heaven*, and *The Flower in the Skull*
are different. These novels represent many religious traditions that have
historically defined the borderlands, rather than one or two, and as they
unfold readers are invited to consider how these religions intersect with
each other in the events and acts of the novels. While Catholicism remains
the predominant religion in the regions traversed by these characters, it is
not the only religious system with a historic or contemporary presence in
the borderlands. These novels include Tarahumara and Opata spirituality
in the region as well as the long-standing Crypto Jewish communities of
Mexico and New Mexico. In Alcalá's work, the region and its populations
are simultaneously a site of conflict and meeting between nations, peoples,
races, and religions—Anzaldúa's Aztlán—and the site of transnational possibility that Anzaldúa's conception of borderlands conveys.[46]

The narrative ethos at work in this trilogy, however, is not merely celebratory of multiple differences but instead echoes Anzaldúa in its emphasis
on a critical assessment of inherited traditions in spiritual mestizaje. The

remembrance of the repression and violence directed against Jews in the Americas by the Inquisition and the ongoing suspicion of Jews evident in acts by Estela's family and the people of Saltillo form part of the narrative's critical assessment. In addition, across the spiritual spectrum and through-out the three novels, characters engage in critical questioning of their inher-ited religious beliefs, sometimes in comparison to others, as when in *Spirits of the Ordinary* Julio wonders about his wife, Mariana's, spirituality, and other times in considering the social implications of particular religious beliefs, as when Margarita questions Father Newman's religious rationale for slavery ("some people are given dominion over others").[47] These novels represent this active engagement with one's spiritual framework positively, as a sign of health, growth, survival, and change.

Because these novels seek to address the lacunae about Judaism in the Americas, and in the borderlands in particular, they address this religion more than others, and Judaism and Kabbalah also undergo critical exami-nation. Zacarías's open critique of his father's religious practice as overly shuttered and secret is echoed by Julio himself as he contemplates the ef-fects of isolation and secrecy on the survival of Judaism: "There were people lighting candles on Friday night who hadn't the faintest idea why they were doing it. Only blind tradition maintained the tenuous thread."[48] Julio cri-tiques not only the long-term suppression that creates the danger of obliv-ion for Judaism, but also the unthinking repetition of ritual—the complete opposite of a critically engaged spiritual practice.

In considering his son's marriage to a non-Jew, Julio's regret over having allowed the marriage is tempered by his awareness of the inevitability of racial and religious mixture: "Half of the families, although they would not admit it, had Jewish blood. The other half, although they would not admit it, dark as they were, had Indian blood. It was only a matter of time, Julio thought, before some had both."[49] The inability of the dominant mestizo society to accept either Jewish or indigenous ancestry and the continued marginalization and racism directed against these groups that such views inevitably signal betray a process of racial formation that naturalizes Jews and Indians as inferior. Julio recognizes this process, and the hypocrisy of those participating in it, in his observation, but he also suggests the inevita-bility of racial/cultural and religious mixture.

Linked in Europe, religion and race remain interconnected in the Ameri-

cas. In New Spain, "whiteness, Catholicism, and civilization"[50] were frequently conflated. After U.S. expansion to what is now called the Southwest, Protestantism replaced Catholicism in the formulation. Although
there were exceptions to both of these predominant perspectives in their
respective eras, neither indigenous nor Crypto Jewish beliefs or communities have enjoyed mainstream acceptance for most of the time since European settlement.[51] The racialized discrimination of anti-Semitism that
Julio addresses resonates for other racial minorities who, as he observes, do
not fit neatly into racially "pure" or superior categories of white, criollo, or
mestizo. From both the dominant and marginal perspectives, race and religion are interconnected, though the natural process of racial intermixture
that Julio envisions will not, as narrative events demonstrate, necessarily
result in religious mixture. Instead, the kind of cross-cultural dialogue that
occurs at Casas Grandes becomes key to the development of spirituality in
the Americas. But Julio's ties to tradition may hamper rather than advance
this project: "Although Julio had been born in Mexico, as had many generations before him, he was a spiritual product of the old world, never quite at
ease in this wild, open space, where the races intermingled freely and a man
could outrun his reputation, if he ran far enough. Julio was rooted to place,
to order, to predictability."[52]

Julio retains Eurocentric views of the land and peoples of the Americas,
ideas that contribute to his unease about his own place and raise questions
about the relationship between European religious traditions and the peoples and landscapes of the New World. Yet while Julio's Crypto Judaism
and the Quintanilla family's dominant Catholicism exist separately, in opposition, Zacarías in *Spirits of the Ordinary* and Estela and Noé in *Treasures
in Heaven* are able to draw upon both religious traditions in confronting
the challenges of life in the borderlands.

Common Ground: Gardens and
the Religious Injunction to Do Good

The religious pluralism of the borderlands is represented in this trilogy
by characters who hail from distinct traditions, yet it also includes the
differing views and practices of individuals who share the same religious
tradition, revealing a heterogeneity of spiritual expression even within established groups or worldviews. The garden, the natural flora and fauna

significant to spiritual accounts of origins, emerges as a potent site of negotiation among the various spiritual perspectives as well as a symbol of common ground. Each of the spiritual traditions represented in these novels
expresses itself, in part, through its relationship to and mythology of the
garden or natural world.[53]

In *Spirits of the Ordinary*, Julio and Mariana Caraval's garden is explicitly portrayed in this way. A private garden that did not give up its secrets
easily for over 400 years, in other words, since Jews settled in the Americas,
the garden is initially described as rich:

> The house, set low against a slight rise, nearly invisible in its lush sur-
> roundings of cedar, jacaranda, bottlebrush and wisteria, did not seem
> to have a front . . . as though it was self-effacing and wished to be
> forgotten. . . .
>
> Within the enclosure was a miniature garden almost gemlike in its
> perfection. Low boxwood hedges hugged the wall on two sides, filling
> the air with their pungent odor. . . . Alongside the portico grew blood
> red roses, almost funereal in their intensity of color. . . .
>
> Huge pots of fuchsias hung from the protruding vigas, catching the
> sun and contrasting sharply with the deep shade against the house.
>
> At the center of the garden, a fountain as squat as the house itself
> gurgled softly. The cold spring water spilled over its thick, green-
> stained lips and ran obediently along channels in the flagstone paving
> to form a shining ribbon that laced the garden in severe Moorish sym-
> metry before disappearing under the hedges. The fountain had run
> steadily since the house was built, the spring within the earth seem-
> ingly inexhaustible.[54]

This garden metaphorically represents the secrecy, skill, beauty, intensity,
order, and deep well of tradition with which Judaism and Jewish people
have survived in the Americas. This description also conveys a rootedness
and energy that, in a different way, we see in Zacarías who, as a miner, becomes expert in reading the landscape. The harmony with which garden
and house coexist and the fullness of the garden itself suggest a blessed relationship with the natural world. But, with echoes of the expulsion from
the garden of Eden, this beautiful landscape is transformed into a severe
and desolate place by Julio's desire to impose his control and will on the

external world, his son, and his wife, Mariana—a desire that he mistakenly sees as divinely inspired. Julio's trimming and pruning and management eventually destroy the garden, and Mariana laments this destruction of the natural world, which she sees as desiring "nurture and co-resplendence."[55] Previously Mariana's special place, the garden becomes a battleground for the contending spiritual visions of Julio and Mariana, for while he avidly seeks the glory of God in intense study and mystical practice, Mariana simply admires this glory as it unfolds every day in the natural world. Julio's desire is, in many ways, for both recognition from the divine and sacred guidance in directing or controlling life's events. Mariana's effortless communion with the sacred betrays no such desires.

Though not a garden in the same sense as that of Julio and Mariana, the care, knowledge, and observation with which Concha describes the landscape of the Opatería also convey a profound and symbolic relationship to the natural world: "In the desert, deep inside the spiny center of the cactus, nests a bird no bigger than my finger. While the sharp thorns fend off animals that would eat the eggs, the parent birds come and go at will. And this was my mother's name, 'living at the heart of the spiny cactus,' Chiri, what others would call Hummingbird."[56] This naming after the natural world suggests an identification with nature parallel to Julio's but more intimate. Rather than controlling nature by attempting to trim, cut, and manage it, the Opatería appear to tailor their farming and living to the capabilities and gifts of the natural world, having learned about it through study, observation, and experience. This reciprocity is part of Opata spirituality, yet it echoes in the spiritual and political perspectives of other characters, such as Membrillo, Manzana, Estela, Zacarías, Noé, and Mariana.

Treasures in Heaven focuses on Estela's, and later Noé's, efforts to improve the lot of poor working women in Mexico City. Set in the historical period of Porfirio Díaz's positivist regime, the novel centers on the emergent feminism of social reformers whose work is made possible, in part, by limitations the Díaz regime imposes on church holdings, institutions, and organizations.[57] *Treasures in Heaven* explores the social reform movement of that era, situating the school for poor women and children that Estela is hired to run, La Paciencia, in an abandoned convent.[58]

Estela's involvement with La Paciencia brings her into contact with the social reform movement and an emergent feminist movement. She brings her religious values to bear in attending to the women and children of La Paciencia; charity and hope flow freely from Estela, but La Paciencia turns out to be a school for her as well, where her own journey of spiritual mestizaje continues. Her experiences in managing and organizing the school, and with the feminist and social reform movements that support it, transform Estela into a confident leader dedicated to improving women's lives. She gains a heightened awareness of the inequalities between women and men—and even sees the shortcomings of the social reform movement in this regard. Estela's active Catholicism is important to her and to her work in aiding the poor women and children of Mexico City, but it is supplemented by her growing political consciousness.

Estela raises her son Noé in Catholicism, attending mass with him regularly throughout their sojourn in Mexico City, but she also shares Noé's spiritual training with his Jewish grandparents, Julio and Mariana Caraval, who, having relocated to Mexico City, become part of a vibrant yet secretive Crypto Jewish community. Julio and Mariana repeatedly provide Estela with assistance in the work of social reform—including education, health care, housing, and workers' rights—acting out of their own religious convictions to do good in the world. This dual religious training creates in Noé the desire to participate in creating a more just society, and as he grows into a young man he becomes increasingly involved in movements for change. He openly credits his Catholic mother and his Jewish grandparents for having "learned the value of the good word," meaning sacred texts and good work, and he refuses to hide either religious tradition from view.

Noé's acceptance of Judaism in his life follows his father's prior return to the Jewish mystical tradition of his parents and ancestors. The experience at Casas Grandes allows Zacarías to see the value of a spiritual tradition that guides one in caring actions for this world and its inhabitants yet also acknowledges an imperfect communion with the ineffable. When his son Gabriel later discovers a manuscript left by Zacarías, he concludes: "From his writings, it was clear that he had undergone a deep and profound change— a revelation if you will—that had shaken him to the very foundation of his soul and brought him back to the traditions of his family."[59] *Spirits of the Ordinary* includes canticles and prayers that form part of a fragmented manuscript left by Zacarías following his experience at Casas Grandes; their presence attests to Zacarías's reintegration into Jewish mysticism. Actually quoting from *Los judios bajo la inquisición en Hispanoamérica* (*Jews under*

17. Book cover of
Treasures in Heaven
by Kathleen Alcalá,
© 2000 Kathleen
Alcalá. Used with
permission of
Chronicle Books LLC,
San Francisco.

the Inquisition in Latin America),[60] the novel incorporates these materials to represent Zacarías's spiritual renewal in the aftermath of Casas Grandes. Eventually, his son Gabriel comes into possession of these pages and finds that the recovered manuscript also contains family stories (presumably the novel we are reading).

An excerpt from the Zohar, a medieval Judaic mystical text, appears between the dedication page and the opening of the novel: "In love is found the secret of divine unity. / It is love that unites the higher / and the lower stages of existence. / That raises the lower to the level of the higher—/ where all become fused into one." This paratextual positioning accords the Zohar a place of importance in interpreting the novel. Indeed, this excerpt reverberates in the novel in a number of ways. Love, including how to love and what kinds of love are socially acceptable, is an important issue. The

Zohar is a key text, long secret, whose authorship and sacredness have been historically debated; in the novel, Zacarías's recovered manuscript takes on the coloration of an analogous text, this one based in the Americas. The Zohar takes an unorthodox form and conveys some of the key tenets of Jewish mysticism, including the idea of reciprocity between God and human; the importance of the imagination in visionary ascent; an understanding of God's unity as one that combines the masculine and feminine divine; and the transformation of the Jewish experience of exile into "symbolic mission."[61] These issues resonate in the novel's exploration of the relationship between humans and the divine from a variety of spiritual perspectives and in its particular interest in how gender and spirituality intersect in the characters' lives and in religious conceptions of God.

To turn one's experience into a "symbolic mission" is to suggest that it offers something to those outside of or beyond the experience; in telling stories about the suppression and renewal of Crypto Jewish and indigenous worldviews, the novels stage a symbolic mission of returning the voices of the marginalized to history, recognizing the multiple spiritualities and sacred texts of the Americas, and opening the door to further spiritual renewals and revisions. The narrative constructions of *Spirits of the Ordinary* as, in part, pages from Zacarías's manuscript, and of *Treasures in Heaven* and *The Flower in the Skull* as stories of spiritual action and reflection—all hidden or lost and later recovered—echo the emergence of this Jewish text which, according to Blumenthal, arose "out of an almost complete, hardly penetrable anonymity and concealment" to become a widely accepted sacred text of Judaism.[62] Ariel notes:

> The *Zohar* is a comprehensive mystical commentary on many sections of the Torah. It presents a reading of the Torah as a novel of the inner life of God and the dynamics of the divine powers. It was the primary literary vehicle through which the mystical teachings and symbolism of the Spanish *Kabbalah* were conveyed along with major innovations in theory and interpretation.[63]

On multiple levels, the Zohar becomes a paradigmatic text for the exploration of new spiritualities in these novels, a status heightened by its history as a text that attests to the formation of new spiritualities from existing traditions with a "symbolic-mythic-poetic dimension."[64]

Indigenous Communities and Spiritualities in the Borderlands

The trilogy also includes Native American characters that engage in spiritual *mestizaje* and create new spiritualities. The Tarahumara and Opata belief systems are perpetuated by oral tradition, performance, and ritual, rather than through literary texts. Tarahumara, Opata, and many other indigenous belief systems underwent transformation as a result of contact with conquerors, settlers, and missionaries—global phenomena often accompanied by environmental changes, economic disruptions, or disease.[65] One example of transformation is the incorporation of Easter Passion Play rituals into native religious performances, melding indigenous and Christian ritual performances.[66] Despite their displacement, these remain important rituals in contemporary indigenous communities, though the separation from traditional lands and ways of life contributes, for some, to the pressure to "forget" the components of native religiosity embedded in these practices and instead read them as strictly Christian.[67] In the first chapter of *The Flower in the Skull*, Concha remembers the ways of her people, the Opata, who are under pressure from the Mexican government's efforts to displace them and other indigenous peoples from their traditional lands. Concha's remembrance is an alternative history of the region, a counter-memory that contests the obscuration of minority histories by dominant society,[68] and also a testimony to a different way of being in the world, one in which humans share a reciprocal relationship with the natural world and women share in communal power. Her description of her naming conveys the status of women among the Opata: "My name at that time was Shark's Tooth from the Sea, which means 'something precious.' . . . my mother's family named me after this rare and beautiful object. It meant that I was strong and fierce and wild and beautiful, all things that the Opata wanted in their baby girls."[69] The defensive wars waged by indigenous peoples in the northwestern part of Mexico, fictionalized in this narrative, take a toll on the continued survival of the Opata. The incursion of Western power and beliefs is symbolically represented in Concha's narrative by the appearance of the black-hatted trader in their villages, who is figured not as an agent of cross-cultural dialogue but as a predator:

El Gusano used to come on horseback to our village to trade. He always
came with a lot of money and brought mescal for the men, and even the
women who wanted it. He would take someone aside and talk in a low
voice so no one could hear, his big black Stetson with the rattlesnake
band pulled low over his eyes, so all you could see was smoke. Pretty
soon that man was nodding, and you could see that they were counting
things up. . . . Once he came and took a girl away, crying.[70]

The materiality of the horse, the mescal, the hat—objects from another
world—represents cultural incursion for Concha, and her account is
saturated with foreboding. Readers witness the further fragmentation of
Opata life and culture in *The Flower in the Skull* when Concha and her
two sisters are sold by their mother, Chiri, to El Gusano as she flees the
devastated Opata village to join in the revival at Casas Grandes described
in *Spirits of the Ordinary*. Concha describes a people under siege who seek
both to practice their way of life and to defend themselves against the Mexican government and Apache raids. Chiri's action in selling her daughters
while keeping Beto, who is gifted with psychic powers but also prone to
uncontrollable seizures, appears perhaps as an unwelcome influence of
cross-cultural contact and a sign of the diminishment of women among
the Opata. The irony of Chiri's action, her desire to join in the community
at Casas Grandes while selling her daughters, both blocks a romantic reading of native peoples and echoes the all-too-human imperfections of other
characters in this trilogy, of whatever religious persuasion. Here we see another aspect of the change that cross-cultural contact—or, more precisely,
the crisis precipitated by that contact—may engender. El Gusano feeds on
the crisis of the disintegrating Opata village as the Mexican government's
war against Indians slowly takes its toll.

The Opata nation joined together in a shared worldview fragments in
Concha's account, disrupting a spiritual cohesion that unifies and constitutes social groups.[71] Before colonial incursion, the Opatería enjoyed the
unity (not to be confused with conflict-free society) of a social group joined
by a shared perspective and ethos. Under pressure from the Mexican national project to assimilate or disappear, the Opata flee, migrate, and move,
their worldview surviving among individuals or in smaller groups. Beto,
Concha's brother, carries this with him, and even Concha remains spiritually Opata, but neither enjoys the communal aspect of their religion, the

18. Book cover of *The Flower in the Skull*, text © by Kathleen Alcalá, cover illustration © 1999 by Nicholas Wilton, reproduced by permission of Houghton Mifflin Harcourt Publishing Company.

ability to worship with others. In this the Opata are not alone; communal worship is also denied to Crypto Jews in the borderlands. In the Jewish mystical tradition, the Zohar emphasizes the significance of congregation and the "aggregate merit" of prayer with others in the synagogue, something denied to Julio, Mariana, Zacarías, and Crypto Jews and anusim in the borderlands.[72] *Spirits of the Ordinary*, *Treasures in Heaven*, and *The Flower in the Skull* reveal how the suppression of Opata and Jewish religious communities serves the consolidation first of a colonial Catholic power and later of a Mexican national and Catholic state in ways that prompt us to consider the link between religion and race in the configuration of the ideal citizen subject, an issue significant not only for Mexico but for the borderlands and beyond.

In *The Flower in the Skull*, Shelly, on assignment in Tucson for her publishing company, discovers her own family's past, or at least part of it, in a private archive of antique photographs that includes photos of her grandmother Concha. Prompted by this to dig deeper, Shelly undertakes research that eventually leads her to San Xavier del Bac Mission, outside of Tucson, where she joins Opata worshippers, and later to an annual Opata pilgrimage and religious observance at Magdalena in northern Mexico. In returning to the Opatería, Shelly returns not to a preserved, "authentic" native past, nor to a "pure" Christianity, but instead to the ritual performance of hybrid religiosity and community that constitutes contemporary Opata spirituality. It is her experience of having to conceal herself to avoid sexual harassment that opens her eyes to the masked ways that the Opatería carried their own spirituality into Christianity at San Xavier; her description of this revelation suggests a kind of Crypto-Opata community in plain sight. This is one of many ironies in these novels, where suppression creates secret lives and communities whose existence necessarily suggests that there is a stark contrast between the imagined community and the actual. The novel renders any hint of nostalgia in Shelly's final return to Magdalena ironic in that she goes back not to an idyllic past but to a recovery of the history of suppression, displacement, exile, and violence that her family has suffered.[73]

The narrative investment in representing multiple religious traditions calls into question the supremacy or primacy of any one religious tradition, imagining instead how spiritual mestizaje unfolds amid the contacts and conflicts of the varied peoples and views of the borderlands. The narrative focus of this trilogy remains on the examination of spirituality as a way of being in the world, that is, the behaviors and interactions that respect for the sacred guides and inspires, the social enactment of belief. In contrast to the texts discussed in chapter 2, where individual journeys of spiritual mestizaje unfold, or the texts of chapter 3, where this critical spirituality occurs communally, in Alcalá's novels the portrayal of characters moving through historic events and migrations with attention to the sacred resonates with Anzaldúa's efforts to understand spiritual mestizaje as a social phenomenon. Here characters discover that love, in its many forms, rather than fear, self-preservation, power, ethnocentrism, or essentialism, is the greatest asset in negotiating conflict and what will come of it. The excerpt from the Zohar above expresses an understanding of love and acting in love that pervades these texts, perhaps most powerfully when it is absent.

Gender and New Spiritual Visions

Each of the novels in this trilogy explores the formation of gender and sexuality quite distinctly. In *Spirits of the Ordinary*, religion plays a major role in policing gender conventions and sexual norms; *scandal* means acting outside of these norms. The strictness of the dominant codes for gender and sexual behavior create, for many characters, a double life and, for others, a violent death. Estela and her daughters face censure for behaving in ways that violate the closeting of women's sexuality in the small town of Saltillo, while the landowner and businesswoman Margarita learns that her economic power shields her from that censure. Estela's twin siblings, Membrillo and Manzana, pose an even greater challenge to the gender and sexual norms of Saltillo and the region. Identical hermaphrodite twins, they are described by their doctor as "an aberration of nature, marica and marimacho," who their father, Horacio, and the rest of the family, nonetheless, accept and raise as perfectly natural, beautiful, refined human beings. The twins, therefore, accept themselves with confidence, as the following passage indicates: Membrillo and Manzana "really did seem to see themselves as the most natural beings in the world, and viewed the rest of humanity with a curious detachment, as though the wide ocean of variable and questionable beings around them were slightly farther away from the peaceful center of the universe upon whose bosom they rested with perfect ease."[74] By virtue of their self-assurance, the twins resist socialization into either of the existing gender categories, instead seemingly calling such categories into question. In their androgyny they are evocative of some of the mythic and mystical beliefs of borderlands peoples—both the two-spirit people that some indigenous groups regard as especially gifted and the feminine and masculine unity of the Sephiroth and Ein Sof of the Kabbalah. Though the twins seem impervious to it, the novel creates a strong image of Membrillo and Manzana as existing on the edge of a social acceptance that could, and eventually does, turn the other way. The twins are, indeed, gifted, spending their adult lives as water diviners throughout the region, but they are, at the novel's end, murdered for their difference by the wave of repression against any nonconformity that accompanies the tragedy at Casas Grandes.

The historical roots of the violence unleashed against native peoples at the ancient settlement and of the gendered and racialized violence directed against native women are the central narrative threads of the third book in the trilogy, *The Flower in the Skull*. Each of the narrators in this novel recounts a violent history: Concha tells about her displacement, exile, and rape by the wealthy Anglo settler George Vaughan; Rosa describes her marginalization and silence; Shelly describes the sexual harassment and rape she suffers at the hands of her boss.[75] The nation, the dominant ethnicity and race, and the inequalities of gender all contribute to the violence that these characters experience. However, the discourses of academe are also implicated. In Shelly's account, a critique of the discourse of anthropology emerges in the portrayal of her workplace, a publishing company that produces coffee-table books that capture and immobilize indigenous women, rendering them as beautiful objects for display—or victimization.

Through her Tucson assignment, Shelly begins to discover previously occluded parts of the story of her people—not present in the books published by the company where she works—and to imagine another story for herself. One gets a strong sense that the genocide, ethnocentrism, and gender discrimination both experienced and practiced by frontera inhabitants will not remain unknown after Shelly's recovery. This is cast as a liberating event for Shelly, who states: "It was just another assignment. Yet I felt as if I had been given a chance to change the direction of my life."[76] Chronologically in the novel, it is after the initial recovery of her family's violent history that Shelly's sexually harassing boss rapes her. In this way the text suggests a contemporary continuation of the violent regimes responsible for the suppression of the stories that Shelly is in the process of investigating.

In contrast to the narratives discussed in previous chapters, where female protagonists predominate, in this trilogy two key male characters emerge, and both learn to embrace partnership, collaboration, and dialogue with women. The first is Zacarías in *Spirits of the Ordinary*, who comes to be viewed as a prophet and healer among the native peoples, and the second is his son Noé in *Treasures in Heaven*, who joins his mother, Estela's, efforts to improve the lot of poor women and children in Mexico City.

Zacarías is initially detached from his family, self-absorbed, and obsessed with mining for gold, and he enjoys the prerogatives of his position as head of the household. Estela's action in legally prohibiting him from draining the family coffers for his adventures forces him to reconsider his life, livelihood, and relations with women. The quiet and tender Zacarías cares for both his parents and his family, yet does not feel drawn to them in the ways they require and desire. Zacarías's parents, wife, and children want him to work in town, and his father, Julio, also wants him to take up religious study, but Zacarías is bent on mining for gold. He benefits from a gender privilege that allows him greater social freedoms than those afforded to his wife. Estela's action in cutting him off from the family finances—her legal prerogative under Mexican law—removes her from the position of wife-in-waiting and frees him from a life he merely tolerates; however, the boldness of her action draws criticism and has enduring consequences. Subsequent narrative events do not simply celebrate her action by, for example, imagining a blissful or triumphant post-marriage life for Estela. The language in which Estela and others consider her situation as a semi-divorced woman suggests not easy resolution but difficult and ongoing negotiation with prevailing gender norms and expectations.

Noé becomes a key character of the second novel in the trilogy, *Treasures in Heaven*, through his collaboration with a group of progressive-minded women and men who publish *La Linterna*, a magazine for "the working women of Mexico, who carry it and all its inhabitants on their backs."[77] The highly secret editorial board of *La Linterna* includes La Señorita, Mejora de Gonga; her lawyer and assistant, Humberto; Noé's mother, Estela; and Gloria Quinque, a teacher from Mérida who turns to journalism after having been banned from the schools because "her students had acquired too many ideas about freedom and their place in the world."[78] As a child, Noé soaks up the atmosphere of social reform that characterizes La Señorita's household and his mother's work, lives amid the working poor for whom Estela works, and benefits from his regular contact with grandparents Julio and Mariana, learning through both observing and sharing in their lives the prayers and meditations of the Kabbalah as well as what it means to live a life of love. As a young man, Noé becomes the messenger to *La Linterna*'s secret printer and later an editor and writer for the magazine. His education and interest in the philosophical, social, ethical, and moral issues of his era combine with his growing activism and he becomes, in the latter part of the novel, the inheritor not only of La Señorita's estate but also of her life's work as he and his new partner, Matilda, take over La Señorita's house and La Paciencia, the school for women.

In its ending, *Treasures in Heaven* plays with reader expectations. Because descriptions of La Señorita throughout the novel emphasize her mysteriousness and timelessness—"she appeared to be of a constant age"—as well as her interest in both utilizing Estela's skills and educating her further in the realities of working women's lives and the routes toward change, the narrative creates the expectation of her eventual demise.[79] By creating Estela's life in Mexico City as one marked by the movement from naïve novice to experienced social reformer, the narrative simultaneously suggests that Estela will inherit La Señorita's legacy. Her return, therefore, to Saltillo and to a quiet life in the company of her sister, older children, and other relatives disrupts reader expectations. Instead of Estela's ascension to La Señorita's place, it becomes Noé's and Matilda's, that is, the future work toward greater gender, sexual, economic, and social equality falls to Estela's feminist son and his feminist partner, Matilda (who is the daughter of Estela's long-standing lover and collaborator in the publication of *La Linterna*, Doctor Carranza).

Gloria Quinque and La Señorita argue that publishing *La Linterna* is necessary in the fight to defend the poor from the massive exploitation brought by industrialization, especially in the henequen plantations. Estela, whose work flows from her Christianity, logically expects that the church would be involved in combating the horrible conditions on the plantations. She is stunned to discover otherwise when Gloria states: "The Church merely promises treasures in heaven."[80] Gloria awakens in Estela a recognition of the divide between her religious motivations for engaging in the work of social justice, what this analysis suggests is spirituality as a way of being in the world, and a religiosity that perpetuates injustice by withdrawing from the world and focusing on interior devotion. *La Linterna*, the group decides, can combat passivity through education but, as Gloria observes, what the magazine can accomplish is limited: "We cannot change the order of things, . . . but we can change their place in it. They will have to change the order themselves."[81] *La Linterna* offers information on women's health and sexuality, a controversial project in Mexico at the beginning of the twentieth century, the novel suggests, but one that has a long history, as the secret printer, M Cardoz, notes when he compares it to the medieval *Tacuinum Sanitatis*.[82] Since the event of *La Linterna*'s publication is not possible without the act of Mariana and Julio finding the printer M Cardoz, rumored to be Jewish, in Mexico City, the story draws the Judaic mystical tradition as one more accepting of sexuality.[83] The publication and circulation of *La Linterna* and the collaborative effort that this entails do not, in the events of the novel, "change the order of things," but both acts make it possible for individuals to begin to change that order.

Noé receives a task not only from La Señorita but also from Estela, when she makes him promise that he will write the story of it all, and at the end of the novel a brief, italicized section begins: "And so I have written this down, just the way my mother, Estela Quintanilla de Carabajál, told it to me, and the way I experienced it, was told it, or imagined the text."[84] In contrast to the imagined female scribes discussed in previous chapters, such as Nena in *Canícula*, Soveida in *Face of an Angel*, and María in *Mother Tongue*, who themselves take up the pen and write their lives, *Treasures in Heaven* centers on the lives of women as told to an imagined male scribe, though it is not until the end that readers know that the narrator is Noé. *Spirits of the Ordinary* ends on a similar note when Gabriel, the eldest son of Estela and Zacarías, returns to the Southwest and receives fragments of a manuscript that includes his family history, apparently penned by his father in the wake of his exile from Casas Grandes and Saltillo. Gabriel's discovery prompts him to return to Saltillo to unearth the family home and reestablish family connections, and this narrative event aptly conveys the twin themes of retrospection and renewal that predominate in this work. As fictions that incorporate both a formal element of the testimonio form—Zacarías writes a first-person witness account, while Estela tells Noé her story for publication—and a thematic element of the testimonio form, the story of a journey toward greater awareness, both *Spirits of the Ordinary* and *Treasures in Heaven* share some commonalities with that form.

Though this trilogy clearly looks to the testimonio, only one of its books fits cleanly into the category of fictional testimonio: *The Flower in the Skull*. Its three first-person accounts of individual and collective journeying together form a narrative of growing consciousness about the historic and continued suppression of Indian women. It also has the most open-ended final scene—Shelly's arrival in Magdalena to continue her search for family and history, a dramatic change in her life and circumstances whose outcome remains uncertain. In contrast, the endings of the other two novels carry a greater degree of certainty; in each case, the ending points back toward the beginning as the narrative represents, metafictionally, its creation as part of the spiritual and political work that Zacarías and Noé continue. While both Zacarías and Noé experience conversions—into scribes, prophets, and feminists—the narratives do not conflate their individual conversions with those of the individuals and collectivities whose stories they write. They reveal collective experiences that impact individual characters, including themselves, differently.

Secrecy and Religious Survival

The historical condition of Jews and indigenous peoples in the borderlands as repressed religious minorities, as diasporan peoples forced to hide their beliefs, required them to practice their faiths with some stealth but, as this fictional trilogy imagines, it may also have created a bridge between them.[85] In these narratives, the history of genocide against indigenous peoples in the Americas meets the history of European pogroms against and persecution of Jewish people, which were brought to the Americas most famously via the Inquisition. Together, the novels assert the continuing legacy of the conquest and colonial moment on religious and racial formation in the Americas, where Jews and Indians are figured as racial Others. The brief period of very limited open recognition of the Jewish community in the Americas, shown by the phrase "only ten years had passed since a Jewish marriage had been allowed in Buenos Aires" and in the description of Zacarías as "the first son in thirteen generations to bear an overtly Jewish name," closes once again when the Mexican government brutally destroys the renewed community of Casas Grandes and circulates the suggestion that the Jewish Zacarías attempted to lead Indian peoples there in insurrection.[86] Not only are Julio and Mariana, Zacarías's parents, forced to flee from the mob violence directed against them, but all those who survive the military attack are also forced to disperse and to hide, once again, their spiritual beliefs and practices. Concha's account in *The Flower in the Skull* begins with a testament to the Opata diaspora: "This is the story of my people, the Opata, who once numbered as many as the saguaro of the desert, and who once farmed many rancherías and had many villages, but are now just a few, and scattered far and wide from their home and the constellations that knew them."[87] That the story of her people is not only a story of exile and displacement, but also a story of continual violence against indigenous women radically recenters the history of the Opata on questions of racialized, gendered, sexual violence, rather than viewing these as an addendum to history, and reads these circumstances as evidence of the continued subjugation of the Opata.

In secrecy, the stories of this trilogy imagine, lies the possibility for survival. Secrecy, observes Daniel C. Matt, remains a significant core of the Zohar, which engages in the revelation of ancient secrets and the creation of new knowledge: "The Kabbalists, as a group, are described as knowing how to 'renew ancient words every day.'"[88] Yet that secrecy might also contribute to further loss and displacement, as it does for the Opata people in *The Flower in the Skull*. Alcalá repeatedly suggests the tenuousness or fragility engendered by secrecy. These novels, therefore, do not celebrate the hidden transcript, that space away from the surveillance of dominant regimes, but imagine the ways that peoples of the Americas have made use of or suffered under that imposed condition and especially how they have managed to engage with others in spiritual mestizaje despite isolation and secrecy in ways that suggest the possibility for further imaginings of, as Alcalá states, "who we will be."[89]

5 *"Bad Religion"*

My purpose here has been to turn attention to the ways that Anzaldúa's perspective of the borderlands centers spiritual transformation as a possibility arising from the meeting of disparate cultures and as a necessary and more conscious element of the critical project of the borderlands. In considering the theory and method of spiritual mestizaje, I created a framework for the analysis of religion and spirituality in borderlands Chicana narratives. These texts imagine and represent the relationship between spirituality, on the one hand, and subject formation and material and social relations, on the other hand, as mutually informing and intersectional, echoing a critical aspect of Anzaldúa's theory and analysis; without her emphasis on the material conditions of the border and its inhabitants, the historical creation of the border, and the histories of marginalization embodied in that border, there would be nothing requiring transformation and the kinds of consciousness that could bring it to fruition. The consciousness she proposes emerges from, rather than mimetically represents, the material conditions of the border. Similarly, the narratives discussed here do not set forth an established border or history—recall that most begin with a different telling of the past or an open questioning of the past—but instead create or imagine characters moving through complex borderlands societies that present both the necessity of and possibility for changes in consciousness. In some ways my study takes up the call by Carl Gutiérrez-Jones for work that examines "how historiography legitimates certain rhetorical modes," since each of the narratives must address historiography in some form in the course of imagining a feminist discourse of spirituality—whether it is a character contesting romantic family stories or a film advancing another view of women's historic worship of Guadalupe or a novel populating the borderlands with the many spiritual traditions it has always held.[1]

In centering spiritual mestizaje, Anzaldúa distances herself from the perspective that a stronger new mestiza consciousness requires jettisoning a reliance on "primitive" folk beliefs, outmoded systems of thought, residual practices, or irrational and superstitious intellectual crutches, as she questions the cultural patrimony that might otherwise support, as Canclini observes, oligarchic or authoritarian systems.[2] Her critical memories of relation, experience, and economies embedded in a particular sociopolitical, cultural, and temporal space model a decolonial practice also adopted in Chicana fictional and documentary narratives here.

This Anzaldúan method for imagining, and then creating, more just forms of social relation brings her to study and recuperate indigenous worldviews in the Americas for a contemporary queer feminist practice. The incorporation of these elements into her mestiza consciousness through spiritual mestizaje follows an imperative that is also characteristic of moves in postcolonial scholarship to recover the indigenous, but without a national project as its aim. Her assertion of indigeneity enacts significant social, cultural, and political change on several levels: it creates a bridge among different groups of the marginalized, rejects a class and race bias, counters an oppressive institutional religion that devalues her as a queer woman, and pursues an epistemology of the Americas. In *Borderlands/La Frontera*, Anzaldúa works to separate spirituality and women's active participation in shaping it from patriarchal norms of gender and sexuality. Her decolonial stance promotes an ongoing critical spiritual praxis informed by the borderlands and an understanding of the history of indigenous peoples on the continent, particularly women and queers. This decolonial stance, following Emma Pérez, clearly and carefully assesses inherited ideas, beliefs, and practices taking special stock of those interstitial spaces where women have historically operated.[3]

Postcolonial and Decolonial Perspectives on Spirituality, Gender, and Nation

Anzaldúa's theory of spiritual mestizaje shares with postcolonial studies roots in an anticolonial or anti-neocolonial location, directly invoked in her discussion of the Anglo settlement and takeover of what was then Mexico in the nineteenth century. In each case, religious configurations shift. For example, in postcolonial India, Hindu religiosity becomes in-

fused with western rationality as a new national and hegemonic culture takes shape that more aptly corresponds to the economic and material shifts engendered by colonialism.[4] This does not appear strange if we consider that a religious rationale also supported colonization.[5] However, as Chicano/a studies has recognized, this new nationalism itself gives rise to another series of exclusions, not the least of which is one based on gender, and establishes new essentialisms. Anzaldúa's implicit critique of the early Chicano/a movement's "nativism" and the exclusions enacted there resonates with postcolonialists' critique of new post-Independence hegemonies of native nationalist classes. For those examining the postcolonial liberal nationalist project, it is apparent that while these new hegemonies reverse the colonialist assertion of superiority over native cultures and belief systems, such projects, in harnessing native cultures and belief systems in the interests of a new nationalist state that also incorporates Western values, remain enmeshed in colonialist ideologies.[6]

However, neither the colonial nor the postcolonial, neither the settler nor the nation-state, succeeds in erasing native worldviews or cultures from memory or practice. Both Ranajit Guha and Ashis Nandy address this in different ways in the Indian context. Guha notes that neither the colonialist project nor the new nationalist project achieved consistent and universal hegemony. Instead, he argues, resistance to hegemonic rule present in the "material and spiritual life" of India under colonialism continues under nationalist rule in the form of "entrenched feudal customs and belief systems, and the compromises imposed by these on official and nonofficial elitist attempts at social reform."[7] The "mythic past" of India, though co-opted for colonialist and nationalist projects, is not completely subsumed by them and remains as an alternative form of native knowledge and culture that resists hegemony. Nandy traces the continuation of Indian conceptions of the feminine, masculine, and native gender norms that differ from those of colonial ideologies in support of his claim that Indian sacred texts and spiritual practices might provide an alternative lens for evaluating and living modernity.[8] Nandy observes that colonialism advances a dichotomy between "history" and "myth" which casts the latter as a form of second-rate consciousness unable to distinguish past from present, whereas mature societies (read: Western culture) are characterized by their distance from the past.[9] In contrast, Nandy values and explores Indian myth. In her study of indigenous worldviews and her remembrance of her grandmother's spiritual practices, Anzaldúa undertakes the kind of excavation central to the critical process of spiritual mestizaje, mining the past for alternative forms of knowledge. Like Nandy, who recognizes the significance of spirituality in resistance to domination but rejects, as a "neo-romantic" stereotype, the notion of the Indian subject as only or primarily spiritual or irrational,[10] Anzaldúa's critical analysis of the interrelations of religion, spirituality, power, and social transformation decidedly shift away from idealized or stereotyped conceptions of the spiritual subject.

The patterns that Anzaldúa examines have a long history in the Americas, where a religious rationale—of superior and civilizing belief systems—presents itself alongside conquering, colonial, and imperial political and economic projects of domination.[11] Scholars have argued that the colonial emergence and establishment of native Catholic saints and holy figures in the Americas dovetails with the growing desire of the criollo classes to assert their religious autonomy from colonial powers, in tandem with political and economic autonomy.[12] In Mexico's postcolonial period, indigenous cultures and mestizo identities are celebrated, differentiating the independent and sovereign Mexican state from a colonial outpost.[13] The recovery and celebration of indigenous culture have not created American societies where equality reigns, but rather tend to empower elite classes or serve as rationalizations for mestizo-identified states where Indians remain marginalized and exploited—though not entirely subsumed by these states' hegemony, as twentieth-century indigenous movements in Chiapas, Guatemala, Bolivia, and Peru demonstrated. Néstor García Canclini's critique of the museumification of indigenous cultures in Mexico trenchantly locates the development of a national mythos of racial and ethnic identity in the rise of Mexico's celebration of its glorious Indian past, a celebration that erases existing communities of native peoples from contemporary consciousness as it provides Mexico with a romantic self-identity that is ostensibly without prejudice.[14]

However, the continued recognition of and devotion to indigenous sacred figures also suggests native peoples' resistance to complete domination through a hybridization of systems or the syncretic fusion of cultures in order to resolve lengthy cross-cultural encounters. Indigenous knowledge remains a part of Mexican and Chicano/a cultures in their everyday, ordinary practices. Like the novels and films that represent Chicana spirituality as partly indigenous, Luis D. León's study of contemporary curandera shops in Los Angeles reveals the continuation of indigenous beliefs and practices in the lives of Mexicans and Mexican Americans, indicating that while the reification and commodification that Canclini describes operate at the levels of both the national state and the national identity and throughout Mexico's culture and tourism industry, they do not completely account for all expressions of indigenous identity or all forms through which native knowledge continues to exist and have impact.[15] An additional lens is necessary for interpreting native or popular spiritual practices.

Anzaldúa's theory of spiritual mestizaje shares with Latin American and South Asian postcolonial analyses of religion, spirituality, and nation a recognition of the particular religiosity that prevails in a specific geographic, temporal, and cultural space—in her case, the borderlands—as well as an appreciation for its historical and material foundation in specific crossroads of cultures. However, her theory of spiritual mestizaje departs from a postcolonial perspective in its recourse to the decolonial as an explanation for the critical potential of spiritual renewal or for the spiritual renewal of critique.[16] Spiritual mestizaje directs itself, Anzaldúa argues, toward the elimination of inequalities, a project which requires the ongoing critique of power. Unlike the colonialist or nationalist projects of fusing values and beliefs from disparate cultures to establish a new hegemony, Anzaldúa's theory proposes a way to resist such hegemonies; she does not fix or reify the components of a particular spiritual mestizaje but instead elaborates a critical process that will serve to contest new reifications. The fictional and documentary narratives discussed here mirror Anzaldúa's description of the intellectual, psychic, emotional, and physical processes of spiritual mestizaje, rendering the actions and discourses of the people depicted in these texts, as well as the texts themselves, as vibrant interventions in culture rather than catalogues or artifacts of culture.

Testimonio and Spiritual Mestizaje

Form and function are inseparable in these narratives. The critique of institutionalized forms and the divergence from them occur both on the aesthetic level in the adaptations of testimonio or in the collage-like or multiple-genre character of some texts, and on the story or content level where characters examine or encounter conflations of religion and power, reconsider received religious instruction, and engage in home-centered spiritual practices. As in Anzaldúa's *Borderlands*, the testimonio form is intrinsically linked to the processes of spiritual mestizaje as represented and enacted in these texts. In *Borderlands*, Anzaldúa's analysis, critique, theorizing, and imagining—what she names autohisteoría—proceed through a first-person account of her experiences, her knowledge, and her status in various groups. The stories of other women in her family, including her aunt and grandmother, figure in this process as well. This is a strategy shared by Cherríe Moraga in *Loving in the War Years* and Ana Castillo in *Massacre of the Dreamers*, both of whom theorize through the recalling and telling of individual and collective experiences. *Borderlands*'s central concern is not simply the recalling of the past but remembrance, that is, not merely the ability to recite a story, an event, a fact, but an act of recognition that involves the assimilation of the past into the present and the hoped-for future; remembrance is an act of interpretation and self-creation.

How Chicana narratives represent and embody the individual, communal, and social transformations that occur through spiritual mestizaje has been my focus. Yet it is important to note that these Chicana explorations of plural and hybrid spiritualities also partake of hemispheric phenomena— the encounter between cultures under domination and the resistance and opposition to that status registered at varied levels and in several forms— apparent in the concerns of other literatures from the Americas wherein we see multiple religiosities with unequal relations to power.[17] While analyses of spirituality in Chicano/a and Latino/a literature and visual culture are relatively new, spiritual issues, values, beliefs, and conundrums and their interactions with discourses of race, class, nation, sexuality, and gender have long been present and are gaining increased critical attention by scholars of literature, film, religion, and art. This is, in part, an aspect of the growth and depth of multiple fields. However, the entry of these texts into mainstream publishing in the United States also prompts one to consider what work these texts might be doing in that broader context, for such inclusion is not without complications and is not a sign of the full incorporation or acceptance of Chicano/as and Chicano/a cultures into the life of the nation.[18]

Social Formation and Power in Literature

In the discourse of religious affiliation and belief, the phrase *religious for-mation* refers to one's education, training, and experience in a particular religion. Because of the term's similarity to contemporary understandings of *social formation*, it is useful to consider whether these ideas are paral-lel or comparable. For many scholars, there is an important distinction be-tween the discursive and rhetorical systems that bring "religion" into being in particular historical moments and in specific forms and a religious per-spective focused strictly on the established discourses of specific religions. To examine a social formation is to consider both the shared identity and the historical conditions, discourses, and other identities through which particular religious formations take shape, historicizing the relations and discourses involved.[19] Religious formation, in contrast, describes a process internal to a particular religion. A focus on religious formation without regard for its intersections with social formation is the purview of theology.

My analytic frame partakes of an interest in social formation, that is, I am interested in how the material, social, political, and economic con-ditions described or represented in Chicana narratives—and alterations or fluctuations in them—become enmeshed in the creation and mainte-nance of religion, gender, race, and sexuality and how these distinct social formations repeatedly intersect and interact with political and economic power in the elaboration of religious identities and communities. At stake is, among other issues, the regulation of female sexuality. In these texts the reassertion of power and control over self or community—an act that nec-essarily centers the raced, gendered, sexualized body—emerges as an act of justice and of healing necessary not only for survival but also for bringing into being a more equitable social order. These narratives frequently anchor the drive for justice and healing and the recognition of individual and com-munal humanity in the materiality and discourse of spirituality, in how a shared belief creates communities of support or how a belief represents a shared history.

In *Face of an Angel* and *Mother Tongue*, the Catholic identity of each protagonist fragments under the impact of movements for greater equal-ity for women, changing sexual mores, and economic and political shifts.

Soveida's narrative chronicles the changes in social and economic power that accompany her critical reevaluation of received religious instruction, thereby historicizing her religion and spirituality rather than naturalizing it as simply belonging to the realm of personal and private experience which merely fades or wanes. Michel Foucault's observation that power does not repress sexuality so much as establish norms for its discipline and practice—its parameters—becomes useful in considering Soveida's chronological narrative:

> What mode of investment of the body is necessary and adequate for the functioning of a capitalist society like ours? From the eighteenth to the early twentieth century I think it was believed that the investment of the body by power had to be heavy, ponderous, meticulous and constant. Hence those formidable disciplinary regimes in the schools, hospitals, barracks, factories, cities, lodgings, families. And then, starting in the 1960s, it began to be realized that such a cumbersome form of power was no longer as indispensable as had been thought and that industrial societies could content themselves with a much looser form of power over the body. Then it was discovered that control of sexuality could be attenuated and given new forms.[20]

The norms of Soveida's childhood authorized her father's sexual desire since he was the working head of the household, while her mother's sexual desire, since she was a woman confined to the house, was subordinated to her husband's whims. In becoming and remaining a waitress, Soveida enters a social and economic realm unknown to the women in her family. In this new setting she confronts prevailing sexual mores and values. While Soveida's narrative confirms Foucault's observation about the shift from the more stringent regulation of the body to a "looser form," María's narrative in *Mother Tongue* forces us to reconsider the universality of this change for she ironically describes herself, initially, as someone free of the operation of "formidable disciplinary regimes" over her body. However, María arrives at an understanding of herself, both as a victim of violence and as a person in solidarity with those subjected to extreme forms of social control over their bodies, as someone still subject to such controls and, therefore, an actor in contesting them. She recognizes that to view oneself as free from these disciplinary mechanisms is to refrain from contesting them. The novel makes much of María's distance from the religion of her forebears, signaling an already divided religious community, a division exacerbated by the differing responses of religious communities to the conflict in El Salvador and the plight of Salvadoran working people. As in *Face of an Angel*, María contests the discourses, including religious, that would impose a second-class status on her; however, through her narrative of involvement in the sanctuary movement, María confronts the inadequacy of her religion in addressing contemporary issues and in confronting power. In front of the plaza church, María's longing betrays the loss of solidity and community she faces: the sanctuary movement is primarily based in Protestant churches; the religious community in which José participates in El Salvador is violently crushed; the nation that absorbed the plaza church within its borders supports the regime inflicting violence on Salvadorans or stands by and does nothing. In short, the crisis she faces is simultaneously social, material, and spiritual. Through the narrative commitment to spiritual mestizaje, represented in these cases as individual journeys of transformation, Soveida and María become subjects creatively engaged in contesting, shaping, and transforming the prevailing social relations and discourses through their individual words and actions as well as through their union with others in struggle.

For the characters of *Canícula* and for the women in *Flowers for Guadalupe* and *Señorita Extraviada*, the violent power of the state and an exploitative economic system are confronted through the mobilization of religious identity and community. Just as economic relations in El Salvador form part of the set of interactions that gives rise to the particular circumstance of Christian-based communities in El Salvador, here the specific shape of a religious community, practice, or belief cannot be disarticulated from the discourses of nation, economy, and gender through which social relations on the frontera are policed or changed.

Canícula's emphasis on an organic, spiritual community that traverses the border, its remembrance of home-centered folk practices and healing powers, and its understated awareness of the power of the state in regulating Chicano/as all subtly unmask the ways that constructions of nation, gender, race, sexuality, ethnicity, and religion intersect with one another. *Flowers* focuses on the ways that the spiritual practices and beliefs of women in relation to Guadalupe contrast with gendered religious and political discourses that subordinate women. Where the latter assign little value to women's work, exclude women's voices and experiences, and understand women's spirituality as superstition, *Flowers* addresses the significance of women's physical, intellectual, and emotional work; women organizing and collaborating; and women's sense of communication with and devotion to Guadalupe in ways that reveal the gendered and racialized character of the prevailing discourses of nation and religion. Indeed, women's spirituality in *Flowers* might be productively viewed as a performance of these alternative ways of understanding themselves. In the massive all-women marches to Tepeyac and the younger women's relay race portrayed in *Flowers*, we see desired social outcomes for women—health, teamwork, collaboration among women, management and organization, self-sufficiency—integrated with the religious values of honor for Guadalupe, honoring tradition, and communal prayer and worship in ways that chip away at or dismantle constraining gender norms. Viewers might observe that the historical genealogy of the march offered in the film discloses the conditions of indigenous culture and its survival and the colonial inequalities addressed in Guadalupe worship, which continue to inform current practices of devotion. And though the lone male voice in the film critiques these manifestations of popular religiosity as divergent from a "true" religious practice, the women in the film make it clear that religion and gender are already united or mutually informing in ways that limit them; their overt women-only activities subvert these limiting associations as they shape a set of practices unique to their era.

Canícula positions itself as a family photo album by setting up the scene in the prologue where family members gather to sort through family photos and to remember family history. Where the photos differ from or contradict the brief stories that surround them, they require further analysis, and where there are no photos, one must imagine and see the story for oneself. Through these home stories and photos, we witness Nena and her family members reading the signs of power that surround them and examining the institutions empowered to act against them, employing their own stories and photos to deconstruct those sign systems and creating new significations for them, a frontera of transnationalist feminism and spirituality. In this way, *Canícula* employs the meta-ideologizing that Chela Sandoval identifies as a key emancipatory technology.[21] Similarly, *Flowers for Gua-*

dalupe reveals women whose devotion to Guadalupe, occurring as it does in the context of economic and gendered inequalities and grounded in an awareness of their social location, takes the form of practices that contrast with those of the ideologies and powers that limit them, and in doing so they create new ways of seeing and understanding Guadalupe devotion.

Señorita Extraviada takes on what seems like an insurmountable task: to critically examine the exploitative economies and states for which women's lives are disposable commodities or tools in a way that moves viewers to action. The film's invocation of the contemporary visual crime investigation genre and its careful presentation of evidence and testimony create a desire in the viewer for a definitive solution or resolution, thereby eliciting audience involvement in the narrative. Rhetorically, it asks us to invest in an answer and promotes an empathetic identification among viewers.[22] Materially, the filmmaker insists on providing contact information for the women's groups mobilized around this issue in Juárez and there are often actions associated with screenings or distribution of the film, further underscoring her aim to promote involvement. The women's groups appeal to the moral conscience of residents of Juárez and the world by employing the pink and black crosses as symbols of their demand for justice. Just as the families of the victims of violence use the occasion of the funeral procession of one victim to publicly protest the lack of serious investigation of all of the women's murders, so the film aims to turn the act of mourning by the viewer into political protest. That the murders continue unsolved, that the maquilas continue to exploit women and their labor, and that conditions at the border worsen attest to the complexity and enormity of the problem facing Voces sin Fronteras, a group that in its name and collaboration with other feminist and social justice groups strives to build a transnational movement for justice in Juárez. Are the women hampered by their inability to meta-ideologize? Their faith is earnest, their demand honest, their subversion evident. At one point, the filmmaker asks a young girl in the colonias whether, given all that has happened, she wants to go to work in the maquilas, and she responds yes, because in doing so she will be able to help her family. Does the girl represent a naïve investment in the maquila industry? Is there no other option for survival? Do religious ideals of how people should interact cloud the recognition of structural inequities? It is apparent in the film that the women of Juárez are aware of the overwhelming structural inequities at various levels of society, yet they have little say in changing these as they are repeatedly ignored, dismissed, silenced.

Fredric Jameson's argument that stylistic innovation constitutes not only a break with the past but also a "projected solution" on the "imaginary level" to a "genuine" social contradiction may be an apt lens for considering the work that *Señorita Extraviada* and the other texts do. The ways that the narratives work to incorporate and authorize multiple perspectives—from the pieces of *Canícula* to the direct and seemingly uninterrupted filming of women's testimonies in *Flowers* and *Señorita*—suggest forms of collective consciousness that, as Jameson notes, cannot be achieved individually.[23] They, thereby, bring social movements into the picture of the borderlands. While some of the narratives in this book represent characters who develop new forms of consciousness of themselves as classed, raced, and gendered individual subjects, other narratives, and the two documentaries in particular, reveal the class or communal consciousness of groups of women. My analysis has not aimed to romanticize these communities, but to recognize communal spiritual movement and agency.

Societies in Motion

In the Alcalá trilogy, both Native American and Jewish peoples struggle to survive under a political and religious order from which they are excluded as equals and which severly limits women's lives. These novels represent the religious rationales that, in part, justify the attacks of the Mexican government that gradually displace indigenous peoples from their lands, fragment their communities, and turn them into exiles in the borderlands, as they also represent the desire for political, social, economic, and spiritual order. While a spiritual gathering of indigenous peoples in *Spirits of the Ordinary* is perceived as a political threat by the Mexican troops—somewhat ironically since readers are aware of the gap between the activities of the assembled Indians and the Mexican army's imagination of their activities— this and other narrative events represent the mutually authorizing fusion of religious and political discourses on both sides. The exile in which the indigenous peoples find themselves is common to the many nontraditional or minority characters in this trilogy and speaks to the intersection of religion and nation in this narrative. Women, adherents of minority religions, Native Americans, practitioners of indigenous spiritualities, and gender-bending characters populate the borderlands too and, though displaced, manage to connect and ally with other marginalized groups. These exiles and displacements appear in the novels not only as individual situations but also as social phenomena with corresponding spiritual ramifications on the populace. How could circumstances creating social change not have an impact on religious beliefs or practices? If religion is a social formation, it is therefore an active and ongoing process.[24] Each of the texts under discussion here, in revealing spiritual mestizaje, engage in the demystification of religion even when they present characters or situations that affirm particular religious beliefs or when they portray the creation or adoption of new spiritual practices. Demystification, McCutcheon suggests, is central to the academic study of religion, which he defines as the "cross-disciplinary study of how human beliefs, behaviors, and institutions construct and contest enduring social identity."[25]

While this book's focus on spiritual mestizaje is consonant with McCutcheon's argument that religious studies scholars must examine both the implications and the causes of religion in order to avoid scholarship that "romanticizes and thereby depoliticizes historical, human interactions and institutions," my analysis departs from McCutcheon's tendency to ignore, in the interests of critically interrogating religious terms and discourses, the role of participants in religion, the agency of religious and cultural actors, and the perspectives and understandings from which they operate in the construction and contestation of discourses of religion and spirituality.[26] The participation, agency, and understandings of religious and spiritual adherents are all elements that we need to take into account. Even when these narratives depict characters for whom religion is a private experience, they do not fail to suggest the "historically distinctive disciplines and forces" contributing to the authority of religion.[27]

The active processes portrayed in the novels discussed here involve a hermeneutics of memory engaged in spiritual mestizaje—whether the critical remembrance of childhood religious training and social relations, or the critical remembrance of inherited history and culture, or the critical remembrance of non-victorious social movements. These narratives suggest an understanding of how social reality is created, in part, by historical social formation. Where they end or where characters end up is not unimportant, yet the narrative focus on spiritual mestizaje suggests not a definitive religious or spiritual answer or particular set of beliefs, but a recognition of contingencies in religious social formation, which is impacted by the intersection of discourses of religion with discourses of nation, class, gender, sexuality, and race. There is also an ethics of memory involved: many of these narratives, in remembering violence against women and against ethnic, racial, and religious minorities and doing so via a variety of strategies of representation, vividly convey the experience of injustice to readers and viewers and, in their testimonial character, aim to have a different impact than simply providing an entertaining story. Richard Kearney, discussing the fictionalization of historical horrors such as the Holocaust, suggests that "sometimes an ethic of memory is obliged to resort to an aesthetic of representation." Kearney, following the work of Paul Ricoeur, also says that "a key function of narrative memory is empathy,"[28] which supports the distinction drawn between testimonio and other literatures in my and other scholarship. Ricoeur considers the ethics of memory against the ritualized commemoration of the past, which emphasizes reverence, and states, "The exercise of memory is here an exercise in *telling otherwise*, and also in letting others tell their own history. . . . It is very important to remember that what is considered a founding event in our collective memory may be a wound in the memory of another." The forward-looking character of the "exemplarity" of remembered events that Ricoeur discusses parallels the hoped-for future impact of the "representativeness" of testimonio literature—in both, "justice is the horizon." Furthermore, he argues, "a basic reason for cherishing the duty to remember is to keep alive the memory of suffering over against the general tendency of history to celebrate the victors." This remembering is, for Ricoeur, most valuable as an ethical and political pedagogical practice:

> That is, the duty to remember consists not only in having a deep concern for the past, but in transmitting the meaning of past events to the next generation. The duty, therefore, is one which concerns the future; it is an imperative directed towards the future, which is exactly the opposite side of the traumatic character of the humiliations and wounds of history. It is a duty, thus, to tell. An example of what is at issue here can be found in Deuteronomy, when the author says "you will tell your children, you will tell them, you will tell them!"[29]

This duty to remember and the corresponding duty to act differently in the future based on this knowledge inflect each of the texts discussed here: one character overtly directs another to remember, a subject testifies to her own experience, while multiple memories are represented in the icons, artifacts, photographs, interviews, and reportage incorporated into these texts.

The critical feminist spiritual renewal that unfolds in each of these narratives requires this, yet the fictional testimonios, despite the creation of an authorizing discourse of memory, arouse suspicion for some readers. The contemporary context of religious conservatism that informs political and social life in the United States in the twenty-first century has had an impact on how these narratives, as well as study and discussion of them, are received. As McCutcheon observes, dominant ideologies have been challenged by the growth of "feminist, race, class, and postmodern studies." He continues, "The tremendous degree of conservative backlash against such fields of study suggests just what is at stake in this debate."[30]

Mother Tongue, Señorita Extraviada, and Shelly's story in *The Flower in the Skull* are set or occur in the twenty-first century. *Canícula, Face of an Angel*, and *Flowers for Guadalupe* take the late 1980s or early 1990s as their temporal setting. *Spirits of the Ordinary* and *Treasures in Heaven* are set in the nineteenth century and the early twentieth. Grouping the texts in this way allows us to consider the three historical periods represented in terms of the spiritual concerns prevalent in a particular era. The narratives set after 2000 share a concern with brutal violence, the erosion of basic human rights, and ethical behavior as well as an interest in or calling to indigenous spiritualities or radically renewed forms of traditional religions. An interest in female-centered spiritual practices or theologies, the feminine divine, and feminist interventions in traditional religions characterize the group of narratives set in the late 1980s or early 1990s, not decades when these areas of inquiry first emerged but when they gained greater legitimacy. The first two historical novels of Alcalá's trilogy imagine the conflicted relations among competing groups and religions in the borderlands at the turn of the twentieth century; however, in their attention to the intersections of gender and sexuality with religion and nation, these novels engage in "telling otherwise," imagining a historical past through the lens of a contemporary sensibility about gender and sexuality. In their contemporary focus, these narratives explore spirituality through perspectives that, as McCutcheon notes, have generated debate and opposition.

Spirituality, Modernity, and the Religious Right

Ultra-conservative religious movements, preachers, and politicians have spread into the mainstream in the United States. Sara Diamond observes that this ultra-conservative religious and political movement promotes the view that "Christians are under siege" and can "reclaim their liberty through collective action," and it has mobilized and unified a constituency to oppose much of the transformation that feminist, race, and class analyses and movements have succeeded in effecting in the United States.[31] However, the ultra-conservative movement's adoption of the position of a disadvantaged constituency, as Steve Bruce notes, differs radically from the claims of racial minorities or victims of gender or sexual bias in that the latter demand greater universalization of the rights and opportunities available to the majority, while the former proposes that their "values and beliefs deserve greater status and advantage in the public sphere."[32] To that end, this religious and political movement has strived to shape political, economic, educational, cultural, and social life in keeping with its minority values and beliefs. Their interests have not been confined to the hot-button issues of abortion and same-sex marriage but also include equal rights for women and minorities, welfare reform, public arts programs, and educational policy. The ferocity of this effort, some would argue, has negatively affected all religious communities in the United States, promoting a monolithic and negative view of religion; one minister I know says that there is "a lot of bad religion out there."

Religious adherents who are not conservatives have responded to the ultra-conservative movement by more strongly claiming a spiritual life dedicated to social justice. Bruce suggests that the Christian Right cannot ultimately succeed, because it stands both in opposition to the stable majority in favor of "regulation of the economy, reproductive rights for women and affirmative action, though without strict quotas," and in opposition to "modernity itself," that is, the continued expansion of economies that fuel migration and social mobility, leading to heterogeneous rather than homogeneous societies as the norm.[33] Under modernity, Bruce notes, religious particularisms increasingly shift from the public sphere to the private as society accommodates the expansion of diversity it experiences. If we understand the relationship between private and public spheres as less dichotomous than typically asserted, as I have argued, and we take seriously the analyses that reveal modernity to indeed have a particular religious inflection if not framework, then the issue becomes more complicated. The work that these narratives do—in claiming public space (but not all space) for "private" popular religiosities and imagining new, non-institutional forms of spirituality—suggests greater public respect for difference, rather than homogeneous religious society.

What does it mean, in this context, to teach and write about literature by an ethnic and racial minority whose very presence in the United States remains the subject of vitriolic argument, whose literature rarely registers an orthodox or conservative religious understanding but nonetheless represents or asserts the significance of religion and spirituality in communal and individual life? Or to do this work from a feminist perspective, attentive to the workings of gender and sexuality as well as the lure of nation? While many students and researchers respond with interest and eagerness to Chicano/a and Latino/a literature's engagement with various spiritualities, a small but vocal minority feels offended by critiques of institutional religion, revisions of sacred stories and figures, or the authority accorded to "superstitious" practices in this literature.[34] Others are unable to grasp the study of religion in literature as anything other than the promotion, advocacy, or embrace of a religious perspective, which they view as regressive. While some have been won over to trying to understand the perspective of the Other on "religion," those who are unable to see past a dogmatic approach, whether of the conservative or the liberal variety, or who are unwilling to accept variations in spirituality, or unable to imagine that religious beliefs, practices, and institutions might change, find support for their views in contemporary political and social debate.

In the course of my research and teaching I have also encountered those who urged, for ideological reasons, particular scholarly approaches: some attach greater value to theologically informed analyses, and others respect only work grounded in European philosophies. I have been cautioned about the negative consequences of critiquing well-established religions, accused of thinking myself above religion, advised to be a "good Catholic," taken to task for a pro-choice essay, mistaken for a conservative religious scholar, accused of proselytizing, sneered at for wearing my Guadalupe/Goddess necklaces, and condescended to for considering the study of representations of religion to be worthy of scholarly attention. I have encountered the academic equivalent of assuming that all Latino/a literature is only autobiography or sociology, that is, that my study of spirituality in literature and film is really a personal search for religion by a confused adherent. These varied responses are as much an indication of how polarizing religion has become in the United States as of the situations Latinas face in the academy. It is hard to segregate the assorted comments proffered by both conservatives and liberals from the political and social era of their utterance; in the twenty-first century, religion has become a battleground. As I worked on this project, I myself was the victim of violence, and of a series of damaging incidents and intrusions into my private life, events which prompted me to consider anew the overlap of religion, education, and government in contemporary conditions.

The question of one's own religious commitments is an interesting one for the field. It has long been a tenet of gender studies that one's social location matters in all kinds of ways.

The novels and films discussed here address complex intersectional identities as well as the historical and social significance of religion and spirituality on the borderlands. A consciousness of how religion and politics have been intertwined in the past, and might be in the future, lies within each of these Chicana narratives. Their exploration, critique, evaluation, and renewal of Chicana forms of spirituality historicize religious discourse and suggest either its vitality and adaptability or lack thereof. Chicana narratives address the contemporary debates about religion in the political, economic, and social spheres not from the perspective of a political agenda but instead from the perspective of complex subjects living in an unjust world whose existence is partially formed or informed by inherited and existing religious discourses. Given the migrations that have expanded the diversity of religious expression in the United States and the degree to which, on a global scale, we all increasingly interact with both diverse religious subjects and diverse spiritualities, the ways that these Chicana narratives critically engage the interactions among gender, sexuality, race, nation, and religion in a project of spiritual mestizaje offer insight into the evolution of religious discourses. These texts affirm a difference with modernity in order to make room for themselves in the project of shaping the contemporary contours of modernity in progressive directions.

While McCutcheon argues for a strong separation between religious studies scholarship and theology, noting the very different methods and purposes of each, I have found it necessary to engage the work of Latino/a theologians not because my aim is to offer a theological reading of literary texts, but because Latino/a theologians make up most of the scholars writing about Latino/a religions today; because Latino/a theology, for the most part, remains a site of critical evaluation of religion; and because some of the novels and films directly engage theological questions. Those working in Latino/a theology speak from the position of adherent, a stance that many of the characters and individuals in these narratives adopt, though that stance is not more important than their locations as gendered, racialized, and sexualized subjects. Finally, it is also essential to distinguish a largely Christian Latino/a theological perspective from that of Anzaldúa, whose spirituality is not defined by adherence to one traditional religion and who offers a strong critique of Catholicism in particular, the religion with which she is most familiar.

Lest we fall into the trap of promoting a view of Anzaldúa as an anomaly, a bitter ex-Catholic, or a radical proponent of a "separatist" borderlands ideology (all of which have been said about her work in one form or another), let us turn to Luis León's article on Cesar Chávez's Buddhism.[35] Yes, Cesar Chávez's Buddhism. Countless articles, essays, stories, and films have focused on Chávez's Catholicism and its role in Chávez's political commitments and his leadership of the United Farm Workers. That his Catholicism, particularly his adherence to its message of social justice, was important to him and to the UFW movement is not an issue. However, what León finds is that this now-canonical view of Chávez omits an important element of his spirituality: the long-overlooked hybrid character of his spirituality as a Catholic Buddhist. León's article is a rare instance of scholarship that departs from the well-worn script of Mexican Americans as long-suffering Catholics. In its exploration of the history of the varieties of spiritual expression and practice among well-known Chicano/as, it offers a much-needed corrective to our understanding of Latino/a religiosity and, in the process, reveals that Chicana writers such as Sandra Cisneros and Denise Chávez, who have defined themselves as Buddhalupists or Catholic Buddhists, are far from some new fringe element but heirs to a legacy of hybrid spirituality in the Americas.

NOTES

Chapter 1: A Theory of Spiritual Mestizaje

1. Anzaldúa, *Borderlands/La Frontera*, 81.
2. Anzaldúa comments on this lacuna in the critical reception of her work in an interview with AnaLouise Keating. See Anzaldúa, "Last Words? Spirit Journeys: An Interview with AnaLouise Keating (1998–1999)," in *Interviews/Entrevistas: Gloria Anzaldúa*, 281–91.
3. Arjun Appadurai refers to "the imagination as a social practice," something that exceeds categorization as fantasy, escape, elite pastime, or contemplation. Instead, he suggests, it "has become an organized field of social practices, a form of work (both in the sense of labor and of culturally organized practice) and a form of negotiation between sites of agency ('individuals') and globally defined fields of possibility." Appadurai, "Disjuncture and Difference in the Global Cultural Economy," 29–30; also see Jameson, *The Political Unconscious*.
4. Hume and McPhillips, *Popular Spiritualities*, xv.
5. Masuzawa, *The Invention of World Religions*.
6. Asad, *Genealogies of Religion*.
7. Anzaldúa employs this contemporary usage in which the term indicates a more inclusive connection to others and the world rather than a particular religious tradition or exclusive worldview. See *Encyclopedia of Religion*, 2nd ed., ed. Lindsay Jones (Detroit: Thomson/Gale, 2005), 13:8718–19.
8. Further reading on important scholarship in this mode might include the work of Mary Daly, Elisabeth Schussler Fiorenza, Virginia Ramey Mollenkott, and Pamela Dickey Young.
9. Yarbro-Bejarano, "Gloria Anzaldúa's *Borderlands/La Frontera*," 13–15, 16.
10. Sandoval, *Methodology of the Oppressed*.
11. García, *Chicana Feminist Thought*. García's introduction places the major trends in Chicana feminist thought within the context of broader political developments with an eye toward reconstructing, as much as possible, the major concerns of each part of the chronology she develops. The majority of the materials García collected originally appeared in journals, newspapers, magazines, and newsletters published in California. Some materials that originated in Texas and New Mexico also are included, but there are only one or two from Colorado or regions outside of the Southwest. This is not to say that a Southwest-based and specifically California-based view of the development

of Chicana feminist thought is inaccurate, but simply to note these limitations. For example, it does not include discussion of the midwestern feminists who worked on the journal *Revista Chicano-Riqueña* in the early 1980s or the Chicana, Latina, and multicultural collective in New York that nourished the emergence of *This Bridge Called My Back*.

12. Anzaldúa, *Borderlands/La Frontera*, 80–81; an internal footnote has been omitted.
13. Sandoval, *Methodology of the Oppressed*, 83.
14. Yarbro-Bejarano, "Gloria Anzaldúa's *Borderlands/La Frontera*," 25.
15. Anzaldúa, "Quincentennial: From Victimhood to Active Resistance," 177; Anzaldúa, "(Un)natural bridges, (Un)safe spaces," 1; Anzaldúa, "Now Let Us Shift . . . The Path of Conocimiento . . . Inner Work, Public Acts," 548.
16. In citing her home experience, Anzaldúa situates herself among others with a similar religious background in the borderlands. As Stevens-Arroyo suggests, "The home-centered aspects of Catholicism are much stronger among Latinos than among Euro-American Catholics, assuming a primacy over clerically dominated and institutionally-based traditions like mass attendance and obedience to the clergy." Stevens-Arroyo, "Latino Catholicism and the Eye of the Beholder," 31.
17. Anzaldúa, "(Un)natural bridges, (Un)safe spaces," 3.
18. Ibid., 3, 4.
19. Embry, "Cholo Angels in Guadalajara," 101.
20. Anzaldúa, "Making Choices: Writing, Spirituality, Sexuality, and the Political," an interview with AnaLouise Keating in *Interviews/Entrevistas*, 164.
21. Pérez-Torres, *Mestizaje*, 51.
22. Alarcón, "Chicana Feminism," 66. Chabram-Dernersesian also challenges the gendering of mestizaje as masculine and the limitations of the Indian/European binary commonly invoked by mestizaje. Chabram-Dernersesian, "Encountering the Other Discourse of Chicano-Mexicano Difference"; Chabram-Dernersesian, "'Chicana! Rican? No, Chicana Riqueña!' Refashioning the Transnational Connection," in *Between Woman and Nation: Nationalisms, Transnational Feminisms, and the State*, 264–95.
23. Delgadillo, "'Angelitos Negros' and Transnational Racial Identifications," 129–43.
24. De Castro, "Richard Rodríguez in 'Borderland.'"
25. Saldívar terms this the "materially hybrid." See *Border Matters*.
26. Luis Dávila observes, "Anzaldúa insists that this borderland is in a constant state of transition, dynamic and vibrant," and rather than suggest a new fixed identity or consciousness, Anzaldúa "tells us that the people of the Border-

lands are free to engage in an authentic course of spiritual or even surrealist action with no guarantee of being culturally right, but rather must heroically try to change that world without losing their sense of creative doubt, loving ambivalence and democratic hope." Dávila, "Gloria Anzaldúa and Octavio Paz," 53–54.

27. Anzaldúa, *Borderlands/La Frontera*, 22.

28. León, *La Llorona's Children*, 58.

29. Shaw and Stewart, *Syncretism/Anti-Syncretism*, 14–15; Burns, *Roman Catholicism after Vatican II*, 125.

30. Virgil Elizondo, a Catholic theologian, has written about a "mestizo spirituality" in which indigenous Nahua and Spanish Christian traditions were fused. Elizondo also employs the term *spiritual mestizaje*; however, for him, it describes something in the past, the colonial era fusion of native and Christian beliefs. The union of indigenous and Spanish occurs, for Elizondo, through the Guadalupe event, which he describes in this way: "the Indian Mother sends the Christian-Indian child to call the Christian Father to become a home-builder." This "new spiritual/Christian mestizaje" is evangelical Christianity in the Americas. Elizondo, *Guadalupe*, 110–11, 107, 129. Anita De Luna, a scholar of Tejano religiosity, employs the terms in a similar manner, recognizing popular religiosity as "mestiza" and "mestiza spirituality" as the historical biological and spiritual union of Indian and Spanish. She cites Anzaldúa in her footnotes. De Luna, *Faith Formation and Popular Religion*, 57. Elizondo, De Luna, and Roberto S. Goizueta take up the everyday, popular practice of religion through which this syncretism finds expression. For example, Goizueta states, "U.S. Hispanic popular religiosity is, by definition, a theopoetic mediation of the historical praxis of an oppressed, marginalized community," an analysis in accord with Anzaldúa's theorization of spirituality born of, in part, the experience of her Mamagrande's folk religion and its place in their collective survival. Goizueta, "U.S. Hispanic Popular Catholicism as Theopoetics," 268.

These theologians share with Anzaldúa a regard for the multiple sources of Mexican and Chicana/o subjectivity and spirituality and an interest in greater appreciation for the indigenous elements of popular religiosity. Yet for both Elizondo and De Luna, spiritual mestizaje is not a present reality but instead signifies a past, historic event—in Elizondo, brought about by divine intervention and in De Luna, created organically through biological mixing.

31. The mujerista theology proposed by Ada María Isasí-Díaz, for example, identifies both mestizaje and mulatez, reading the former as a mixture of white and indigenous and the latter as a mixture of white and black, as its *locus*

202 ❖ *Notes to Chapter One*

theologicus. A mujerista theology grounds itself in the daily lived experience of Hispanic women and regards that shared experience as hermeneutically and epistemologically significant in the development of a liberatory praxis for Hispanic women within Catholicism and other Christian traditions—an approach similar to Anzaldúa's excavation of knowledge and method from the history, experience, and mythos of Chicanas in the borderlands. Isasí-Díaz rejects the term *feminism*, arguing that it is both hopelessly associated with the middle-class, Anglo American women's movement and was unpopular among women at the time of her writing in the 1990s; instead, she adopts *mujerista* to denote the "for-women" aspect of this theology. An extension of the liberation theology project, mujerista theology is directed toward three goals: first, serving Hispanic women by enabling recognition of the specific forms of oppression they face and the necessity for combating it; second, reforming the Church into an institution that respects difference and pluralism generally and accepts the particular religiosity of Hispanic women specifically; and third, enabling "Hispanic women to understand the centrality of eschatology in the life of every Christian." Isasí-Díaz, *Mujerista Theology*, 62–63.

Jeanette Rodríguez and María Pilar Aquino explicitly cite Gloria Anzaldúa as an influence in their theological work. Rodríguez takes from Anzaldúa a recognition of a particularly Hispanic and Latino spirituality that may combine traditional religiosity with indigenous spiritual traditions, a mestiza spirituality in which inclusiveness reigns. Rodríguez, "Latina Activists," 126–27. Like Anzaldúa and other Chicana feminists, Aquino sees her work in the context of "a social milieu that has produced a systemic, articulated, and multifaceted oppression of women." Aquino, "The Collective 'Dis-covery' of Our Own Power," 250. Aquino's Latina feminist theology strongly aligns itself with Anzaldúa's project, yet focuses its energy on the Christian and Catholic arena. Accepting of "divine revelation as its fundamental principle of knowledge and discernment" and valuing the everyday expressions of Latina spirituality in popular religiosity, Aquino adopts the method of spiritual mestizaje for her denomination-specific theological work. Aquino thereby firmly embraces the feminist moniker and cause, situates her theology within the Christian liberation theology movement, and incorporates aspects of Anzaldúa's thought into her own theology. For example, she defines the "five preconditions" for "theologians everywhere" as "entering *nepantla*; fostering *la facultad*; *honesty* with the real; *empapamiento* of hope; and an *evolving* truth." Aquino's view of Latina and Chicana feminisms synthesizes several perspectives, including Anzaldúa's; she describes her feminism as a "*mestiza* theory, method, spirituality, and praxis that has egalitarian social relations in everyday life as its principle of coherence, and it seeks to intervene in concrete reality for the historical actualization of social justice." Like Isasí-Díaz and Rodríguez, Aquino's work is directed toward the full incorporation of Latinas and Chicanas into primarily Catholic institutions, including fostering greater awareness of Latina and Chicana issues in these spaces and the inclusion of Latinas and Chicanas in church and theological leadership. Aquino suggests that linking "theology and spirituality in feminist terms" remains an urgent task for the liberation of Latinas and, reflecting her partisanship, for the prevention of their recruitment into other Christian groups with less respect for the "reasoned dimensions of religious faith." Aquino, "Latina Feminist Theology," 151, 149, 136, 147–48, 154.

Gloria Inés Loya also advances a "mestiza feminist theology" for Protestant and Catholic women who work from within the church yet feel disconnected from it. Loya consciously draws from Anzaldúa and also from Adelaida Del Castillo and Norma Alarcón. From Loya's theological perspective, "a *mestiza* feminist theology must be grounded in Guadalupe" and in revised understandings of Malinche/Malinalli Tenepal. Jeanette Rodríguez also explicitly cites Anzaldúa as influential to the theological work of understanding the significance of Guadalupe in image, in history, and in Latina lives. Loya, "Pathways to a *Mestiza* Feminist Theology," 217–40; Rodríguez, *Our Lady of Guadalupe*, 62.

32. Anzaldúa, *Borderlands/La Frontera*, 19, 36–37.

33. There are a number of religious studies scholars whose work critically examines sacred texts and the institutional history of homosexuality in efforts to renew a variety of religious traditions. See Comstock and Henking, *Que(e)-rying Religion*.

34. For example, Lara Medina documents new formations of women's spiritual circles in which a commitment prevails to the negotiation or synthesis of multiple religious traditions to create a more inclusive rather exclusive practice that can nurture Chicanas. Medina, "Los Espíritus Siguen Hablando," 189–213.

35. Castillo, *Massacre of the Dreamers*, 145.

36. Throughout this work, I use *spiritual mestizaje* to designate the process that Anzaldúa theorizes in *Borderlands* and *mestizo/a spirituality* to designate the mixture or blending of spiritualities in specific practice or belief.

37. Conner, "Santa Nepantla."

38. Keating, "Introduction," in *Entre Mundos/Among Worlds*, 9–10.

39. Keating, "Shifting Perspectives," 242.

40. Keating, *Women Reading Women Writing*, 39, 71, 122, 136.

41. Alexander, *Pedagogies of Crossing*, 286.

42. Ibid., 269.

43. Ibid., 280.

44. Ibid., 296–99, 294.

45. Anzaldúa, "Writing: A Way of Life," interview with María Henríquez Betancor (1995) in *Interviews/Entrevistas*, 242.

46. Yarbro-Bejarano's analysis notes the significance of personal stories, memories, and theories in *Borderlands*: "One axis for the enactment of *mestiza* consciousness in Anzaldúa's text is the use of personal histories and private memories that necessarily entail a context of political struggle. Another privileged site for the construction of border consciousness is Coatlicue, Lady of the Serpent Skirt, a pre-Columbian deity similar to India's Kali in her nondualistic fusion of opposites—both the destruction and creation, male and female, light and dark." Yarbro-Bejarano, "Gloria Anzaldúa's *Borderlands/La Frontera*," 19.

47. Alarcón, "Anzaldúa's *Frontera*," 358.

48. Counter-memory, according to Amritjit Singh, Joseph T. Skerrett Jr., and Robert E. Hogan, stands in contrast to "a dominant historiography that fails to represent the whole picture." *Memory and Cultural Politics*, 14.

49. Anzaldúa, *Borderlands/La Frontera*, 1.

50. Alarcón has also noted this aspect of Anzaldúa's project in recognizing that the self that Anzaldúa creates "becomes a cross-roads, a collision course, a clearinghouse, an endless alterity who, once she emerges into language and self-inscription, so belated, appears as a tireless peregrine collecting all the parts that will never make her whole. Such a hunger forces her to recollect in excess, to remember in excess, to labor to excess, and produce a text layered with inversions and disproportions, which are effects of experienced dislocations." Alarcón, "Anzaldúa's *Frontera*," 367.

51. Anzaldúa, *Borderlands/La Frontera*, 4.

52. Lipsitz, *Time Passages*, 213.

53. For a discussion of status and the self at stake in according validity to memories, see Edwall, "Comment," 16.

54. Alexander describes her effort to recall the early visions of women-of-color feminism in just this way, as recalling spirits into the present that must be fed—memory as writing as alchemy. Alexander, *Pedagogies of Crossing*, 278. The issue of whether memory is a kind of data bank versus a social phenomenon has been discussed extensively in the literature on memory, with new biological research adding twists to the ongoing debate.

55. Halbwachs, *On Collective Memory*, 52.

56. Ibid., 53.

57. Rogers, "Comment," 85.

58. Thompson, "Believe It or Not," 1–13.

59. Halbwachs, *On Collective Memory*, 182–83.

60. Anzaldúa, "Writing: A Way of Life," interview with María Henríquez Betancor (1995) in *Interviews/Entrevistas*, 239–40.

61. Anzaldúa, "Quincentennial: From Victimhood to Active Resistance," 177; Anzaldúa, "(Un)natural bridges, (Un)safe spaces," 1; Anzaldúa, "Now Let Us Shift... The Path of Conocimiento... Inner Work, Public Acts," 548.

62. Alexander, *Pedagogies of Crossing*, 278.

63. Anzaldúa, "(Un)natural bridges, (Un)safe spaces," 1–5, 3.

64. Anzaldúa, *Borderlands/La Frontera*, 27.

65. Ibid., 27.

66. Yarbro-Bejarano, "Gloria Anzaldúa's *Borderlands/La Frontera*," 17.

67. Carrasco notes that the discovery of the Templo Mayor in downtown Mexico City in the 1970s was "among the most significant archaeological discoveries in this century." Carrasco, *Religions of Mesoamerica*, 14. For information on reinterpretations of the significance of female goddess figures at Teotihuacan, see Pasztory, *Teotihuacan*; Berlo, *Art, Ideology, and the City of Teotihuacan*.

68. Anzaldúa and Keating, *This Bridge We Call Home*, 546.

69. Alarcón, "Chicana Feminism," 66–67; internal notes deleted.

70. Anzaldúa, *Borderlands/La Frontera*, 35.

71. Goizueta suggests that such popular religious practices engage in a historicized theopoetics that dynamically links imagination and affect to praxis. Goizueta, "U.S. Hispanic Popular Catholicism as Theopoetics," 265. León suggests that Guadalupe devotion "lends itself to the tactics and strategies of religious poetics" precisely because it is a "border tradition, straddling and blurring lines of religious demarcation." León, *La Llorona's Children*, 63.

72. Cisneros, *Woman Hollering Creek and Other Stories*, 17–20.

73. Anzaldúa, *Borderlands/La Frontera*, 28.

74. Rodríguez, *Our Lady of Guadalupe*, xviii, 45; Rodríguez, "Sangre llama a sangre," 117–33; Elizondo, *Guadalupe*, 84, 110–14; Goizueta, "Our Lady of Guadalupe," 145.

75. Lafaye, *Quetzalcóatl y Guadalupe*; Brading, *Mexican Phoenix*.

76. Brady, *Extinct Lands, Temporal Geographies*, 121.

77. Anzaldúa, *Borderlands/La Frontera*, 30.

78. Moraga, *Loving in the War Years*, ii.

79. Cisneros, "Little Miracles, Kept Promises," in *Woman Hollering Creek and Other Stories*, 127.

80. Mora, *Agua Santa/Holy Water*, 71.

81. Sandoval, *Methodology of the Oppressed*.

82. Mora, *Agua Santa/Holy Water*, 71.

83. Ibid., 73.

84. Castillo, "Extraordinarily Woman," 72–78.

85. Ibid., 75.
86. Castillo, *Massacre of the Dreamers*, 101, 110–11.
87. Alfaro, "The Doll," 184–86.
88. Ibid., 184.
89. For further discussion on Chicana feminist and lesbian investments in the figure of Guadalupe, see Esquíbel, *With Her Machete in Her Hand*.
90. Martí, "Our America," 882.
91. Anzaldúa, *Borderlands/La Frontera*, 68.
92. Ibid., 86; Saldívar, *The Dialectics of Our America*.
93. Saldívar-Hull, *Feminism on the Border*, 47, 170–71.
94. Ibid., 162–66, 171. Other critics who address women's writing and testimonio include Tey Diana Rebolledo, who grounds her reading of links between Chicana and Latin American women's writing in their shared commitment to the personal witness of social struggle and repression, and Sidonie Smith and Julia Watson, who suggest that among the forms of writing about one's life are "narratives of ethnic identity and community" and "testimonios," but they also suggest that many forms of life writing combine varied discourses, particularly a text like Rigoberta Menchú's. Rebolledo, *Women Singing in the Snow*, 158; Smith and Watson, *Reading Autobiography*.
95. Sommer notes the uniqueness of the testimonial "I": it "represents the plural not because it replaces or subsumes the group but because the speaker is a distinguishable part of the whole. In rhetorical terms, whose political consequences should be evident in what follows, there is a fundamental difference here between the *metaphor* of autobiography and heroic narrative in general, which assumes an identity by substituting one (superior) signifier for another (I for we, leader for follower, Christ for the faithful), and *metonymy*, a lateral identification through relationship, which acknowledges the possible differences among 'us' as components of the whole." Sommer suggests that women's testimonios extend the domestic sphere into the political sphere, in contrast to the heroic narratives of male-authored testimonio, and reveal the heterogeneity in networks of people. Similarly, women testimonio subjects do not shy away from confronting and denouncing male gender privilege. Sommer, " 'Not Just a Personal Story,' " 108–10, 121–22, 125, 129.
96. As a form, the testimonio has multiple literary antecedents, including the picaresque novel, documentary fiction, *crónica*, and the revolutionary memoir, yet, as George Yúdice suggests, its combination of pragmatism and aesthetics is not one that adheres "to the definitions of the literary as legitimized by dominant educational, publishing, and professional institutions." Discussing the dismissal of testimonio, Yúdice notes that the "modern institution of literature traditionally has functioned as a gatekeeper, permitting certain classes of

individuals to establish standards of taste within the public sphere and excluding others," whose texts are marked as "substandard discursive forms." Yúdice, "Testimonio and Postmodernism," 46–47.

Marc Zimmerman's analysis of the forms that influence testimonio emphasizes its syncretic spiritual nature: "The testimonio is also a mode that precedes Catholic confession as an attribute of Mayan culture. But it is a mode that then reemerges with the force of the return of the repressed, at a time of Catholic transformation . . . [and] simultaneously reaffirms a mode that is both Mayan and Catholic, sacred and yet fully social." Zimmerman reads Menchú's narrative as a Mayan and Catholic form of speech that asserted itself in a period of change in which traditional religious leadership was felt to be insufficient. Zimmerman follows John Beverley in conceiving of testimonio as inaugurating new forms of literary production, altering the cultural authority of the literary enterprise, and representing social movements for change. Beverley suggests that these are all interrelated since "literature cannot be simply appropriated by this or that social project. It is deeply marked by its own historical and institutional entanglements, its 'tradition of service,' so to speak." Zimmerman, "Testimonio in Guatemala," 101, 113; Beverley, "Through All Things Modern: Second Thoughts on Testimonio" (1991), in *Testimonio*, 58.

Critics skeptical of what they see as the canonization of testimonio include Alberto Moreiras, who questions the radical possibility ascribed to testimonio and challenges its possible fetishization in its induction into the literary-critical apparatus, and Georg M. Gugelberger, who suggests that "testimonio has been the salvational dream of a declining cultural left in hegemonic countries." Gugelberger, like Moreiras, wonders about the consequences of institutionalization. In response, Beverley questions deconstructive readings such as these insofar as they reproduce "the fixity of relations of power." Moreiras, "The Aura of Testimonio," 192–224; Gugelberger, "Introduction," in *The Real Thing*, 7, 14; Beverley, "The Real Thing" (1996), in *Testimonio*, 67–68.

Critical work on women, women's writing, and testimonio by Doris Sommer and María Josefina Saldaña-Portillo also bears on the significance of this genre for Chicana narrative. Saldaña-Portillo's work identifies within the genre a kind of testimonio that refuses the lure of developmental models of economic and individual formation, citing Rigoberta Menchú's text in contrast to the masculinist narratives of Che Guevara and Mario Payeras, finding in Menchú not an anonymous collective subject but instead, following Doris Sommer, an individual subject consciously working within given conventions to tell a collective story that unfolds through varied registers. In contrast to Sommer's view that testimonio suggests a respect for difference in its insistence on keeping secrets and Beverley's view that it aims for solidarity between narrator and reader, Saldaña-Portillo suggests that Menchú's testimonio critiques and challenges its reader "to recognize his or her own subjection to this neocolonial culture." Menchú's effort at revolutionary speech, according to Saldaña-Portillo, "recounts a repetitive and continual process of conscience/consciousness birth that defies the unilinear, messianic model of revolutionary transformation." Saldaña-Portillo, *The Revolutionary Imagination in the Americas and the Age of Development*, 154, 167, 174; Sommer, "No Secrets," 157; Beverley, "The Margin at the Center: On Testimonio" (1989), in *Testimonio*, 27.

Testimonio critics acknowledge the influence of various literary forms and discourses on this genre; however, Sommer also points to an intellectual shift in the United States—the turn toward oral histories—as a factor in the emergence and validation of testimonio. Writing about the incorporation of women into histories of the West in the United States, Susan Armitage notes that until the oral history movement of the mid-1970s, women were generally absent from dominant historical narratives of the region. Armitage credits the success of the largely community-based movement to document women's experiences and accomplishments through oral histories with leading to its acceptance in academia and to the growth of both archival collections and research in this area. As she documents, early efforts were collaborative projects with specific communities—work that seemed to want to have an immediate impact in the same way that testimonio does—while later work turned to expanding and amplifying the category of "women" with research on racial and ethnic communities of women. Within the field of oral histories, Armitage observes that few oral histories of indigenous women exist, in part because Indian women are no longer willing to be anthropologized in the form of the life history common in that field. Maureen E. Shea describes the shift in Latin American letters: "Worlds previously unknown may be discovered through oral history and recorded in the form of testimonial literature." Sommer's brief note suggesting feminist transnational influence in shifting the direction of history and literature in the Americas is tantalizing in that it raises many possibilities for future investigations on the routes of feminist exchange and collaboration in the Americas. Sommer, "'Not Just a Personal Story,'" 110; Armitage, "Here's to the Women," 556; Shea, "Latin American Women and the Oral Tradition," 141.

97. Saldívar, *Chicano Narrative*.

98. This view of fictional testimonio, based as it is on the identification of formal attributes that correspond to those of testimonio (such as an individual subject who speaks from and about a collective context or bears witness to such in a multilayered narrative whose arc is toward the acquisition of a greater

concientización), differs from the distance or proximity to fact that governs the definition of the "testimonial novel" offered by Linda J. Craft. However, Craft's discussion of the Central American testimonial novel provides an excellent discussion of the genre's preoccupation with voice, justice, and nation. Craft, *Novels of Testimony and Resistance from Central America.*

99. Grewal suggests, "It is imperative for us to examine new forms of subjectivity that are radically different from this European imperialist and state-nationalist subject that is binarily constructed and essentialist." Grewal names Anzaldúa and Alarcón as key theorists in pointing us toward a heterogeneous or multiply defined subject and Anzaldúa's theory of mestiza consciousness as a key move in this project. In her discussion of autobiographies by women of color, Grewal notes that "for those termed minorities, it is not the resolution of identity that is necessary for political action, but oppositional mobilization and coalitional, transnational, feminist practice." Grewal, "Autobiographic Subjects and Diasporic Locations," 233, 251.

100. Alarcón, "Traduttora, Traditora," 126.

101. Saldívar describes this as Chicano/a literature's "difference from and resistance to American cultural norms." Saldívar, *Chicano Narrative,* 5.

102. Pérez, "*El desorden,* Nationalism, and Chicana/o Aesthetics," 19–20.

Chapter 2: Bodies of Knowledge

1. Martínez, *Mother Tongue,* 81.

2. Chávez, *Face of an Angel,* 304.

3. García, *Chicana Feminist Thought.*

4. The essays do, however, sometimes present a monolithic view of "la Chicana," which was not uncommon in this early stage of Chicana feminism as women grappled with defining themselves and recognizing the differences among themselves.

5. For example, see Vásquez, "The Woman of La Raza," in García, *Chicana Feminist Thought,* 29–31; Chávez, "Women of the Mexican American Movement," ibid., 36–39; and Elizabeth Olivárez, "Women's Rights and the Mexican-American Woman," ibid., 131–36.

6. See also Martínez, "La Chicana—Legacy of Suffering and Self-Denial"; Anna Nieto Gomez, "Chicana Feminism"; and Sister Teresita Basso, "The Emerging 'Chicana,'" all in Medina, *Las Hermanas.*

7. Spain, *Gendered Spaces,* 235. Linda McDowell cautions that although "the home is one of the most strongly gendered spatial locations, it is important not to take the associations for granted, nor to see them as permanent and unchanging." McDowell, *Gender, Identity and Place,* 93.

8. Ibid., 8–9.

9. Ibid., 265.

10. In this, they share some similarities with Chicano texts of the 1970s that also turned to indigenous spiritualities and epistemologies and contrasted them with dominant Catholicism.

11. Chávez, *Face of an Angel*, 4.

12. Martínez, "Nuevas voces Salvadoreñas," 117.

13. Hedges and Fishkin are paraphrasing and highlighting the innovations of Tillie Olsen's *Silences* (1978) in their introduction to *Listening to Silences*, 3.

14. Adams, "Northamerican Silences," 131.

15. Chávez, *Face of an Angel*, 4.

16. *Webster's Ninth New Collegiate Dictionary.*

17. Personal conversation with Amalia Delgadillo.

18. In his introduction to Fernando Ortiz's important work, Fernando Coronil explains, "A contrapuntal perspective, by illuminating the complex interaction between the subaltern and the dominant, should make it difficult to absorb one into the other, completing, however unwittingly, the work of domination." Coronil, "Introduction to the Duke University Press Edition," xl.

19. Jara states: "La intimidad no es privada, le pertenece a todos, y por ello la externaliza en la exhibición del dolor y la angustia, le vejación y el heroismo." My translation: "From the perspective of the narrator [of testimonio], intimacy is not private but concerns all, and for this reason the narrator makes it public in the exhibition of sorrow, anguish, oppression and heroism." Jara, "Introduction," 3.

20. Jara states that testimonio is "un golpe a las conciencias" that produces "una deconstrucción brutal de las versiones tranquilizadoras que emanan de los departamentos de estado" at the same time that it ruptures "los límites entre lo público y lo privado." Ibid., 3.

21. See Beverley's discussion of the difference between the texts of the personal experience of a marginalized subject and testimonio. Beverley, *Against Literature*, 69–72.

22. Ibid., 73. Rice-Sayre notes that an emphasis on moral and human rights, even when these are not enforceable, exposes the danger of relying on positive law when that law often represents "the received ideas of powerful groups of men at particular times." Rice-Sayre, "Witnessing History," 48–72, 63.

23. Chávez, *Face of an Angel*, 125.

24. Ibid., 127.

25. Rebolledo, *Women Singing in the Snow*, 117.

26. Ibid., 153, 158.

27. "Despojarse de su individualidad, sí, pero para asumir la de su informante, la de la colectividad que éste representa. Flaubert decía: 'Madame Bovary, c'est moi.' El author de novela-testimonio debe decir junto con su protagonists: 'Yo soy la época.'" Barnet points to the novel testimonio form as particular to the contemporary period; however, other aspects of his definition of the novel testimonio, including its emphasis on representing historic and epic movements and "objectivity" do not take into account women's testimonios. Barnet, "La Novela Testimonio," 288.

28. Chávez, *Face of an Angel*, 11.

29. Quintana, *Home Girls*, 82–83.

30. John Beverley emphasizes this soberness in arguing that as a form of narrative bearing witness to struggle, pain, and danger, testimonio conveys urgency and danger in what he has described as both its "truth effect" and its sincerity. Critics such as Sklowdowska and Saldaña-Portillo emphasize that this should not diminish recognition of the form as a crafted narrative. See Beverley, *Subalternity and Representation: Arguments in Cultural Theory* (Durham: Duke University Press, 1999); and Beverley, *Testimonio.: On the Politics of Truth* (Minneapolis: University of Minnesota Press, 2004).

31. Hernández, *Chicano Satire: A Study in Literary Culture* (Austin: University of Texas Press, 1991), 5.

32. Chávez, *Face of an Angel*, 11.

33. Ibid., 85–91.

34. Ibid., 114.

35. As Hutcheon notes, contemporary parody does not always reflect negatively on its target for, as she explains, "parodic art both deviates from an aesthetic norm and includes that norm within itself as backgrounded material. Any real attack would be self-destructive." Hutcheon, *A Theory of Parody*, 44.

36. Ball, *Satire and the Postcolonial Novel* (New York: Routledge, 2003), 27; Hutcheon, *A Theory of Parody*, 44.

37. Chávez, *Face of an Angel*, 211.

38. Ibid., 217.

39. Romero, *Maid in the U.S.A.*, 93.

40. Ibid., 26–27.

41. Hondagneu-Sotelo, *Doméstica*, 94.

42. Ibid., 10–11.

43. Ibid., 11.

44. Ibid., 35.

45. Chávez, *Face of an Angel*, 214.

46. Romero, *Maid in the U.S.A.*, 1–4, 92.

47. Ehrenreich and Hochschild, "Introduction," 1–13.
48. Zavella, *Women's Work and Chicano Families*, 10.
49. Chávez, *Face of an Angel*, 451.
50. Romero discusses this book as a popular mid-twentieth-century manual for employers of domestic labor in the U.S. Romero, *Maid in the U.S.A.*
51. Hawkins, Soper, and Henry, *Your Maid from Mexico*, 2.
52. Chávez, *Face of an Angel*, 171.
53. Moraga, *Loving in the War Years*, 103.
54. Chávez, *Face of an Angel*, 270.
55. As a descriptive term for literature, *metafiction* refers to literature that self-consciously represents the imaginative or writing process, thereby setting out a framework for its reading that calls forth an engaged response centered on "the imaginative process (of storytelling), instead of on that of the product (the story told), and it is the new role of the reader that is the vehicle of this change." Hutcheon, Introduction, in her *Narcissistic Narrative*.
56. Hutcheon suggests that metafiction's ability to make literature strange and unfamiliar for readers who have perhaps become complacent in their knowledge of its strategies and, therefore, inattentive and uncritical enables it to lay claim to both "be[ing] a genre rooted in the realities of historical time and geographical space" and "only narrative, as its own reality—that is, as artifice." Hutcheon, *A Theory of Parody*, 31.
57. This is the mutilated Nahua goddess figure who in Chicana feminist perspective has come to represent the violent suppression of women. Coyolxauhqui's representation was discovered at what is now known as the Templo Mayor site in Mexico City and remains a central attraction of this museum.
58. Moraga, *Loving in the War Years*, 132.
59. Molly Hite, discussing female fiction, calls this "turning a product of the dominant meaning system into a producer of meanings." Hite, "Writing—and Reading—the Body," 122.
60. Mitchell, "An Interview with W. J. T. Mitchell," 247.
61. Ibid., 247–48. This reading of the visual in literature, according to Mitchell, also allows greater interpretive insight on "imagination, memory, fantasy" for "all the psychological notions of vision—interior vision, imagining, dreaming, remembering, etc.—are activated by visual and literary means."
62. Morgan states that "the material culture of religion is widely understood to sacralize space" in his study of religious imagery. Morgan, *Visual Piety*, 182.
63. Carrasco, *Religions of Mesoamerica*, 156.
64. Mitchell, "An Interview with W. J. T. Mitchell," 245.
65. Morgan, *Visual Piety*, 31, 202.
66. Some parallels between Nahua pictographs and icons and milagrito images

might also suggest that the latter represent a syncretic adaptation of the former. Ellen McCracken observes that Latina narratives frequently represent popular religious practices and that doing so allows them to engage in a "rearticulation of Catholicism" that shares something with orthodox religion but is not congruent with it. McCracken, *New Latina Narrative*, 96.

67. Personal interview with Denise Chávez, October 22, 2008.
68. For further reading on this, see Fields and Zamudio-Taylor, *The Road to Aztlan*; Pérez-Torres, *Movements in Chicano Poetry*.
69. Carrasco, *Religions of Mesoamerica*, 156.
70. Rodriguez, *Brown Gumshoes*, 53.
71. Moraga, *Heroes and Saints and Other Plays*, 35.
72. Rodriguez, *Brown Gumshoes*, 53.
73. Chávez says that "angels have always played an important part in my life, from the Catholic, as helpers—those luminous helpers throughout our lives." Describing her own spirituality, Chávez says, "I grew up as a Catholic and am Catholic and Buddhist." Personal interview with Denise Chávez, October 22, 2008.
74. Chávez, *Face of an Angel*, 403, 375.
75. Ibid., 318.
76. Ibid., 465.
77. Ibid., 457.
78. Ibid., 416.
79. Alarcón, "Chicana Feminism," 63–71, 69.
80. Elizabeth Dore says that several studies of Latin American households since the 1970s have found "surprising" numbers of female-headed households, and she suggests that what we might learn from this is the power of misperceptions and that the story of the traditional patriarchal Latin American family is a myth, primarily a feature of the dominant classes. What needs to be addressed in building on Dore's research is the appeal of or desire for this myth among all classes, the mechanisms by which it is perpetuated, and the consequences. Dore, "The Holy Family," 101–17.
81. Alarcón, "Chicana Feminism," 69.
82. Butler, *Gender Trouble*, 11.
83. Butler suggests that transformation might be possible through the "subversive repetition enabled by those constructions" or the non-repetition of the "discursive practices that give those terms the intelligibility that they have" in order to produce a "radical proliferation of gender" that might "displace the very gender norms that enable the repetition itself." Ibid., 188–89.
84. Ibid., 94.
85. Ibid., 98; Butler, *Bodies That Matter*, 10.

86. In making the film *Señorita Extraviada*, Lourdes Portillo specifically rejected any focus on graphic scenes of dismemberment, the pornographic gaze that would make the murders of women in Juárez sensational and lurid. Personal conversation with Lourdes Portillo, Detroit, October 2001.

87. Kaplan suggests that a feminist transnational politics can only succeed if hegemonic use of gender or essentialist, nostalgic intimacies among women across borders are discarded: it must be a politics that points toward coalition rather than universalism. Kaplan, "The Politics of Location as Transnational Feminist Critical Practice," 139.

88. Martínez, *Mother Tongue*; Martínez, "The Writer as Witness."

89. Wuthnow, *After Heaven*, 111, 73–75, 4.

90. For more on the history of the Salvadoran war, liberation theology movements in El Salvador, U.S. support for the war, political and guerrilla organizations in El Salvador, and the solidarity movement in the U.S., see Gettleman et al., *El Salvador*; Binford, "Peasants, Catechists, Revolutionaries, Organic Intellectuals in the Salvadoran Revolution," 105–25.

91. Martínez, *Mother Tongue*, 8.

92. Singh, Skerrett, and Hogan describe the necessity for multiethnic literatures to contest a "dominant historiography that fails to represent the whole picture." Singh, Skerrett, and Hogan, "Introduction" to their *Memory and Cultural Politics*, 14.

93. Saldívar-Hull, "Feminism on the Border: From Gender Politics to Geopolitics," 203–20.

94. Martínez, *Mother Tongue*, 115–16.

95. Greene, "Feminist Fiction and the Uses of Memory," 296. Greene argues that the feminist fiction she describes is no longer written, confined to texts produced in the 1960s and 1970s. It may be that, for white feminist writers, issues of memory and history no longer surface as principal concerns in their work, yet her observations on memory in feminist fiction and especially feminist metafiction continue to resonate in the contemporary work of Chicana and other women-of-color fiction not because these remain bound by a feminist consciousness that mainstream white feminism has already superseded but because memory and history remain significant in deciphering racial and sexual formation, and intersectional identities, in contemporary contexts. These contemporary texts create new forms of metafiction that nonetheless have something in common with the metafiction of previous generations of women writers.

96. Martínez, *Mother Tongue*, 13.

97. Ibid., 119.

98. Ibid., 70.

99. Beverley notes: "Romanticizing victimization would tend to confirm the Christian narrative of suffering and redemption that underlies colonial or imperialist domination in the first place." Beverley, *Subalternity and Representation*, 73.

100. Several critical takes on this text have focused on María's witness to the war in El Salvador and the novel's examination of justice and love.

101. Martínez, *Mother Tongue*, 17.

102. Adapting Omi and Winant's theory of racial formation, with qualifications, to the category of gender allows for the integration of theory, material realities, and historical specificity. See Omi and Winant, *Racial Formation in the United States*.

103. In their reading of this novel, Debra A. Castillo and María Socorro Tabuenca Córdoba note the multiple and conflicting identities that the text attempts to explicate via the trope of language, translation, mother tongue. While Castillo and Tabuenca focus on ethnic and national difference, my reading concurs with their analysis of the contrapuntal and partial quality of *Mother Tongue*'s revelations. Castillo and Tabuenca, *Border Women*, 168–88.

104. Martínez, *Mother Tongue*, 79.

105. Ibid., 78.

106. Ibid., 77–78, 99.

107. Ibid., 75, 78.

108. Martínez, "Nuevas voces Salvadoreñas," 114–15.

109. Butler, *Bodies That Matter*, 15.

110. Foucault, *Power/Knowledge*, 55–57, 61.

111. Although this narrative mentions only two, seventeen religious were killed in El Salvador between 1977 and 1982. See Morkovsky, "*Guerrilleros*, Political Saints, and the Theology of Liberation."

112. Rodríguez, *Women, Guerrillas, and Love*, 23.

113. Ibid., 19, 24.

114. Stasiulis suggests the necessity of "a conceptual apparatus that can analytically deal with not merely the *plurality* but also and more importantly the *positionality* of different nationalisms, racisms, ethnocultural movements, and feminisms *in relation to one another*." Stasiulis, "Relational Positionalities of Nationalisms, Racisms, and Feminisms," 183.

115. Foucault states, "Power must be analysed as something which circulates, or rather as something which functions in the form [of] a chain.... And not only do individuals circulate between its threads; they are always in the position of simultaneously undergoing and exercising this power." Foucault, *Power/Knowledge*, 98.

116. Martínez, *Mother Tongue*, 52.

117. Ibid., 4.

118. Ibid., 16.
119. Ibid., 15, 33–34, 25, 43.
120. Ibid., 35, 102.
121. Greene, "Feminist Fiction and the Uses of Memory," 293.
122. Ibid., 292–93.
123. Martínez, *Mother Tongue*, 59.
124. Keating, "Myth Smashers, Myth Makers," 81; Steele, *We Heal from Memory*, 87–90.
125. Scott, *Domination and the Arts of Resistance*, 190–91.
126. Martínez, "The Writer as Witness," 44–45.
127. Torres, "The Construction of Self in U.S. Latina Autobiographies," 275.
128. This stands in contrast to universalist conceptions of morality, justice, and equality as Rafael Pérez-Torres notes in his discussion of resistant versus reactionary postmodernism. Pérez-Torres, "Nomads and Migrants," 168.
129. Morkovsky, "*Guerrilleros*, Political Saints, and the Theology of Liberation."
130. My thanks to Katharina Albrecht for her seminar paper on the figure of the Mother of the Disappeared in *Mother Tongue* (Latino/a Literature Seminar, 2004), which offered a unique interpretation of the more universal appeal of this figure for all Catholics.
131. Cisneros, "Guadalupe the Sex Goddess," 45.
132. Studies cite the classic *Nican Mopohua* as well as other accounts of Guadalupe's appearance with varying degrees of skepticism about the authenticity of her manifestation and of the accounts. The accuracy of the reports of the appearance and the dates are settled for the church but not for historians, whose research is driven in part by inquiry into the extant and integral link between Guadalupe (sacred) and Mexico (nation). See Brading, *Mexican Phoenix*; Poole, *Our Lady of Guadalupe*; Lafaye, *Quetzalcóatl y Guadalupe*.
133. Rodríguez, *Our Lady of Guadalupe*.
134. Brading, *Mexican Phoenix*, 75; Lafaye, *Quetzalcóatl y Guadalupe*, 324–31.
135. Brading, *Mexican Phoenix*, 75.
136. Poole, *Our Lady of Guadalupe*, 29.
137. Becker, *Setting the Virgin on Fire*, 9.
138. Ibid., 21–23.
139. Ibid., 18.
140. Ibid., 66–67, 37–38, 157.
141. Ibid., 101.
142. Ibid., 160–62.
143. The image of Guadalupe today retains some continuity with her historical meanings—as symbol of church and nation, as protective Indian mother—and takes on new dimensions in its continued renewal by the faithful. Chicana

artists Ester Hernandez and Yolanda López, in their paintings in the 1970s, offered new visions of Guadalupe that included Hernandez's interpretation of Guadalupe's powers of protection in the battle for Chicano/a rights and López's portrayal of herself, her mother, her grandmother, and the Aztec goddess Coatlicue as Guadalupes, emphasizing the presence, intimacy, and empowerment of Guadalupe in the lives of brown-skinned and working-class women who continually remake her in their devotion and faith. Lucy Lippard suggests that López revises an idealized image of social control in her view of Guadalupe. Chabram-Dernersesian notes how much Chicana artistic revisions of Guadalupe challenge nationalist, culturalist, and sexist paradigms of Chicano identity. Lippard, *Mixed Blessings*, 42; Chabram-Dernersesian, "I Throw Punches for My Race, but I Don't Want to Be a Man."

144. Canclini states, "That group of goods and traditional practices that identify us as a nation or as a people is valued as a gift, something we receive from the past that has such symbolic prestige that there is no room for discussing it. The only operations that are possible—to preserve it, restore it, disseminate it—are the most secret basis of the social simulation that keeps us together as a group. . . . it occurs to almost no one to think about the social contradictions that they express. . . . For that very reason, it is in the patrimony that the ideology of the oligarchic sectors—that is, substantialist traditionalism—survives best today." Canclini, *Hybrid Cultures*, 108.

145. Medina's work on Las Hermanas also reveals the significance of revising androcentric images of God for the members of this feminist, Chicana religious organization. See Medina, *Las Hermanas*, 142.

146. "Demetria Martínez," in *A Poet's Truth*, 85.

147. Elizabeth Olivárez, "Women's Rights and the Mexican-American Woman," in García, *Chicana Feminist Thought*, 131–36.

148. Sandoval, *On the Move*, 81.

149. Boff and Boff, *Introducing Liberation Theology*, 14.

150. Aquino, "The Collective 'Dis-covery' of Our Own Power," 252–53.

151. Perhaps in tracing its genealogy through struggles against colonial and neocolonial domination in Latin America, liberation theology cements the union of nation and theology that leaves women, and any challenge to normative gender and sexuality, outside its boundaries. The struggles against neocolonial national oppression that emerged in Latin America between the 1960s and 1980s embodied a Latin American historic revolutionary spirit which liberation theology also represented. Ibid., 256.

The United States government also recognized this connection. As the Boffs note, the "Santa Fe Document, produced by advisors to President Reagan in 1982," explicitly states: "American foreign policy must begin to counterattack (and not just react against) liberation theology." Boff and Boff, *Introducing Liberation Theology*, 86.

The year 1982 is significant. That is the year that José Luis sees María primarily as a subject of the nation that attacks his country and people, and the year that María believes she can remain innocently free of politics.

152. Martínez, *Mother Tongue*, 90.

153. Katzenstein, "Feminism within American Institutions."

154. Scott, *Domination and the Arts of Resistance*, 123.

155. Martínez, *Mother Tongue*, 7.

156. Scott, *Domination and the Arts of Resistance*, 111.

157. Martínez, *Mother Tongue*, 4–7, 12.

158. Agosín, *Tapestries of Hope, Threads of Love*, 8–10; Dandavati, *The Women's Movement and the Transition to Democracy in Chile*, 50–54.

159. Hanh, *The Heart of the Buddha's Teaching*, 64–67.

160. Sommer, "Taking a Life," 936. My characterization of these two novels as fictional testimonios coincides to some degree with Craft's category of "pseudo-testimony," which is an invented "eyewitness account that resembles testimony and incorporates testimonial function[s]." Craft's analysis closely examines history, or "the real," in testimonial literature and focuses on struggles for national liberation in fiction, while my work explores the interrogation of history and hegemonies (nation, class, race, gender, sexuality) in fictional testimonios through the self-conscious invocation of memory. This is also why the term *fictional testimonio* fits this analysis over *pseudo-testimony*, which may appear to suggest the primacy of the real, autobiographical, or historical and certainly the national. Craft's continuum between testimonio and pseudo-testimony offers a framework for considering the varieties of this genre. Within the testimonial functions, Craft includes "resistance, heterogeneity, multiplicity of voices, and decentering of the authorial figure" as well as the use of modes that disrupt the "traditional valorization of *haute literature*." Craft, *Novels of Testimony and Resistance from Central America*, 189, 191.

161. Cubitt and Greenslade in discussing the public-private sphere issue in Latin America observe, "Reliance on this dichotomized framework has resulted in an essentialized version of women's subjectivity and reinforces the simplistic equation 'public man/private woman.'" The novels discussed here further break down this dichotomy by exploring how public discourses affect private lives and by representing characters whose participation in both realms demands awareness of subordinating discourses (rather than freedom from them in social movement or work). Cubitt and Greenslade, "Public and Private Spheres," 53.

162. Fred Pfeil suggests a great divide between fiction that acknowledges difference

and that which maintains "in-difference," arguing that the former works to find a "way *through* difference via a praxis whose goal is neither the totalitarian effacement of difference nor the delirious celebration of a limitless and ever-proliferating 'in-difference,' but the construction of flexible, practical relations of *solidarity*." Pfeil, "No Basta Teorizar," in *Scattered Hegemonies*, 225.

163. Sandoval, *Methodology of the Oppressed*.

164. Ortiz describes transculturation and its parts as follows: "*transculturation* better expresses the different phases of the process of transition from one culture to another because this does not consist merely in acquiring another culture ... the process also necessarily involves the loss or uprooting of a previous culture, which could be defined as deculturation. In addition it carries the idea of the consequent creation of new cultural phenomena, which could be called neoculturation." Ortiz, *Cuban Counterpoint*, 102–3.

165. Canclini has described this with respect to the art of several Latin American artists: "they are not fleeing from an inhospitable present; they want to incorporate the fullness of history into the modern gaze." Canclini, *Hybrid Cultures*, 79.

166. Morgan notes: "In fact, the sacred happens in the recounting of the past generally, for it is in such acts of memory that believers encounter the social world of relationships, anxieties, and desires that structure their worlds." Morgan, *Visual Piety*, 202.

167. Here I echo Greene's observation that feminist fiction creates something new out of the past. Greene, "Feminist Fiction and the Uses of Memory," 292. However, Canclini and others take the view that this is "the ongoing condition of all human cultures, which contain no zones of purity because they undergo continuous processes of transculturation." Canclini, *Hybrid Cultures*, xv.

Chapter 3: Sacred Fronteras

1. Woman from village in Los Tuxtlas region speaking in a group interview in Gleason et al.'s *Flowers for Guadalupe/Flores para Guadalupe*.

2. Beverley, *Testimonio*, xiii.

3. In countering the rhetoric about the border, it becomes, in part, narrative as rhetoric, which is, according to James Phelan, an action: "the telling of a story by someone to someone on some occasion for some purpose" that involves "complex, multilayered processes of writing and reading, processes that call upon our cognition, emotions, desires, hopes, values, and beliefs." Phelan, *Narrative as Rhetoric*, 8, 19.

4. Padilla, *My History, Not Yours*, 232, 4, 10, 20–21, 25.

5. Ibid., 238.
6. Fraser, "Rethinking the Public Sphere."
7. Miranda, *Homegirls in the Public Sphere*, 80.
8. This reconsideration of the domestic sphere owes much to Scott's theorization of the "hidden transcript" versus the "public transcript" as distinct sites of social interaction with differing audiences and aims. See Scott, *Domination and the Arts of Resistance.*
9. Holler, "Exploring the Popular Religion of U.S. Hispanic/Latino Ethnic Groups," 23.
10. Anzaldúa, *Borderlands/La Frontera*, 81.
11. The theologian Elizondo identifies the fusion of indigenous and Spanish cultural traditions as a central feature of mestizo Christianity in Latin America. In Anzaldúa's work these elements do not exist in a smooth fusion but rather as different strands of an inherited spiritual legacy—a hybrid spirituality. The reevaluation of that inheritance constitutes part of the work of spiritual mestizaje in renewing one's relation to the sacred, the world, and others. Elizondo, *Galilean Journey*; Elizondo, *Guadalupe*; Anzaldúa, *Borderlands/La Frontera*, 80–81.
12. Holler, "Exploring the Popular Religion of U.S. Hispanic/Latino Ethnic Groups," 5.
13. Noriega and López suggest that Latino/a film and media deserve to be read "through the filter of a number of competing disciplines, traditions, histories." I suggest that religion, spirituality, testimonio, and gender are some of the discourses through which these films can be productively read. Noriega and López, "Introduction," ix.
14. Gutiérrez, *A Theology of Liberation*, 151.
15. In Boff, *Faith on the Edge*, 22.
16. The women who are active in this struggle are a spiritual community, but the film prompts one to wonder where the official church, of any denomination, is in all of this—what statements have been made, what positions expressed in support of women, what organized material and advocacy support have been offered. While there are some who argue that the killings represent a general breakdown of the family and religious values in society, there are others who wonder if perhaps an activist church guided by liberation theology were the norm, such out-of-control and senseless violence would not exist, that is, that in retrospect perhaps there has been a real cost to the turn away from liberation theology.
17. Mohanty, *Feminism without Borders*, 40.
18. Braziel and Mannur, "Nation, Migration, Globalization: Points of Contention in Diaspora Studies," in their *Theorizing Diaspora*, 8.

19. Saldívar, *Border Matters*, 14.
20. For discussion of *Canícula*'s "double-cross" of the border, see Brady, *Extinct Lands, Temporal Geographies*, 70–73. For more on *Canícula* as a genre-busting autobiography, see Adams, "'Heightened by Life' vs. 'Paralyzed by Fact'"; and Castillo and Tabuenca Córdoba, *Border Women*, 93–100. Castillo and Tabuenca Córdoba note the influence of the testimonio form on this text, an observation I share.
21. Delgadillo, "Hybrid Spiritualities," 176.
22. Adams's observation of several discrepancies between photos and text is valuable here. He cites Genaro Padilla on the need to expand individualist notions of autobiography yet remains committed to reading *Canícula* as an autobiography characterized by "transcription," or identity life writing, which stands implicitly in contrast to literary life writing. In his reading, the photographs are authenticating material. See Adams, "'Heightened by Life' vs. 'Paralyzed by Fact.'"
23. Cantú, *Canícula*, 2.
24. Halbwachs, *On Collective Memory*, 38–40, 171–73.
25. Fusco, *English Is Broken Here*, 36–38.
26. Barthes, *Camera Lucida*, 82.
27. Ibid., 82.
28. Barthes, *Camera Lucida*, 27–28.
29. Or, they lend themselves to varied uses, they can be read in a variety of ways. As Elizabeth Edwards and Janice Hart explain, "photographs are both images *and* physical objects that exist in time and space and thus in social and cultural experience." Edwards and Hart, "Introduction: Photographs as Objects," 1.
30. Lalvani employs a Foucauldian "critique of the discourses and technologies by which people have been classified, normativized, and produced as subjects with an identity." Lalvani, *Photography, Vision, and the Production of Modern Bodies*, 40.
31. Barthes, *Camera Lucida*.
32. Nancy M. Shawcross observes that Barthes introduces the terms *studium* and *punctum* "to denote the copresence of two discontinuous elements in the photograph": "studium represents the world of codes, of culture, of conventionalized context" while punctum "speaks to that quality or state in the photograph that is not exclusively anchored in a cultural response (message) that has been engineered (structured) in the manner of a traditional 'sign.'" A punctum is rooted in individual perceptions, "shifts between one viewer and another" or "within one viewer's response over time"; it is "not a thing but rather a condition that arises from the *noeme* of the unique medium of photography" as evidence of what has been. However, explains Shawcross, "if one

does not understand or respond to the cultural context (the studium of the photograph), the lacerating detail and the photograph's potential for pathos remain obscured: without a frame or setting, there is nothing to be exceeded, nothing to be pierced." Shawcross, *Roland Barthes on Photography*, 83, 85, 84.

33. Cantú, *Canícula*, 117.

34. Shawcross notes that, in discussing aura, Barthes's focus is on the subject of the photo whereas Benjamin's is on the object of the photo and its distance from original or authentic art. Shawcross, *Roland Barthes on Photography*, 103. While Benjamin suggests that "the cult of remembrance of loved ones, absent or dead, offers a last refuge for the cult value of the picture," Barthes posits that one way of reading the photograph is to "confront in it the wakening of intractable reality." Benjamin, *Illuminations*, 226; Barthes, *Camera Lucida*, 119. As Keenan notes, both view the photograph as an object that serves forgetting, though Keenan takes up Benjamin's discussion of narrative inspired by photograph to suggest that "it is possible to claim that because the photograph depicts a loaded, personal subject initially stripped of aura, this is what spurs us to configure our memories in terms of this photograph and thus to invest it with aura." Keenan, "On the Relationship between Personal Photographs and Individual Memory," 61–62.

35. Shawcross, *Roland Barthes on Photography*, 45, 103.

36. Ibid., 65.

37. Ibid., 67–68.

38. Halbwachs, *On Collective Memory*, 171.

39. This follows Henri Lefebvre's view of social space as a social product, one created through the various interrelations "constitutive of capitalism," which generate knowledge out of spatial practice, representations of space, and representational spaces. Lefebvre, *The Production of Space*.

40. Cantú, *Canícula*, 3.

41. Ibid., 4.

42. De Luna, *Faith Formation and Popular Religion*, 38–39.

43. Cantú, *Canícula*, 4.

44. Ibid., 5.

45. De Luna notes that "Hispanic/Latino spirituality *mística* emerges out of a culturally rich religious pre-Columbian background. This spirituality in its indigenous roots had a deeply imbedded presence of the divine, which held that life was sacred and the spiritual was the essence of the cosmic and human harmony in a life-death cycle." De Luna, *Faith Formation and Popular Religion*, 13, 14, 38. This theological understanding is further supported by Sue Marasco's analyses of "how religious practices tied to the earth were or-

ganic and could adapt to the local religious environment" in Latino and Native American religions. Marasco, "Cosmology," 121.

46. Cantú, *Canícula*, 10, 13, 15.

47. *Canícula* does not, however, address the frontera as a social space shared with native peoples in contrast to Gloria Anzaldúa's theorization of the borderlands as a site of interaction between Chicanos, indigenous peoples, and blacks where racial formations emerge out of the tension between existing racial and national borders. Anzaldúa, *Borderlands/La Frontera*, 3. *Canícula*'s emphasis on constructed sites of worship differs from the understanding of sacred place in many indigenous traditions, an additional factor that points to the colonial legacies that inform its frontera faith community. For more on sacred places in native traditions, see Arnold, "Sacred Landscapes of New York State and the Problem of Religion in America."

48. Nevins makes a valuable distinction between the terms *border* or *border region*, as marking that place where two nations intersect, and *boundary*, which is a "territorial, juridical, and ideological divide." Nevins, *Operation Gatekeeper*, 15.

49. Taylor, *The Archive and the Repertoire*, 18–19.

50. McDannell, *Material Christianity*, 39.

51. Ibid., 45.

52. Ibid., 57, 98 (for discussion of decorative and materialist meanings of religious items).

53. Cantú, *Canícula*, 35.

54. Ibid., 63.

55. Ibid., 64.

56. Roberto Goizueta holds that popular religion mixes both private and public. See De Luna, *Faith Formation and Popular Religion*, 47.

57. Broyles-González, "Indianizing Catholicism," 117.

58. Cantú, *Canícula*, 25.

59. Adams, " 'Heightened by Life' vs. 'Paralyzed by Fact,' " 4.

60. Cantú, *Canícula*, 70.

61. Ibid., 69–70.

62. Robert T. Trotter and Juan Antonio Chavira note that earlier research on curanderismo viewed it as "a mass-cultural phenomenon, not as a coherent system," and that such an approach "tends to make any discussion of the topic nontheoretical, at least in terms of expecting or eliciting an emic theory of *curanderismo*, because while systems (for example, medical, educational, and scientific systems) are easily recognized as depending on theory, mass-cultural phenomena are generally thought of as having themes or unifying elements,

but not theories. Mass-cultural phenomena are something one has theories about, but they are not theoretical systems themselves." Trotter and Chavira, *Curanderismo*, 6–7.

63. Ana Castillo reads the recollection and enactment of curandera practices as a feminist activism that remembers the "folkways of the grandmothers while altering the Catholic faith of their devout mothers," and she considers the varieties of curandera practice in her analysis of this form of healing. Castillo, *Massacre of the Dreamers*, 152. Luis D. León says that curanderismo is "situated in that paradoxical space—the border that connects yet divides Catholicism and indigenous Mexican ritual." León, "Soy una curandera y soy una Católica," 95.

64. Medina and Cadena, "Día de los Muertos," 88.

65. Cantú, *Canícula*, 83.

66. Ibid., 116.

67. Lippard, *Mixed Blessings*, 42.

68. Anzaldúa, *Borderlands/La Frontera*, 27, 30.

69. Gil and Vazquez, *The Maria Paradox*.

70. Lafaye also notes that the new Mexican nation adopted Guadalupe's colors as the national colors. Lafaye, *Quetzalcóatl y Guadalupe* and *Abismo de conceptos*, 378–79.

71. Lafaye, *Quetzalcóatl y Guadalupe*, 171.

72. Brading, *Mexican Phoenix*, 201–27. See also Lafaye, *Quetzalcóatl y Guadalupe*.

73. Castillo, *Goddess of the Americas*; Burkhart, "The Cult of the Virgin of Guadalupe in Mexico"; Rodríguez, *Our Lady of Guadalupe*; Becker, *Setting the Virgin on Fire*.

74. Video jacket of Gleason et al., *Flowers for Guadalupe/Flores para Guadalupe*.

75. The documentary form parallels the testimonio in significant ways. Its central elements, as outlined by Nichols, include informing logic, rhetoric or argument, an economy of problem and solution, and reliance on spoken word. Rabinowitz notes that a pervasive feature of documentary is to "induce feeling, thought and action," often through an "appeal to emotion." Nichols, *Representing Reality*, 18–21; Rabinowitz, *They Must Be Represented*, 8.

76. Mulvey, *Visual and Other Pleasures*, 14–26; Nichols, *Representing Reality*, 176.

77. Hansen, Needham, and Nichols argue that ethnography satisfies our desire "to know" and yet also "to know it *as strangeness*." Hansen, Needham, and Nichols, "Pornography, Ethnography, and the Discourses of Power," 201–28, 225, 228.

78. Brading cites Juan de Torquemada's work of 1615, which describes indigenous worship of Tonantzin at Tepeyac that predates the Spanish conquest. Lafaye dates pilgrimage to the basilica at Tepeyac to at least 1620 and notes successive expansions of the basilica to accommodate ever-growing numbers of wor-

shippers. Brading, *Mexican Phoenix*, 43; Lafaye, *Quetzalcóatl y Guadalupe*, 181, 360.

79. Mesa-Bains, "Curatorial Statement," 7–8.

80. Bill Nichols distinguishes "the interactive mode" of documentary filmmaking from expository, observational, or reflexive modes. Nichols, *Representing Reality*, 44–56.

81. Nichols calls this moving from the "author-centered voice of authority to a witness-centered voice of testimony." Ibid., 48.

82. Ibid., 144, 141.

83. Ibid., 54–55.

84. For a discussion of the differences between attentive and negative silences, see Cheung, *Articulate Silences*, 114.

85. Nichols observes that "the interview is an overdetermined structure." Though off-camera, the filmmaker mediates, determining, in the unheard questions asked, as Nichols suggests, or in the editing of interviews, as David Mac-Dougall suggests, what information viewers will receive. Nichols, *Representing Reality*, 50–51, 52; MacDougall, *Transcultural Cinema*, 118.

86. Ortiz, *Cuban Counterpoint*.

87. Vargas, *Proletarians of the North*; Rosales, *Chicano/a!*

88. Brading, *Mexican Phoenix*, 363.

89. Stepick, "God Is Apparently Not Dead."

90. Warner, "Introduction: Immigration and Religious Communities in the United States."

91. For further discussion of the narratives of the Puritan ethos and the ideal immigrant in relation to Mexicans, Chicano/as, and their literature, see Aranda, *When We Arrive*, 121–60.

92. Aldama, "Millennial Anxieties," 15.

93. Ibid.

94. Nevins, *Operation Gatekeeper*, 140.

95. Rodríguez, "Sangre llama a sangre," 123.

96. Boff, *Faith on the Edge*, 56.

97. Rabinowitz notes that "ethnography as a historical practice in which white people look at and (through cinema) display people of color maintains imperialist relations of domination." Rabinowitz, *They Must Be Represented*, 174.

98. Nichols notes, "When both filmmaker and social actor coexist within the historical world but only one has the authority to represent it, the other, who serves as subject of the film, experiences a displacement." Nichols, *Representing Reality*, 91.

99. Hansen, Needham, and Nichols, "Pornography, Ethnography, and the Discourses of Power," 227.

100. MacDougall, *Transcultural Cinema*, 121.
101. Gleason et al., *Flowers for Guadalupe.*
102. Gutiérrez, *A Theology of Liberation*, 152.
103. Fregoso, *MeXicana Encounters*, 27.
104. Ibid., 25–26, 20–22.
105. Nevins quotes INS commissioner Doris Meissner in testimony in 1993 acknowledging that the implementation of NAFTA would create greater immigration from Mexico and, therefore, require stronger border enforcement. Meissner's comments also indicate that U.S. officials were well aware of how NAFTA would spur migration within Mexico northward to the maquilas. Nevins, *Operation Gatekeeper*, 138.
106. Zuniga and Fout, "King on the Mountain"; Gonzalez, "Enjoy the View at Cristo Rey."
107. Dorfman, "June 25, 1983," 248–49.
108. Biemann, "Performing the Border," 102.
109. Fregoso, "Introduction: Tracking the Politics of Love," 8.
110. In Marti, "Mystery on the Border."
111. Ibid.
112. Portillo, "A Conversation with Lourdes Portillo," in *Lourdes Portillo*, 68.
113. Portillo, "Interview with Lourdes Portillo (1990)," in *Lourdes Portillo*, 64.
114. Ibid., 68.
115. She says, "So it's inclusion, and inclusion of a dialogue that starts with the crew ends with the product itself, and ultimately when it comes to the audience speaks to them and they respond to it." Portillo, "Interview with Lourdes Portillo (1998)," in *Lourdes Portillo*, 39.
116. Fregoso, "Introduction: Tracking the Politics of Love," 11.
117. Nichols terms "sacramental" "those practices or events that are not what they seem" and applies it to nonvisible experiences that film cannot capture, as in communion or trance. Nichols, *Representing Reality*, 146–47.
118. See Hansen, Needham, and Nichols, "Pornography, Ethnography, and the Discourses of Power," 209.
119. Rodríguez, *Brown Gumshoes*, 125.
120. Portillo, "Director's Statement."
121. Halbwachs states: "To the extent that the dead retreat into the past, this is not because the material measure of time that separates them from us lengthens; it is because nothing remains of the group in which they passed their lives, and which needed to name them, that their names slowly become obliterated." Halbwachs, *On Collective Memory*, 171, 73–74.
122. Fregoso discusses several examples of this in *MeXicana Encounters*. Another book that reports on the murders in this vein is Ronquillo's *Las muertas de Juárez.*

123. Fusco, *The Bodies That Were Not Ours and Other Writings*, 22, 77–81, 78.
124. Ibid., 61–77, 76, 75.
125. Biemann, "Performing the Border," 106.
126. Thompson, "In Mexico's Murders, Fury Is Aimed at Officials."
127. Ferriss, "Women's Murders Remain Unsolved in Guatemala," A17.
128. Martínez, "Choirs of Angles Join the Geometry of Clan."
129. Sandoval, "U.S. Third World Feminism," 87.

Chapter 4: Border Secrets

1. Pérez, *The Decolonial Imaginary*, 27.
2. Ibid., 124.
3. The reviews are overwhelmingly positive on the magic, realism, intermixture, and hope throughout the trilogy. *Publishers Weekly* notes: "In the tradition of Latin American literary fabulism, Alcalá's seductive writing mixes fatalism and hope, logic and fantasy, to create moral, emotional and political complexities. But her characterizations and plot sparkle with a freshness that is an apt fit for the new social order she writes about with a multicultural vision notable for its lack of preachiness." *Publishers Weekly*, Review of *Spirits of the Ordinary*, 54. *Booklist* notes: "Alcala has conjured a culturally and metaphysically complex world." Seaman, Review of *Spirits of the Ordinary*, 924. *Booklist* describes *The Flower in the Skull* as "a quietly riveting story of three brave souls often buffeted by forces beyond their control." Wilkinson, Review of *Flower in the Skull*, 1719. Another reviewer describes it as "the stories of three generations of strong, heroic women." Erazo, Review of *Flower in the Skull*, 72–73. *Booklist* describes *Treasures in Heaven* as "a mesmerizing tale of heartbreak, redemption, and self-actualization." Flanagan, Review of *Treasures in Heaven*, 416.
4. For a quick summary of the major events, see James D. Henderson, Helen Delpar, and Maurice P. Brungardt, eds., *A Reference Guide to Latin American History* (Armonk, N.Y.: Sharpe, 2000).
5. This branch of mystic Judaism has been spelled in a variety of ways. The novel spells it "Cabala"; I will employ the more common contemporary spelling "Kabbalah."
6. Alcalá, *Treasures in Heaven*, 46. Kabbalists hold that the world originated in a divine withdrawal or contraction significant enough to give rise to the spiritual and material realms of which we form a part. It is within the spiritual and material realms that the work of restoration and repair that will eventually heal us from the absence of good is necessary. Jewish mysticism and its relationships with movements for social change thereby merge in Mariana's reading of, and the novel's emphasis upon, the shared link with her Catho-

lic daughter-in-law as a spiritual one in addition to a relational one (affiliated through marriage). Laenen, *Jewish Mysticism.*

7. Donnelly, Review of *Spirits of the Ordinary*, 45.

8. Saldívar, *Chicano Narrative*, 5.

9. Ricoeur, *Memory, History, Forgetting*, 147.

10. In Dubrava, "Fountains Out of the Roots," 9.

11. White, *The Content of the Form*, 74–75.

12. Ibid., 44.

13. In Mazurek, "Metafiction, the Historical Novel and Coover's *The Public Burning*," 194–205.

14. Brooks, "Served Well by Plunder," 24, 27.

15. Saldívar, *Chicano Narrative*, 211; Pérez, *The Decolonial Imaginary*, 26, 127.

16. Hedrick, *Mestizo Modernism.*

17. Macías, *Against All Odds*, 3–24, 36.

18. Ibid., xiii–xv.

19. Pérez, *The Decolonial Imaginary*, 6–7.

20. The theologian María Pilar Aquino concurs with Pérez by suggesting that Latin American women's movements for social and political rights at the turn of the twentieth century "could be rightfully claimed by today's Latina American critical feminism as a necessary moment in our feminist tradition." For Aquino this claim is based on the centrality of women's control over their own bodies in a Latina feminist theology attentive to women, which includes an "awareness of the political character of the biological, the sexual, and the domestic." Aquino, "The Collective 'Dis-covery' of Our Own Power," 249, 256.

21. Marta Cotera explores the history of the Mexican feminist movement as a precursor to Chicana feminism in a speech recorded as "Our Feminist Heritage" (1973) in García, *Chicana Feminist Thought*, 41–44.

22. Anzaldúa, *Borderlands/La Frontera*, vii. George G. Sanchez's note is evident in this trilogy also: "Mestizo America, I would agree with Anzaldúa, is just as likely to produce cultural conflict as it is to generate individual liberation and collective equality." Sanchez, "Y Tú, ¿Qué? (Y2K)," 281.

23. Anzaldúa, *Borderlands/La Frontera*, 194.

24. Alcalá, *Spirits of the Ordinary*, 165.

25. Ibid., 106.

26. Ibid., 138.

27. Ibid., 180.

28. Ibid., 181.

29. Laenen explains that in Kabbalah, "the whole material creation is thus an external manifestation of a single process which is at work both above and below." Laenen, *Jewish Mysticism*, 52. Scholem says the Sephiroth are not in-

termediaries but "planes in the manifestation of Divinity." Scholem, *Major Trends in Jewish Mysticism*, 208–9.

30. Alcalá, *The Flower in the Skull*, 4.

31. Clifford Geertz defines *religion* as a system of symbols that both expresses an understanding of the world and shapes it. Geertz, "Religion as a Cultural System," in his *The Interpretation of Cultures*, 91, 95. Also see Bal, *Narratology*.

32. Arteaga, *An Other Tongue*, 18.

33. Alcalá, *Spirits of the Ordinary*, 182–83.

34. Nieto, *Religious Experience and Mysticism*, 138–39.

35. Ariel, *The Mystic Quest*, 12; Nieto, *Religious Experience and Mysticism*, 139; Laenen, *Jewish Mysticism*.

36. Laenen, *Jewish Mysticism*. Zacarías is reminiscent of Cabeza de Vaca, a Spanish explorer whose account of his journey through and transformation in the Americas chronicles his blending of Christian and indigenous rituals, but Alcalá's character remains in the borderlands. Cabeza de Vaca, *Adventures in the Unknown Interior of America*.

37. Alcalá, *Spirits of the Ordinary*, 225–26.

38. Archaeologists have identified Casas Grandes as a major center of culture and trade between North and South in the pre-Hispanic period. See Reyman, *The Gran Chichimeca*; and Vanpool and Vanpool, *Religion in the Prehispanic Southwest*.

39. Scott observes, in his analysis of forms of resistance and domination, that these social sites are never given but rather "won, cleared, built and defended," and as such they represent a powerful counterweight to totalitarian domination. Scott, *Domination and the Arts of Resistance*, 126.

40. Alcalá, *The Flower in the Skull*, 153.

41. Alcalá, *Treasures in Heaven*, 103–4.

42. Laenen, *Jewish Mysticism*, 52.

43. Blumenthal, *Understanding Jewish Mysticism*, 154, 156.

44. Rosa Linda Fregoso notes the significance of spirituality in Chicano/a film in *The Bronze Screen*.

45. Delgadillo, "Hybrid Spiritualities."

46. Anzaldúa, *Borderlands/La Frontera*. For Anzaldúa, as for Martí a hundred years earlier, that transnational possibility rests on a deeper study of the cultures, histories, and languages of the Americas. Alcalá's historical fictional testimonio engages these ideas but with a keen sense, also, of power and domination in the borderlands. For more on Martí, see Acosta-Belén and Santiago, "Merging Borders," 29–42; Belnap and Fernández, *José Martí's "Our America."*

47. Alcalá, *Spirits of the Ordinary*, 75.

48. Ibid., 85.
49. Ibid.
50. O'Hara, "'In Search of Souls, in Search of Indians,'" 157–80.
51. Sander Gilman has written extensively on the Old World anti-Semitism through which Jews were demonized, which traveled to the Americas via the Inquisition. Elizabeth McAlister suggests that anti-Semitism proliferated in the Americas via Passion Play ceremonies. Gilman, *The Jew's Body*; McAlister, "The Jew in the Haitian Imagination," 61–82.
52. Alcalá, *Spirits of the Ordinary*, 88.
53. Raquel Rubio Goldsmith discusses the significance of norteño gardens for Christians in contrast to indigenous views of the desert. Goldsmith, "Civilization, Barbarism, and Norteña Gardens," in Aiken et al., *Making Worlds*, 274–87.
54. Alcalá, *Spirits of the Ordinary*, 20–21.
55. Ibid., 92.
56. Alcalá, *The Flower in the Skull*, 3.
57. Mexico's reform laws in 1873 created a separation of church and state, prevented the church from holding property, eliminated religious instruction in schools, and prohibited religious attire in public. James D. Henderson, Helen Delpar, and Maurice P. Brungardt, eds., *A Reference Guide to Latin American History* (Armonk, N.Y.: Sharpe, 2000).
58. As historian Anna Macías notes, education for women was largely unavailable. Macías, *Against All Odds*.
59. Alcalá, *Spirits of the Ordinary*, 240.
60. Alcalá found this book on a research trip to Mexico City and the translations are her own. See Dubrava, "Fountains Out of the Roots," 9.
61. Laenen discusses the history of the Zohar and mystical currents in Judaism as well as reciprocity, emanation, and female divinity in Kabbalah. Laenen, *Jewish Mysticism*. Blumenthal discusses the secrecy of and in the Zohar, reciprocity, and exile. Blumenthal, *Understanding Jewish Mysticism*. McGinn discusses love in Jewish mysticism. McGinn, "The Language of Love in Christian and Jewish Mysticism." Wolfson suggests that the imagination, rather than the intellect, plays a key role in visionary ascent, and this is perhaps part of the significance of the Zohar for these novels, which attempt to imagine new spiritualities. Wolfson, "Forms of Visionary Ascent as Ecstatic Experience in the Zoharic Literature."
62. Blumenthal, *Understanding Jewish Mysticism*, 105.
63. Ariel, *The Mystic Quest*, 34.
64. Blumenthal, *Understanding Jewish Mysticism*, 183.

65. Nandy comments on the significance of environmental crises and colonial intrusion in religious change. Nandy, *Exiled at Home*, 3–4.

66. Bahr, *Pima and Papago Ritual Oratory*; Spicer and Crumrine, *Performing the Renewal of Community*.

67. Alvarado, "An Opata Holy Week Ceremonial Complex." In describing her father's participation in the Easter pascola dances, Concha acknowledges the Jesuit influence: "This is the way it had always been, even before the priests like Father Kino came and gave many new names to the old things, or tried to get rid of them altogether." Alcalá, *The Flower in the Skull*, 14.

68. Singh, Skerrett, and Hogan, "Introduction" to their *Memory and Cultural Politics*, 3–18.

69. Alcalá, *The Flower in the Skull*, 3–4.

70. Ibid., 19.

71. Émile Durkheim suggests that the social group is central to what constitutes religion. Durkheim, *The Elementary Forms of Religious Life*, 46.

72. Ariel, *The Mystic Quest*, 145.

73. Hutcheon, "Irony, Nostalgia, and the Postmodern."

74. Alcalá, *Spirits of the Ordinary*, 47.

75. Castañeda, "Sexual Violence in the Politics and Policies of Conquest"; Alarcón, "Traduttora, Traditora." Alarcón suggests that in the Malinche image we can see a violent history of colonization played out over women's bodies. Malinche is a symbol of women exiled from home by subjugation, a fitting description of Shelly in *The Flower in the Skull*.

76. Alcalá, *The Flower in the Skull*, 169.

77. Alcalá, *Treasures in Heaven*, 95.

78. Ibid.

79. Ibid., 21.

80. Ibid., 96.

81. Ibid., 98.

82. Citizenship for women, as a legal state, "begins . . . in the recognition of the full control of our bodies," notes Ileana Rodríguez in her discussion of nation and gender in Latin American literature. Rodríguez, *House/Garden/Nation*, 18. The fictional *La Linterna* project both provides necessary and otherwise unavailable health and sexuality information and also educates women for citizenship.

83. McGinn notes, "Jewish mystics were more successful in drawing out the positive aspects of the human sexual relationship in itself." McGinn, "The Language of Love in Christian and Jewish Mysticism," 226.

84. Alcalá, *Treasures in Heaven*, 211.

85. In this case, the diasporas are concomitant with transnationalism as characters from both groups cross borders. Braziel and Mannur, *Theorizing Diaspora*.
86. Alcalá, *Spirits of the Ordinary*, 140, 22.
87. Alcalá, *The Flower in the Skull*, 5.
88. Matt, "'New-Ancient Words,'" 181.
89. Alcalá, "A Woman Called Concha."

Chapter 5: "Bad Religion"

1. Gutiérrez-Jones, *Rethinking the Borderlands*, 30.
2. Canclini, *Hybrid Cultures*, 108–10.
3. Pérez's decolonial approach focuses on the critical engagement of social and ideological paradigms that further colonialist projects or new hegemonies; studies in this vein have explored, among others, transnational historical subjects, alternative and hybrid spiritualities, and reification of national subjectivities. Pérez, *The Decolonial Imaginary*, 6–7.
4. Chatterjee, *The Nation and Its Fragments*.
5. Van Der Veer, "The Moral State."
6. Guha, *Dominance without Hegemony*, 80, 98, 154, 3, 11.
7. Ibid., 19–20, 80.
8. Nandy, *The Intimate Enemy*.
9. Nandy, *The Intimate Enemy: Loss and Recovery of Self Under Colonialism*, 58–60.
10. Ibid., 81, 113.
11. The religious rationale—the conversion of "heathens" to Christianity—of the Spanish Crown's conquest of the Americas is well known. Vera Kutzinski notes that Alejo Carpentier and others "perceived Afro-Cuban secular and religious culture as a cultural alternative to North-Americanization and as a political vehicle for national integrity and survival." Kutzinski, *Sugar's Secrets*, 142.
12. Poole and Brading explore these issues.
13. Canclini discusses these issues.
14. Canclini, *Hybrid Cultures*. In general terms, there is a similar dynamic at play in the historical pressures for the Americanization of minorities or their dissolution into the "melting pot" of the United States, where there is still not a concomitant acceptance of a U.S. identity informed by multiple cultures and races.
15. León, "Soy una curandera y soy una Católica."
16. Gutiérrez-Jones defines the theoretical as "a form of discourse which comments on its own and other forms of discourse." Gutiérrez-Jones, *Rethinking*

the Borderlands, 29. McCutcheon proposes that we recognize theorizing as "a meta-activity, a higher-order cognitive map designed to provide a rational, explanatory account for just this or that series of experiences, observations, and *events that we as scholars deem important, puzzling, or curious.*" McCutcheon further defines a theory as "(i) a set of related propositions (ii) that possess predictive capability and can therefore be tested empirically (iii) that function to explain the causes of (iv) empirically observable events or processes. Although such theories can never be confirmed, based on their predictive capabilities, they can at least be tested, critiqued, and possibly discarded." McCutcheon, *Critics Not Caretakers*, 112.

17. For example, writing about the significance of African spirituality to the work of Nicolás Guillén in Cuba, Vera Kutzinski observes that the ability to perform an indigenous ritual or to describe its performance in literature is a liberating act in that the "religious beliefs of the participants" are thereby accorded a public presence. Guillén's work "dislocates . . . the formal manifestations of authoritative (and authoritarian) institutions, be they cultural, literary, or political." Kutzinski, *Against the American Grain*, 142, 149. Since the participants of the particular religiosities Kutzinski discusses are otherwise marginalized by virtue of their race, ethnicity, and class, the enjoyment of this public presence is, indeed, liberating. However, as Kutzinski and the music scholar Robin Moore also note, the entry of Afro-Cuban culture into the public mainstream is not, in every case, a liberating movement.

18. Kutzinski suggests that the development of Afro-Cubanism in the late nineteenth century and the early twentieth forms part of a nation-building project, "signifies an active desire to be Cuban" that validates the male mestizo as the desired national subject. Similarly, Robin Moore's work explores the multiple effects of the adoption or appropriation of Afro-Cuban musics into the national canon—some democratizing, some not—and observes that "the mass acceptance of certain forms of black music and dance by Cuban society did not necessarily imply greater social equality for or empowerment of Afrocubans themselves." Kutzinski, *Sugar's Secrets*, 142; Moore, *Nationalizing Blackness*, 5.

19. McCutcheon, *Critics Not Caretakers*, 25, 16, 85.
20. Foucault, *Power/Knowledge*, 58.
21. Sandoval, *Methodology of the Oppressed*, 109–11.2.
22. Phelan, *Narrative as Rhetoric*, 8; Bal, *Narratology*, 168.
23. Jameson, *The Political Unconscious*, 225, 283.
24. McCutcheon, *Critics Not Caretakers*, 26–27.
25. Ibid., 16.
26. Ibid., 85.

27. Asad, *Genealogies of Religion*, 47, 54.

28. Kearney, "Narrative and the Ethics of Remembrance," 30.

29. Ricoeur, "Memory and Forgetting," 9–10.

30. McCutcheon, *Critics Not Caretakers*, 90.

31. Diamond, *Not by Politics Alone*, 77.

32. Bruce, *The Rise and Fall of the New Christian Right*, 190.

33. Ibid., 166, 184, 189.

34. Culler suggests that "religious discourse and religious belief seem to occupy a special, privileged place, as though it went without saying that any sort of challenge or critique were improper, in bad taste." Culler, *Framing the Sign*, 71.

35. Luis D. León, "Cesar Chávez in American Religious Politics: Mapping the New Global Spiritual Line."

BIBLIOGRAPHY

Acosta-Belén, Edna, and Carlos E. Santiago. "Merging Borders: The Remapping of America." In *The Latino Studies Reader: Culture, Economy and Society*, edited by Antonia Darder and Rodolfo D. Torres, 29–42. Oxford: Blackwell, 1998.

Adams, Kate. "Northamerican Silences: History, Identity, and Witness in the Poetry of Gloria Anzaldúa, Cherríe Moraga, and Leslie Marmon Silko." In *Listening to Silences: New Essays in Feminist Criticism*, edited by Elaine Hedges and Shelley Fisher Fishkin, 130–45. New York: Oxford University Press, 1994.

Adams, Timothy Dow. " 'Heightened by Life' vs. 'Paralyzed by Fact': Photography and Autobiography in Norma Cantú's *Canícula*." *Biography: An Interdisciplinary Quarterly* 24, no. 1 (2001): 57–71.

Agosín, Marjorie. *Tapestries of Hope, Threads of Love: The Arpillera Movement in Chile, 1974–1994*, translated by Celeste Kostopulos-Cooperman. Albuquerque: University of New Mexico Press, 1996.

Alarcón, Daniel Cooper. *The Aztec Palimpsest: Mexico in the Modern Imagination*. Tucson: University of Arizona Press, 1997.

Alarcón, Norma. "Traduttora, Traditora: A Paradigmatic Figure of Chicana Feminism." In *Scattered Hegemonies: Postmodernity and Transnational Feminist Practices*, edited by Inderpal Grewal and Caren Kaplan, 110–33. Minneapolis: University of Minnesota Press, 1994.

———. "Chicana Feminism: In the Tracks of 'the' Native Woman." In *Between Woman and Nation: Nationalisms, Transnational Feminisms, and the State*, edited by Caren Kaplan, Norma Alarcón, and Minoo Moallem, 63–71. Durham: Duke University Press, 1999.

———. "Anzaldúa's *Frontera*: Inscribing Gynetics." In *Chicana Feminisms: A Critical Reader*, edited by Gabriela F. Arredondo, 354–69. Durham: Duke University Press, 2003.

Alcalá, Kathleen. *Spirits of the Ordinary: A Tale of Casas Grandes*. San Diego: Harvest/Harcourt Brace, 1998.

———. *The Flower in the Skull*. San Diego: Harvest/Harcourt Brace, 1999.

———. "A Woman Called Concha." January 19, 1999. Author's possession.

———. *Treasures in Heaven*. San Francisco: Chronicle, 2000.

Aldama, Arturo J. "Millennial Anxieties: Borders, Violence, and the Struggle for Chicana and Chicano Subjectivity." *Decolonial Voices: Chicana and Chicano*

Cultural Studies in the 21st Century, edited by Arturo J. Aldama and Naomi H. Quiñonez, 11–29. Bloomington: Indiana University Press, 2002.

Aldama, Frederick Luis. *Brown on Brown: Chicano/a Representations of Gender, Sexuality and Ethnicity.* Austin: University of Texas Press, 2005.

Alexander, M. Jacqui. *Pedagogies of Crossing: Meditations on Feminism, Sexual Politics, Memory, and the Sacred.* Durham: Duke University Press, 2005.

Alfaro, Luis. "The Doll." In *Goddess of the Americas: Writings on the Virgin of Guadalupe*, edited by Ana Castillo, 184–86. New York: Riverhead, 1996.

Allen, Paula Gunn. *The Sacred Hoop: Recovering the Feminine in American Indian Traditions.* Boston: Beacon, 1992 [1986].

Alvarado, Anita L. "An Opata Holy Week Ceremonial Complex." In *Performing the Renewal of Community: Indigenous Easter Rituals in North Mexico and Southwest United States*, edited by Rosamond B. Spicer and N. Ross Crumrine, 289–315. Lanham, Md.: University Press of America, 1996.

Anderson, Benedict. *Imagined Communities: Reflections on the Origin and Spread of Nationalism.* London: Verso, 1991 [1983].

Anderson, Pamela Sue. *A Feminist Philosophy of Religion.* Oxford: Blackwell, 1998.

Anzaldúa, Gloria. *Borderlands/La Frontera: The New Mestiza Consciousness.* San Francisco: Aunt Lute, 1987.

———. "Chicana Artists." In *The Latino Studies Reader: Culture, Economy and Society*, edited by Antonia Darder and Rodolfo D. Torres, 163–69. Oxford: Blackwell, 1998.

———. *Interviews/Entrevistas: Gloria Anzaldúa*, edited by AnaLouise Keating. New York: Routledge, 2000.

———. "Now Let Us Shift . . . The Path of Conocimiento . . . Inner Work, Public Acts." In *This Bridge We Call Home: Radical Visions for Transformation*, edited by Gloria E. Anzaldúa and AnaLouise Keating, 540–78. New York: Routledge, 2002.

———. "Quincentennial: From Victimhood to Active Resistance." In *Gloria E. Anzaldúa: Interviews/Entrevistas*, edited by AnaLouise Keating, 177–94. New York: Routledge, 2000.

———. "(Un)natural bridges, (Un)safe spaces." In *This Bridge We Call Home: Radical Visions for Transformation*, edited by Gloria E. Anzaldúa and AnaLouise Keating, 1–5. New York: Routledge, 2002.

Anzaldúa, Gloria, ed. *Making Face, Making Soul/Haciendo Caras: Creative and Critical Perspectives by Feminists of Color.* San Francisco: Aunt Lute, 1999.

Anzaldúa, Gloria, and Cherríe Moraga, eds. *This Bridge Called My Back: Writings by Radical Women of Color.* New York: Women of Color, 1981.

Anzaldúa, Gloria, and AnaLouise Keating, eds. *This Bridge We Call Home: Radical Visions for Transformation.* New York: Routledge, 2002.

Aparicio, Frances R., and Susana Chávez Silverman, eds. *Tropicalizations: Transcultural Representations of Latinidad.* Hanover, N.H.: Dartmouth College Press, 1997.

Appadurai, Arjun. "Disjuncture and Difference in the Global Cultural Economy." In *Theorizing Diaspora: A Reader,* edited by Jana Evans Braziel and Anita Mannur, 25–48. Oxford: Blackwell, 2003.

Aquino, María Pilar. "The Collective 'Dis-covery' of Our Own Power: Latina American Feminist Theology." In *Hispanic/Latino Theology: Challenge and Promise,* edited by Ada María Isasí-Díaz and Fernando F. Segovia, 240–60. Minneapolis: Fortress, 1996.

———. "Latina Feminist Theology: Central Features." In *A Reader in Latina Feminist Theology: Religion and Justice,* edited by María Pilar Aquino, Daisy L. Machado, and Jeanette Rodríguez, 133–60. Austin: University of Texas Press, 2002.

Aranda, José F., Jr. *When We Arrive: A New Literary History of Mexican America.* Tucson: University of Arizona Press, 2003.

Ariel, David S. *The Mystic Quest: An Introduction to Jewish Mysticism.* Northvale, N.J.: Jason Aronson, 1988.

Armitage, Susan. "Here's to the Women: Western Women Speak Up." *Journal of American History* 83, no. 2 (September 1996): 551–59.

Armstrong, Nancy. *Fiction in the Age of Photography: The Legacy of British Realism.* Cambridge: Harvard University Press, 1999.

Arnold, Philip P. "Sacred Landscapes of New York State and the Problem of Religion in America." In *Sacred Landscapes and Cultural Politics,* edited by Philip P. Arnold and Ann Grodzins Gold, 167–86. Burlington, Vt.: Ashgate, 2001.

Arrizón, Alicia. *Latina Performance: Traversing the Stage.* Bloomington: Indiana University Press, 1999.

Arteaga, Alfred, ed. *An Other Tongue: Nation and Ethnicity in the Linguistic Borderlands.* Durham: Duke University Press, 1994.

Asad, Talal. *Genealogies of Religion: Discipline and Reasons of Power in Christianity and Islam.* Baltimore: Johns Hopkins University Press, 1993.

Avalos, Hector, ed. *Introduction to the U.S. Latina and Latino Religious Experience.* Boston: Brill, 2004.

Bahr, Donald M. *Pima and Papago Ritual Oratory: A Study of Three Texts.* San Francisco: Indian Historian Press, 1975.

Bal, Mieke. *Narratology: Introduction to the Theory of Narrative*, 2nd ed. Toronto: University of Toronto Press, 1997.

Ball, John Clement. *Satire and the Postcolonial Novel*. New York: Routledge, 2003.

Barnet, Miguel. "La Novela Testimonio." In *Testimonio y literatura*, edited by René Jara and Hernán Vidal, 280–302. Minneapolis: Institute for the Study of Ideologies and Literature, 1986.

Barthes, Roland. *Camera Lucida: Reflections on Photography*, translated by Richard Howard. New York: Hill and Wang, 1981.

Bassard, Katherine Clay. *Spiritual Interrogations: Culture, Gender, and Community in Early African American Women's Writing*. Princeton: Princeton University Press, 1999.

Becker, Marjorie. *Setting the Virgin on Fire: Lázaro Cárdenas, Michoacán Peasants, and the Redemption of the Mexican Revolution*. Berkeley: University of California Press, 1995.

Belnap, Jeffrey, and Raúl Fernández, eds. *José Martí's "Our America": From National to Hemispheric Cultural Studies*. Durham: Duke University Press, 1998.

Benjamin, Walter. *Illuminations*. New York: Schocken, 1985 [1955].

Berlo, Janet Catherine, ed. *Art, Ideology, and the City of Teotihuacan*. Washington: Dumbarton Oaks Research Library and Collection, 1992.

Beverley, John. *Against Literature*. Minneapolis: University of Minnesota Press, 1993.

——. *Subalternity and Representation: Arguments in Cultural Theory*. Durham: Duke University Press, 1999.

——. *Testimonio: On the Politics of Truth*. Minneapolis: University of Minnesota Press, 2004.

Biemann, Ursula. "Performing the Border: On Gender, Transnational Bodies, and Technology." In *Globalization on the Line: Culture, Capital, and Citizenship at U.S. Borders*, edited by Claudia Sadowski-Smith, 99–118. New York: Palgrave, 2002.

Binford, Leigh. "Peasants, Catechists, Revolutionaries, Organic Intellectuals in the Salvadoran Revolution, 1980–1992." In *Landscapes of Struggle: Politics, Society, and Community in El Salvador*, edited by Aldo Lauria-Santiago and Leigh Binford, 105–25. Pittsburgh: University of Pittsburgh Press, 2004.

Blumenthal, David R. *Understanding Jewish Mysticism: A Source Reader*. New York: Ktav, 1978.

Boff, Leonardo. *Faith on the Edge: Religion and Marginalized Existence*. San Francisco: Harper and Row, 1989.

Boff, Leonardo, and Clodovis Boff. *Introducing Liberation Theology*, translated by Paul Burns. Maryknoll, N.Y.: Orbis, 1987.

Bouvard, Marguerite Guzman. *Revolutionizing Motherhood: The Mothers of the Plaza de Mayo*. Wilmington, Del.: Scholarly Resources, 1994.

Brading, D. A. *Mexican Phoenix: Our Lady of Guadalupe: Image and Tradition across the Centuries*. Cambridge: Cambridge University Press, 2001.

Brady, Mary. *Extinct Lands, Temporal Geographies: Chicana Literature and the Urgency of Space*. Durham: Duke University Press, 2002.

Braziel, Jana Evans, and Anita Mannur, eds. *Theorizing Diaspora: A Reader*. Oxford: Blackwell, 2003.

Brooks, James F. "Served Well by Plunder: *La Gran Ladronería* and Producers of History astride the Río Grande." *American Quarterly* 52, no. 1 (March 2000): 23–58.

Brooks, Joanna. *American Lazarus: Religion and the Rise of African-American and Native American Literatures*. Oxford: Oxford University Press, 2003.

Broyles-González, Yolanda. *El Teatro Campesino: Theater in the Chicano Movement*. Austin: University of Texas Press, 1994.

———. "Indianizing Catholicism: Chicana/India/Mexicana Indigenous Spiritual Practices in Our Image." In *Chicana Traditions: Continuity and Change*, edited by Norma E. Cantú and Olga Najera-Ramírez, 117–32. Urbana: University of Illinois Press, 2002.

Bruce, Steve. *The Rise and Fall of the New Christian Right: Conservative Protestant Politics in America 1978–1988*. Oxford: Clarendon, 1988.

Burkhart, Louise M. "The Cult of the Virgin of Guadalupe in Mexico." In *South and Meso-American Native Spirituality: From the Cult of the Feathered Serpent to the Theology of Liberation*, edited by Gary H. Gossen in collaboration with Miguel León Portilla. New York: Crossroad, 1993.

Burns, Robert A. *Roman Catholicism after Vatican II*. Washington: Georgetown University Press, 2001.

Butler, Judith. *Bodies That Matter: On the Discursive Limits of "Sex."* New York: Routledge, 1993.

———. *Gender Trouble: Feminism and the Subversion of Identity*. New York: Routledge, 1999 [1990].

Cabeza de Vaca, Alvar Nuñez. *Adventures in the Unknown Interior of America*, 3rd ed. Albuquerque: University of New Mexico Press, 1983.

Calderón, Héctor. *Narratives of Greater Mexico: Essays on Chicano Literary History, Genre, and Borders*. Austin: University of Texas Press, 2004.

Canclini, Néstor García. *Hybrid Cultures: Strategies for Entering and Leaving*

Modernity, translated by Christopher L. Chiappari and Silvia L. López. Minneapolis: University of Minnesota Press, 1995.

Cantú, Norma Elia. *Canícula: Snapshots of a Girlhood en la Frontera*. Albuquerque: University of New Mexico Press, 1995.

Carrasco, David. *Religions of Mesoamerica: Cosmovision and Ceremonial Centers*. Prospect Heights, Ill.: Waveland, 1990.

Castañeda, Antonia I. "Sexual Violence in the Politics and Policies of Conquest: Amerindian Women and the Spanish Conquest of Alta California." In *Building with Our Hands: New Directions in Chicana Studies*, edited by Adela de la Torre and Beatríz M. Pesquera, 15–33. Berkeley: University of California Press, 1993.

Castillo, Ana. *Massacre of the Dreamers: Essays on Xicanisma*. New York: Plume, 1995.

———. "Extraordinarily Woman." In *Goddess of the Americas: Writings on the Virgin of Guadalupe*, edited by Ana Castillo, 72–78. New York: Riverhead, 1996.

Castillo, Debra A., and María Socorro Tabuenca Córdoba. *Border Women: Writing from la Frontera*. Minneapolis: University of Minnesota Press, 2002.

Chabram-Dernersesian, Angie. "I Throw Punches for My Race, but I Don't Want to Be a Man: Writing Us—Chica-nos (Girl, Us)/Chicanas—into the Movement Script." In *Cultural Studies*, edited by Lawrence Grossberg, Cary Nelson, and Paula A. Treichler, 81–95. New York: Routledge, 1992.

———. "'Chicana! Rican? No, Chicana Riqueña!' Refashioning the Transnational Connection." In *Between Woman and Nation: Nationalisms, Transnational Feminisms, and the State*, edited by Caren Kaplan, Norma Alarcón, and Minoo Moallem, 264–95. Durham: Duke University Press, 1999.

———. "En-Countering the Other Discourse of Chicano-Mexicano Difference." *Cultural Studies* 13, no. 2 (1999): 263–89.

Chatterjee, Partha. *The Nation and Its Fragments: Colonial and Postcolonial Histories*. Princeton: Princeton University Press, 1993.

Chávez, Denise. *Face of an Angel*. New York: Farrar, Straus and Giroux, 1994.

Chávez-García, Miroslava. *Negotiating Conquest: Gender and Power in California, 1770s to 1880s*. Tucson: University of Arizona Press, 2004.

Cheung, King-Kok. *Articulate Silences: Hisaye Yamamoto, Maxine Hong Kingston, Joy Kogawa*. Ithaca, N.Y.: Cornell University Press, 1993.

Chow, Rey. *Writing Diaspora: Tactics of Intervention in Contemporary Cultural Studies*. Bloomington: Indiana University Press, 1993.

Cisneros, Sandra. *Woman Hollering Creek and Other Stories*. New York: Random House, 1991.

————. "Guadalupe the Sex Goddess." *Ms.*, July–August 1996, 43–46.

Comstock, Gary David, and Susan E. Henking, eds. *Que(e)rying Religion: A Critical Anthology.* New York: Continuum, 1997.

Conner, Randy. "Santa Nepantla: A Borderlands Sutra." Paper presented at El Mundo Zurdo: An International Conference on the Life and Work of Gloria E. Anzaldúa, sponsored by the Society for the Study of Gloria Anzaldúa and the Women's Studies Institute. University of Texas, San Antonio, May 15–17, 2009.

Connerton, Paul. *How Societies Remember.* New York: Cambridge University Press, 1989.

Coronil, Fernando. "Introduction to the Duke University Press Edition: Transculturation and the Politics of Theory: Countering the Center, Cuban Counterpoint." In *Cuban Counterpoint: Tobacco and Sugar,* by Fernando Ortiz, translated by Harriet de Onís. Durham: Duke University Press, 1995 [1947].

Craft, Linda J. *Novels of Testimony and Resistance from Central America.* Gainesville: University Press of Florida, 1997.

Crenshaw, Kimberlé Williams. "Mapping the Margins: Intersectionality, Identity Politics, and Violence against Women of Color." In *Critical Race Theory: The Key Writings That Formed the Movement,* edited by Kimberlé Crenshaw, Neil Gotanda, Gary Peller, and Kendall Thomas, 357–83. New York: New Press, 1995.

Cubitt, Tessa, and Helen Greenslade. "Public and Private Spheres: The End of Dichotomy." In *Gender Politics in Latin America: Debates in Theory and Practice,* edited by Elizabeth Dore, 52–64. New York: Monthly Review Press, 1997.

Culler, Jonathan. *Framing the Sign: Criticism and Its Institutions.* Oxford: Basil Blackwell, 1988.

Daly, Mary. *The Church and the Second Sex.* Boston: Beacon, 1986 [1968].

————. *Beyond God the Father: Toward a Philosophy of Women's Liberation.* Boston: Beacon, 1993 [1973].

Dandavati, Annie G. *The Women's Movement and the Transition to Democracy in Chile.* New York: Peter Lang, 1996.

Dávila, Luis. "Gloria Anzaldúa and Octavio Paz: The Borderlands Redux." *Indiana Journal of Hispanic Literatures* 12 (1998): 51–57.

De Castro, Juan E. "Richard Rodríguez in 'Borderland': The Ambiguity of Hybridity." *Aztlán* 26, no. 1 (spring 2001): 101–26.

De la Mora, Sergio. *Cinemachismo: Masculinities and Sexuality in Mexican Film.* Austin: University of Texas Press, 2006.

Del Castillo, Adelaida. "Malintzín Tenepal: A Preliminary Look Into a New Perspective." In *Chicana Feminist Thought: The Basic Historical Writings,* edited by Alma M. García, 122–26. New York: Routledge, 1997.

Delgadillo, Theresa. "Hybrid Spiritualities: Resistance and Religious Faith in Contemporary Chicano/a Fiction, Drama, and Film." Ph.D. diss., University of California, Los Angeles, 2000.

———. "'Angelitos Negros' and Transnational Racial Identifications." In *Rebellious Reading: The Dynamics of Chicana/o Cultural Literacy*, edited by Carl Gutiérrez-Jones, 129–43. Santa Barbara: Center for Chicano Studies, 2004.

De Luna, Anita. *Faith Formation and Popular Religion: Lessons from the Tejano Experience*. Lanham, Md.: Rowman and Littlefield, 2002.

Diamond, Sara. *Not by Politics Alone: The Enduring Influence of the Christian Right*. New York: Guilford, 1998.

Díaz-Stevens, Ana María, and Anthony M. Stevens-Arroyo. *Recognizing the Latino Resurgence in U.S. Religion: The Emmaus Paradigm*. Boulder, Colo.: Westview, 1998.

Donnelly, Margarita. "In Search of El Dorado." Review of *Spirits of the Ordinary: A Tale of Casas Grandes*. *Women's Review of Books* 14, no. 1 (July 1997): 45–46.

Dore, Elizabeth. "The Holy Family: Imagined Households in Latin American History." In *Gender Politics in Latin America: Debates in Theory and Practice*, edited by Elizabeth Dore, 101–17. New York: Monthly Review Press, 1997.

Dorfman, Ariel. "June 25, 1983: Fictionalizing the Truth in Latin America." In *Cinema Nation*, edited by Carl Bromley, 242–49. New York: Thunder's Mouth/Nation, 2000.

Dubrava, Patricia. "Fountains Out of the Roots: A Profile of Kathleen Alcalá." *Bloomsbury Review* 20, no. 3 (May–June 2000): 9.

Durkheim, Emile. *The Elementary Forms of Religious Life*, translated by Carol Cosman. Oxford: Oxford University Press, 2001 [1912].

Edwall, Glenace E. "Comment." In *Memory and History: Essays on Recalling and Interpreting Experience*, edited by Jaclyn Jeffrey and Glenace Edwall, 13–15. Lanham, Md.: University Press of America, 1994.

Edwards, Elizabeth, and Janice Hart. "Introduction: Photographs as Objects." In *Photographs Objects Histories: On the Materiality of Images*. London: Routledge, 2004.

Ehrenreich, Barbara, and Arlie Russell Hochschild. "Introduction." In *Global Woman: Nannies, Maids, and Sex Workers in the New Economy*, edited by Barbara Ehrenreich and Arlie Russell Hochschild, 1–13. New York: Holt, 2002.

Elizondo, Virgil. *Galilean Journey: The Mexican American Promise*. Maryknoll, N.Y.: Orbis, 1983.

———. *Guadalupe: Mother of the New Creation*. Maryknoll, N.Y.: Orbis, 1997.

Embry, Marcus. "Cholo Angels in Guadalajara: The Politics and Poetics of

Anzaldúa's *Borderlands/La Frontera.*" *Women and Performance: A Journal of Feminist Theory* 8, no. 2 (1996): 87–108.

Erazo, Edward. Review of *Flower in the Skull. Multicultural Review* 8, no. 2 (June 1999): 72–73.

Esquíbel, Catriona Rueda. *With Her Machete in Her Hand: Reading Chicana Lesbians.* Austin: University of Texas Press, 2006.

Fernandez, Eleazar S., and Fernando F. Segovia, eds. *A Dream Unfinished: Theological Reflections on America from the Margins.* Maryknoll, N.Y.: Orbis, 2001.

Ferriss, Susan. "Women's Murders Remain Unsolved in Guatemala: Violent Crime Wave Similar to Slayings of Hundreds in Mexican City of Juarez." *Austin American-Statesman*, May 30, 2004, § A, 17.

Fields, Virginia M., and Victor Zamudio-Taylor. *The Road to Aztlan: Art from a Mythic Homeland.* Los Angeles: Los Angeles County Museum of Art, 2001.

Fiorenza, Elisabeth Schüssler. *In Memory of Her: A Feminist Theological Reconstruction of Christian Origins.* New York: Crossroad, 1994.

Flanagan, Margaret. Review of *Treasures in Heaven. Booklist* 97, no. 4 (October 15, 2000): 416.

Foucault, Michel. *Power/Knowledge: Selected Interviews and Other Writings, 1972–1977*, edited by Colin Gordon. New York: Pantheon, 1980.

———. *The History of Sexuality.* Vol. 1, *An Introduction.* New York: Vintage, 1990 [1976].

———. *Discipline and Punish: The Birth of the Prison.* New York: Vintage, 1995 [1975].

Fraser, Nancy. "Rethinking the Public Sphere: A Contribution to the Critique of Actually Existing Democracy." In *Habermas and the Public Sphere*, edited by Craig Calhoun, 109–42. Cambridge: MIT Press, 1992.

Fregoso, Rosa Linda. *The Bronze Screen: Chicana and Chicano Film Culture.* Minneapolis: University of Minnesota Press, 1993.

———. "Introduction: Tracking the Politics of Love." In *Lourdes Portillo: The Devil Never Sleeps and Other Films*, edited by Rosa Linda Fregoso. Austin: University of Texas Press, 2001.

———. *MeXicana Encounters: The Making of Social Identities on the Borderlands.* Berkeley: University of California Press, 2003.

Fregoso, Rosa Linda, and Angie Chabram-Dernersesian. "Chicana/o Cultural Representations: Reframing Alternative Critical Discourses." *Cultural Studies* 4, no. 3 (October 1990): 203–12.

Fusco, Coco. *English Is Broken Here: Notes on Cultural Fusion in the Americas.* New York: New Press, 1995.

———. *The Bodies That Were Not Ours and Other Writings*. London: Routledge, 2001.

García, Alma M., ed. *Chicana Feminist Thought: The Basic Historical Writings*. New York: Routledge, 1997.

Gates, Henry Louis, ed. *"Race," Writing, and Difference*. Chicago: University of Chicago Press, 1986.

Geertz, Clifford. *The Interpretation of Cultures*. New York: Basic, 1973.

Gettleman, Marvin E., et al., eds. *El Salvador: Central America in the New Cold War*. New York: Grove, 1987.

Gil, Rosa Maria, and Carmen Inoa Vazquez. *The Maria Paradox*. New York: Putnam, 1996.

Gilman, Sander. *The Jew's Body*. New York: Routledge, 1991.

Gleason, Judith, with the Colectivo Feminista de Xalapa and Elisa Mereghetti, dirs. *Flowers for Guadalupe/Flores para Guadalupe* (video recording). New York: Filmmakers Library, 1995.

Goff, Philip, and Paul Harvey, eds. *Themes in Religion and American Culture*. Chapel Hill: University of North Carolina Press, 2004.

Goizueta, Roberto S. "U.S. Hispanic Popular Catholicism as Theopoetics." In *Hispanic/Latino Theology: Challenge and Promise*, edited by Ada María Isasí-Díaz and Fernando F. Segovia. 261–88. Minneapolis: Fortress, 1996.

———. "Our Lady of Guadalupe: The Heart of Mexican Identity." In *Religion and the Creation of Race and Ethnicity: An Introduction*, edited by Craig R. Prentiss, 140–51. New York: New York University Press, 2003.

Goldsmith, Raquel Rubio. "Civilization, Barbarism, and Norteña Gardens." In *Making Worlds: Gender, Metaphor, Materiality*, edited by Susan Hardy Aiken, Ann Brigham, Sallie A. Marston, and Penny Waterstone, 274–87. Tucson: University of Arizona Press, 1987.

Gonzalez, Maria Cortés. "Enjoy the View at Cristo Rey." *El Paso Times*, http://www.elpasotimes.com.

Greene, Gayle. "Feminist Fiction and the Uses of Memory." *Signs: Journal of Women in Culture and Society* 16, no. 21 (1991): 290–321.

Grewal, Inderpal. "Autobiographic Subjects and Diasporic Locations: *Meatless Days* and *Borderlands*." In *Scattered Hegemonies: Postmodernity and Transnational Feminist Practices*, edited by Inderpal Grewal and Caren Kaplan, 231–54. Minneapolis: University of Minnesota Press, 1994.

Griffith, R. Marie. *God's Daughters: Evangelical Women and the Power of Submission*. Berkeley: University of California Press, 1997.

Guerrero, Andrés G. *A Chicano Theology*. Maryknoll, N.Y.: Orbis, 1987.

Gugelberger, Georg M. "Introduction." In *The Real Thing: Testimonial Discourse and Latin America*, edited by Georg M. Gugelberger, 1–19. Durham: Duke University Press, 1996.

Guha, Ranajit. *Dominance without Hegemony: History and Power in Colonial India*. Cambridge: Harvard University Press, 1998.

Gutiérrez, David G. *Walls and Mirrors: Mexican Americans, Mexican Immigrants, and the Politics of Ethnicity*. Berkeley: University of California Press, 1995.

Gutiérrez, Gustavo. *A Theology of Liberation: History, Politics, and Salvation*, translated by Sister Caridad Inda and John Eagleson. Maryknoll, N.Y.: Orbis, 1988 [1971].

———. *Essential Writings*, edited by James B. Nickoloff. Maryknoll, N.Y.: Orbis, 1996.

Gutiérrez-Jones, Carl. *Critical Race Narratives: A Study of Race, Rhetoric, and Injury*. New York: New York University Press, 2001.

Gutiérrez-Jones, Carl, ed. *Rebellious Reading: The Dynamics of Chicana/o Cultural Literacy*. Santa Barbara: Center for Chicano Studies, University of California, 2004.

Habell-Pallán, Michelle. *Loca Motion: The Travels of Chicana and Latina Popular Culture*. New York: New York University Press, 2005.

Habell-Pallán, Michelle, and Mary Romero, eds. *Latino/a Popular Culture*. New York: New York University Press, 2002.

Halbwachs, Maurice. *On Collective Memory*, edited and translated by Lewis A. Coser. Chicago: University of Chicago Press, 1992 [1941].

Hanh, Thich Nhat. *The Heart of the Buddha's Teaching*. New York: Broadway, 1999.

Hansen, Christian, Catherine Needham, and Bill Nichols. "Pornography, Ethnography, and the Discourses of Power." In *Representing Reality: Issues and Concepts in Documentary*, edited by Bill Nichols, 201–28. Bloomington: Indiana University Press, 1991.

Hawkins, Gladys, Jean Soper, and Jane Henry. *Your Maid from Mexico*. San Antonio: Naylor, 1959.

Hedges, Elaine, and Shelley Fisher Fishkin, eds. *Listening to Silences: New Essays in Feminist Criticism*. New York: Oxford University Press, 1994.

Hedrick, Tace. *Mestizo Modernism: Race, Nation, and Identity in Latin American Culture, 1900–1940*. New Brunswick, N.J.: Rutgers University Press, 2003.

Hernández, Guillermo E. *Chicano Satire: A Study in Literary Culture*. Austin: University of Texas Press, 1991.

Hirsch, Marianne, and Valerie Smith. "Feminism and Cultural Memory: An Introduction." *Signs* 28, no. 1 (autumn 2002): 1–19.

Hite, Molly. "Writing—and Reading—the Body: Female Sexuality and Recent Feminist Fiction." *Feminist Studies* 14, no. 1 (1988): 121–42.

Holland, Sharon Patricia. *Raising the Dead: Readings of Death and (Black) Subjectivity*. Durham: Duke University Press, 2000.

Holler, Stephen. "Exploring the Popular Religion of U.S. Hispanic/Latino Ethnic Groups." *Latino Studies Journal* 6, no. 3 (September 1995): 3–29.

Hondagneu-Sotelo, Pierrette. *Doméstica: Immigrant Workers Cleaning and Caring in the Shadows of Affluence*. Berkeley: University of California Press, 2001.

Hume, Lynne, and Kathleen McPhillips, eds. *Popular Spiritualities: The Politics of Contemporary Enchantment*. Aldershot, England: Ashgate, 2006.

Hutcheon, Linda. *Narcissistic Narrative: The Metafictional Paradox*. London: Routledge, 1984 [1980].

———. *A Theory of Parody: The Teachings of Twentieth-Century Art Forms*. New York: Methuen, 1985.

———. "Irony, Nostalgia, and the Postmodern." In *Methods for the Study of Literature as Cultural Memory*, edited by Raymond Wervliet and Anne Marrie Estor, 189–207. Amsterdam: Rodopi, 2000.

Isasí-Díaz, Ada María. *Mujerista Theology*. Maryknoll, N.Y.: Orbis, 1996.

Jameson, Fredric. *The Political Unconscious: Narrative as a Socially Symbolic Act*. Ithaca, N.Y.: Cornell University Press, 1981.

Jara, René. "Introduction." In *Testimonio y literatura*, edited by René Jara and Hernán Vidal, 1–7. Minneapolis: Institute for the Study of Ideologies and Literature, 1986.

Kaplan, Caren. "The Politics of Location as Transnational Feminist Critical Practice." In *Scattered Hegemonies: Postmodernity and Transnational Feminist Practices*, edited by Inderpal Grewal and Caren Kaplan, 137–52. Minneapolis: University of Minnesota Press, 1994.

Katzenstein, Mary Fainsod. "Feminism within American Institutions: Unobtrusive Mobilization in the 1980s." *Signs* 16, no. 1 (1990): 27–54.

Kearney, Richard. "Narrative and the Ethics of Remembrance." In *Questioning Ethics: Contemporary Debates in Philosophy*, edited by Richard Kearney and Mark Dooley, 18–32. London: Routledge, 1999.

Keating, AnaLouise. "Myth Smashers, Myth Makers: (Re)Visionary Techniques in the Works of Paula Gunn Allen, Gloria Anzaldúa, and Audre Lorde." In *Critical Essays: Gay and Lesbian Writers of Color*, edited by Emmanuel S. Nelson, 73–95. New York: Haworth, 1993.

———. *Women Reading Women Writing: Self-Invention in Paula Gunn Allen, Gloria Anzaldúa and Audre Lorde*. Philadelphia: Temple University Press, 1996.

———. "Introduction: Shifting Worlds, una Entrada." In *Entre Mundos/Among*

Worlds: New Perspectives on Gloria E. Anzaldúa, edited by AnaLouise Keating, 1–12. New York: Palgrave Macmillan, 2005.

———. "Shifting Perspectives: Spiritual Activism, Social Transformation, and the Politics of Spirit." In *Entre Mundos/Among Worlds: New Perspectives on Gloria E. Anzaldúa*, edited by AnaLouise Keating, 241–54. New York: Palgrave Macmillan, 2005.

Keenan, Catherine. "On the Relationship between Personal Photographs and Individual Memory." *History of Photography* 22, no. 1 (spring 1998): 60–64.

Klor de Alva, J. Jorge. "Aztlán, Borinquen, and Hispanic Nationalism in the United States." In *The Latino Studies Reader: Culture, Economy and Society*, edited by Antonia Darder and Rodolfo D. Torres, 63–82. Oxford: Blackwell, 1998.

Kutzinski, Vera. *Against the American Grain: Myth and History in William Carlos Williams, Jay Wright, and Nicolás Guillén*. Baltimore: Johns Hopkins University Press, 1987.

———. *Sugar's Secrets: Race and the Erotics of Cuban Nationalism*. Charlottesville: University of Virginia Press, 1993.

Laenen, J. H. *Jewish Mysticism: An Introduction*, translated by David E. Orton. Louisville: Westminster John Knox, 2001.

Lafaye, Jacques. *Quetzalcóatl y Guadalupe: La formación de la conciencia nacional*. Mexico City: Cultura Económica, 1985 [1977].

———. *Abismo de conceptos: Identidad, nación, Mexicano*. Mexico City: Cultura Económica, 2002.

Lalvani, Suren. *Photography, Vision, and the Production of Modern Bodies*. Albany: State University of New York Press, 1996.

Lee, James Kyung-Jin. *Urban Triage: Race and the Fictions of Multiculturalism*. Minneapolis: University of Minnesota Press, 2004.

Lefebvre, Henri. *The Production of Space*, translated by Donald Nicholson-Smith. Malden, Mass.: Blackwell, 1991 [1974].

León, Luis D. "Cesar Chávez in American Religious Politics: Mapping the New Global Spiritual Line." *American Quarterly* 59, no. 3 (2007): 857–81.

———. "Soy una curandera y soy una Católica: The Poetics of a Mexican Healing Tradition." In *Horizons of the Sacred: Mexican Traditions in U.S. Catholicism*, edited by Timothy Matovina and Gary Riebe-Estrella, 95–118. Ithaca, N.Y.: Cornell University Press, 2002.

———. *La Llorona's Children: Religion, Life, and Death in the U.S.–Mexican Borderlands*. Berkeley: University of California Press, 2004.

Lewis, Reina, and Sara Mills, eds. *Feminist Postcolonial Theory: A Reader*. New York: Routledge, 2003.

Limón, José. *American Encounters: Greater Mexico, the United States, and the Erotics of Culture*. Boston: Beacon, 1998.

Lippard, Lucy R. *Mixed Blessings: New Art in a Multicultural America*. New York: Pantheon, 1990.

Lipsitz, George. *Time Passages: Collective Memory and American Popular Culture*. Minneapolis: University of Minnesota Press, 1990.

Loya, Gloria Inés. "Pathways to a *Mestiza* Feminist Theology." In *A Reader in Latina Feminist Theology: Religion and Justice*, edited by María Pilar Aquino, Daisy L. Machado, and Jeanette Rodríguez, 217–40. Austin: University of Texas Press, 2002.

MacDougall, David. *Transcultural Cinema*. Princeton: Princeton University Press, 1998.

Macías, Anna. *Against All Odds: The Feminist Movement in Mexico to 1940*. Westport, Conn.: Greenwood, 1982.

Marasco, Sue. "Cosmology." In *Themes in Religion and American Culture*, edited by Philip Goff and Paul Harvey, 99–128. Chapel Hill: University of North Carolina Press, 2004.

Marti, Carmen. "Mystery on the Border: Filmmaker Seeks Justice for Slain Mexican Women." *Chicago Tribune*, August 28, 2002, § 8, 3.

Martí, José. "Our America." In *The Heath Anthology of American Literature*, edited by Paul Lauter, 879–86. Boston: Houghton Mifflin, 2002.

Martínez, Demetria. *Mother Tongue*. Tempe, Ariz.: Bilingual Press/Editorial Bilingue, 1994.

———. "The Writer as Witness." Interview by Argie J. Manolis. *Hayden's Ferry Review 24* (summer 1999): 37–51.

———. "Choirs of Angles Join the Geometry of Clan." *National Catholic Reporter*, November 22, 2002.

———. "Demetria Martínez." In *A Poet's Truth: Conversations with Latino/Latina Poets* by Bruce Allen Dick, 81–90. Tucson: University of Arizona Press, 2003.

Martínez, Elizabeth Coonrod. "Nuevas voces Salvadoreñas: Sandra Benítez and Demetria Martínez." In *Reflexiones: Ensayos sobre escritoras hispanoamericanos contemporaneous*, edited by Priscilla Gac-Artigas, 109–19. Fair Haven, N.J.: Nuevo Espacio Colección Academia, 2002.

Masuzawa, Tomoko. *The Invention of World Religions; or, How European Universalism Was Preserved in the Language of Pluralism*. Chicago: University of Chicago Press, 2005.

Matovina, Timothy, and Gary Riebe-Estrella, eds. *Horizons of the Sacred: Mexican Traditions in U.S. Catholicism*. Ithaca, N.Y.: Cornell University Press, 2002.

Matt, Daniel C. "'New-Ancient Words': The Aura of Secrecy in the Zohar." In *Gershom Scholem's Major Trends in Jewish Mysticism 50 Years After: Proceedings of the Sixth International Conference on the History of Jewish Mysticism*, edited by Peter Schäfer and Joseph Dan, 181–207. Tübingen: J. C. B. Mohr (Paul Siebeck), 1993.

May, Lary. *Screening Out the Past: The Birth of Mass Culture and the Motion Picture Industry.* Chicago: University of Chicago Press, 1983 [1980].

Mazur, Eric Michael. *The Americanization of Religious Minorities: Confronting the Constitutional Order.* Baltimore: Johns Hopkins University Press, 1991.

Mazurek, Raymond A. "Metafiction, the Historical Novel and Coover's *The Public Burning.*" In *Metafiction*, edited by Mark Currie, 194–205. London: Longman, 1995.

McAlister, Elizabeth. "The Jew in the Haitian Imagination: A Popular History of Anti-Judaism and Proto-Racism." In *Race, Nation, and Religion in the Americas*, edited by Henry Goldschmidt and Elizabeth McAlister, 61–82. Oxford: Oxford University Press, 2004.

McCracken, Ellen. *New Latina Narrative: The Feminine Space of Postmodern Ethnicity.* Tucson: University of Arizona Press, 1999.

McCutcheon, Russell L. *Critics Not Caretakers: Redescribing the Public Study of Religion.* Albany: State University of New York Press, 2001.

McDannell, Colleen. *Material Christianity: Religion and Popular Culture in America.* New Haven: Yale University Press, 1995.

McDowell, Linda. *Gender, Identity and Place: Understanding Feminist Geographies.* Minneapolis: University of Minnesota Press, 1999.

McGinn, Bernard. "The Language of Love in Christian and Jewish Mysticism." In *Mysticism and Language*, edited by Steven T. Katz, 202–35. New York: Oxford University Press, 1992.

Medina, Lara. "Los Espíritus Siguen Hablando: Chicana Spiritualities." In *Living Chicana Theory*, edited by Carla Trujillo, 189–213. Berkeley: Third Woman, 1998.

———. *Las Hermanas: Chicana/Latina Religious-Political Activism in the U.S. Catholic Church.* Philadelphia: Temple University Press, 2004.

Medina, Lara, and Gilbert R. Cadena. "Día de los Muertos: Public Ritual, Community Renewal, and Popular Religion in Los Angeles." In *Horizons of the Sacred: Mexican Traditions in U.S. Catholicism*, edited by Timothy Matovina and Gary Riebe-Estrella, 67–94. Ithaca, N.Y.: Cornell University Press, 2002.

Menchú, Rigoberta. *I, Rigoberta Menchú: An Indian Woman in Guatemala*, edited by Elisabeth Burgos-Debray, translated by Ann Wright. London: Verso, 1984.

Mesa-Bains, Amalia. "Curatorial Statement." In *Ceremony of Memory: New Expressions in Spirituality among Contemporary Hispanic Artists*, 7–8. Santa Fe: Center for Contemporary Arts of Santa Fe, 1988.

Miles, Angela. "Introduction: Reading the Rainbow." In *Sisterhood, Feminisms, and Power: From Africa to the Diaspora*, edited by Obioma Nnaemeka, 1–35. Trenton, N.J.: Africa World, 1998.

Miranda, Marie "Keta." *Homegirls in the Public Sphere*. Austin: University of Texas Press, 2003.

Mitchell, W. J. T. "An Interview with W. J. T. Mitchell." In *Visual Culture: The Study of the Visual after the Cultural Turn* by Margaret Dikovitskaya. Cambridge: MIT Press, 2005.

Mohanty, Chandra Talpade. *Feminism without Borders: Decolonizing Theory, Practicing Solidarity*. Durham: Duke University Press, 2003.

Mollenkott, Virginia Ramey. *The Divine Feminine: The Biblical Imagery of God as Female*. New York: Crossroad, 1984.

Moore, Robin. *Nationalizing Blackness: Afrocubanismo and Artistic Revolution in Havana, 1920–1940*. Pittsburgh: University of Pittsburgh Press, 1997.

Mora, Pat. *Agua Santa/Holy Water*. Boston: Beacon, 1995.

Moraga, Cherríe. *Loving in the War Years: Lo Que Nunca Pasó por Sus Labios*. Boston: South End, 1983.

———. *Heroes and Saints and Other Plays*. Albuquerque: West End, 1994.

Moreiras, Alberto. "The Aura of Testimonio." In *The Real Thing: Testimonial Discourse and Latin America*, edited by Georg M. Gugelberger, 192–224. Durham: Duke University Press, 1996.

Morgan, David. *Visual Piety: A History and Theory of Popular Religious Images*. Berkeley: University of California Press, 1998.

Morkovsky, Mary Christine. "*Guerrilleros*, Political Saints, and the Theology of Liberation." In *South and Meso-American Native Spirituality: From the Cult of the Feathered Serpent to the Theology of Liberation*, edited by Gary H. Gossen in collaboration with Miguel León Portilla, 526–47. New York: Crossroad, 1993.

Moya, Paula M. L. *Learning from Experience: Minority Identities, Multicultural Struggles*. Berkeley: University of California Press, 2001.

Mulvey, Laura. *Visual and Other Pleasures*. Bloomington: Indiana University Press, 1989.

Nandy, Ashis. *Exiled at Home*. Oxford: Oxford University Press, 1998.

———. *The Intimate Enemy: Loss and Recovery of Self under Colonialism*. Oxford: Oxford University Press, 1999.

Nevins, Joseph. *Operation Gatekeeper: The Rise of the "Illegal Alien" and the Making of the U.S.–Mexico Boundary.* New York: Routledge, 2002.

Nichols, Bill. *Representing Reality: Issues and Concepts in Documentary.* Bloomington: Indiana University Press, 1991.

Nieto, John C. *Religious Experience and Mysticism: Otherness as Experience of Transcendence.* Lanham, Md.: University Press of America, 1997.

Noriega, Chon A. *Shot in America: Television, the State, and the Rise of Chicano Cinema.* Minneapolis: University of Minnesota Press, 2000.

Noriega, Chon A., ed. *Chicanos and Film: Representation and Resistance.* Minneapolis: University of Minnesota Press, 1992.

Noriega, Chon A., and Ana M. López, eds. Introduction. In *The Ethnic Eye: Latino Media Arts,* ix–xxi. Minneapolis: University of Minnesota Press, 1996.

O'Hara, Julia Cummings. "'In Search of Souls, in Search of Indians': Religion and the 'Indian Problem' in Northern Mexico." In *Race, Nation, and Religion in the Americas,* edited by Henry Goldschmidt and Elizabeth McAlister, 157–80. Oxford: Oxford University Press, 2004.

Olmos, Margarite Fernández, and Lizabeth Paravisini-Gebert, eds. *Sacred Possessions: Voudou, Santería, Obeah, and the Caribbean.* New Brunswick, N.J.: Rutgers University Press, 1997.

Omi, Michael, and Howard Winant. *Racial Formation in the United States: From the 1960s to the 1990s.* New York: Routledge, 1994.

Ortiz, Fernando. *Cuban Counterpoint: Tobacco and Sugar.* Durham: Duke University Press, 1995 [1947].

Padilla, Genaro. *My History, Not Yours: The Formation of Mexican American Autobiography.* Madison: University of Wisconsin Press, 1993.

Pasztory, Esther. *Teotihuacan: An Experiment in Living.* Norman: University of Oklahoma Press, 1997.

Pérez, Emma. *The Decolonial Imaginary: Writing Chicanas into History.* Bloomington: Indiana University Press, 1999.

Pérez, Laura Elisa. "*El desorden,* Nationalism, and Chicana/o Aesthetics." In *Between Woman and Nation: Nationalisms, Transnational Feminisms, and the State,* edited by Caren Kaplan, Norma Alarcón, and Minoo Moallem, 19–46. Durham: Duke University Press, 1999.

Pérez-Torres, Rafael. "Nomads and Migrants: Negotiating a Multicultural Postmodernism." *Cultural Critique* 4 (1993): 161–89.

———. *Movements in Chicano Poetry: Against Myths, against Margins.* Cambridge: Cambridge University Press, 1995.

———. "Chicano Ethnicity, Cultural Hybridity, and the Mestizo Voice." In

Mixing Race, Mixing Culture: Inter-American Literary Dialogues, edited by Monika Kaup and Debra J. Rosenthal, 163–84. Austin: University of Texas Press, 2002.

——. *Mestizaje: Critical Uses of Race in Chicano Culture*. Minneapolis: University of Minnesota Press, 2006.

Pfeil, Fred. "No Basta Teorizar." In *Scattered Hegemonies: Postmodernity and Transnational Feminist Practices*, edited by Inderpal Grewal and Caren Kaplan, 197–230. Minneapolis: University of Minnesota Press, 1994.

Phan, Peter C. "A Common Journey, Different Paths, the Same Destination: Method in Liberation Theologies." In *A Dream Unfinished: Theological Reflections on America from the Margins*, edited by Eleazar S. Fernandez and Fernando F. Segovia, 129–51. Maryknoll, N.Y.: Orbis, 2001.

Phelan, James. *Narrative as Rhetoric: Technique, Audiences, Ethics, Ideology*. Columbus: Ohio State University Press, 1996.

Poole, Stafford. *Our Lady of Guadalupe: The Origins and Sources of a Mexican National Symbol, 1531–1797*. Tucson: University of Arizona Press, 1995.

Portillo, Lourdes. *Señorita Extraviada*. Xochitl Films/Independent Television Service Production, 2001.

——. "Director's Statement." In *"Señorita Extraviada, Missing Young Woman, A Women Make Movies Press Kit."* [10 pages, unnumbered, no date]

——. "Interview with Lourdes Portillo (1998)." By Rosa Linda Fregoso. In *Lourdes Portillo: The Devil Never Sleeps and Other Films*, edited by Rosa Linda Fregoso, 27–39. Austin: University of Texas Press, 2001.

——. "Interview with Lourdes Portillo (1990)." By Kathleen Newman and B. Ruby Rich. In *Lourdes Portillo: The Devil Never Sleeps and Other Films*, edited by Rosa Linda Fregoso, 48–73. Austin: University of Texas Press, 2001.

——. "A Conversation with Lourdes Portillo." Interview by Hector A. Torres. *Film and History* 34, no. 1 (2004): 66–72.

Publishers Weekly. Review of *Spirits of the Ordinary*. *Publishers Weekly* 243, no. 52 (December 30, 1996): 54–55.

Quintana, Alvina E. *Home Girls: Chicana Literary Voices*. Philadelphia: Temple University Press, 1996.

Rabinowitz, Paula. *They Must Be Represented: The Politics of Documentary*. London: Verso, 1994.

Rajan, Rajeswari Sunder. *Real and Imagined Women: Gender, Culture and Post-colonialism*. London: Routledge, 1993.

Randall, Margaret. *Christians in the Nicaraguan Revolution*. Vancouver: New Star, 1983.

Rebolledo, Tey Diana. *Women Singing in the Snow: A Cultural Analysis of Chicana Literature*. Tucson: University of Arizona Press, 1995.

Reyman, Jonathan E., ed. *The Gran Chichimeca: Essays on the Archaeology and Ethnohistory of Northern Mesoamerica*. Aldershot, England: Avebury, 1995.

Rice-Sayre, Laura P. "Witnessing History." In *Testimonio y literatura*, edited by René Jara and Hernán Vidal, 48–72. Minneapolis: Institute for the Study of Ideologies and Literature, 1986.

Ricoeur, Paul. "Memory and Forgetting." In *Questioning Ethics: Contemporary Debates in Philosophy*, edited by Richard Kearney and Mark Dooley, 5–11. London: Routledge, 1999.

———. *Memory, History, Forgetting*, translated by Kathleen Blamey and David Pellauer. Chicago: University of Chicago Press, 2004.

Rodríguez, Ileana. *House/Garden/Nation: Space, Gender, and Ethnicity in Postcolonial Latin American Literatures*, translated by Robert Carr and Ileana Rodríguez. Durham: Duke University Press, 1994.

———. *Women, Guerrillas, and Love: Understanding War in Central America*, translated by Ileana Rodríguez with Robert Carr. Minneapolis: University of Minnesota Press, 1996.

Rodríguez, Jeanette. *Our Lady of Guadalupe: Faith and Empowerment among Mexican-American Women*. Austin: University of Texas Press, 1994.

———. "Sangre llama a sangre: Cultural Memory as a Source of Theological Insight." In *Hispanic/Latino Theology: Challenge and Promise*, edited by Ada María Isasí-Díaz and Fernando F. Segovia, 117–33. Minneapolis: Fortress, 1996.

———. "Latina Activists: Toward an Inclusive Spirituality of Being in the World." In *A Reader in Latina Feminist Theology: Religion and Justice*, edited by María Pilar Aquino, Daisy L. Machado, and Jeanette Rodríguez, 114–30. Austin: University of Texas Press, 2002.

Rodriguez, Ralph E. *Brown Gumshoes: Detective Fiction and the Search for Chicana/o Identity*. Austin: University of Texas Press, 2005.

Rodriguez, Richard. *Brown: The Last Discovery of America*. New York: Viking Penguin, 2002.

Rogers, Kim Lacy. "Comment." In *Memory and History: Essays on Recalling and Interpreting Experience*, edited by Jaclyn Jeffrey and Glenace Edwall, 84–88. Lanham, Md.: University Press of America, 1994.

Romero, Mary. *Maid in the U.S.A.* New York: Routledge, 1992.

Ronquillo, Victor. *Las muertas de Juárez: Crónica de los crímenes más despiadados e impunes en México*. Mexico City: Planeta Mexicana, 1999.

Rosales, F. Arturo. *Chicano! The History of the Mexican American Civil Rights Movement*. Houston: Arte Público, 1997.

Rothberg, Donald. *The Engaged Spiritual Life: A Buddhist Approach to Trans-forming Ourselves and the World*. Boston: Beacon, 2006.

Saldaña-Portillo, María Josefina. *The Revolutionary Imagination in the Americas and the Age of Development*. Durham: Duke University Press, 2003.

Saldívar, José David. *The Dialectics of Our America: Genealogy, Cultural Critique, and Literary History*. Durham: Duke University Press, 1991.

———. *Border Matters: Remapping American Cultural Studies*. Berkeley: University of California Press, 1997.

Saldívar, Ramón. *Chicano Narrative: The Dialectics of Difference*. Madison: University of Wisconsin Press, 1990.

Saldívar-Hull, Sonia. "Feminism on the Border: From Gender Politics to Geopolitics." In *Criticism in the Borderlands: Studies in Chicano Literature, Culture, and Ideology*, edited by Hector Calderón and José David Saldívar, 203–20. Durham: Duke University Press, 1991.

———. *Feminism on the Border: Chicana Gender Politics and Literature*. Berkeley: University of California Press, 2000.

Sanchez, George G. "Y Tú, ¿Qué? (Y2K): Latino History in the New Millennium." In *"Mixed Race" Studies: A Reader*, edited by Jayne O. Ifekwunigwe, 276–82. London: Routledge, 2004.

Sánchez, Rosaura. *Telling Identities: The Californio Testimonios*. Minneapolis: University of Minnesota Press, 1995.

Sandoval, Chela. *Methodology of the Oppressed*. Minneapolis: University of Minnesota, 2000.

———. "U.S. Third-World Feminism: The Theory and Method of Oppositional Consciousness in the Postmodern World." In *Feminist Postcolonial Theory: A Reader*, edited by Reina Lewis and Sara Mills, 75–102. New York: Routledge, 2003.

Sandoval, Moises. *On the Move: A History of the Hispanic Church in the United States*. Maryknoll, N.Y.: Orbis, 1990.

Scholem, Gershom. *Major Trends in Jewish Mysticism*. New York: Schocken, 1961.

Scott, James C. *Domination and the Arts of Resistance: Hidden Transcripts*. New Haven: Yale University Press, 1990.

Seaman, Donna. Review of *Spirits of the Ordinary*. *Booklist* 93, no. 11 (February 1, 1997): 924–25.

Segovia, Fernando. "Introduction: Minority Studies and Christian Studies." In *A Dream Unfinished: Theological Reflections on America from the Margins*, edited by Eleazar S. Fernandez and Fernando F. Segovia, 1–33. Maryknoll, N.Y.: Orbis, 2001.

Shaw, Rosalind, and Charles Stewart, eds. *Syncretism/Anti-Syncretism: The Politics of Religious Synthesis*. New York: Routledge, 1994.

Shawcross, Nancy M. *Roland Barthes on Photography: The Critical Tradition in Perspective*. Gainesville: University Press of Florida, 1997.

Shea, Maureen E. "Latin American Women and the Oral Tradition: Giving Voice to the Voiceless." *Critique* 34, no. 3 (spring 1993): 139–54.

Singh, Amritjit, Joseph T. Skerrett Jr., and Robert E. Hogan. Introduction. In *Memory and Cultural Politics: New Approaches to American Ethnic Literatures*, edited by Amritjit Singh, Joseph T. Skerrett Jr., and Robert E. Hogan, 3–18. Boston: Northeastern University Press, 1996.

Smith, Sidonie, and Julia Watson. *Reading Autobiography: A Guide for Interpreting Life Narratives*. Minneapolis: University of Minnesota Press, 2001.

Smith, Valerie. *Not Just Race, Not Just Gender: Black Feminist Readings*. New York: Routledge, 1998.

Sommer, Doris. " 'Not Just a Personal Story': Women's *Testimonios* and the Plural Self." In *Life/Lines: Theorizing Women's Autobiography*, edited by Bella Brodzki and Celeste Schenck, 107–30. Ithaca, N.Y.: Cornell University Press, 1988.

———. *Foundational Fictions: The National Romances of Latin America*. Berkeley: University of California Press, 1991.

———. "Taking a Life: Hot Pursuit and Cold Rewards in a Mexican Testimonial Novel." *Signs: Journal of Women in Culture and Society* 20, no. 4 (1995): 913–40.

———. "No Secrets." In *The Real Thing: Testimonial Discourse and Latin America*, edited by Georg M. Gugelberger, 130–57. Durham: Duke University Press, 1996.

Sontag, Susan. *On Photography*. New York: Farrar, Straus and Giroux, 1977.

Spain, Daphne. *Gendered Spaces*. Chapel Hill: University of North Carolina Press, 1992.

Spicer, Rosamond B., and N. Cross Crumrine, eds. *Performing the Renewal of Community: Indigenous Easter Rituals in North Mexico and Southwest United States*. Lanham, Md.: University Press of America, 1996.

Stasiulis, Daiva K. "Relational Positionalities of Nationalisms, Racisms, and Feminisms." In *Between Woman and Nation: Nationalisms, Transnational Feminisms, and the State*, edited by Caren Kaplan, Norma Alarcón, and Minoo Moallem, 182–218. Durham: Duke University Press, 1999.

Steele, Cassie Premo. *We Heal from Memory: Sexton, Lorde, Anzaldúa and the Poetry of Witness*. New York: Palgrave, 2000.

Stepick, Alex. "God Is Apparently Not Dead: The Obvious, the Emergent, and the Still Unknown in Immigration and Religion." In *Immigrant Faiths: Trans-*

forming Religious Life in America, edited by Karen I. Leonard, Alex Stepick, Manuel A. Vasquez, and Jennifer Holdaway, 11–37. Lanham, Md.: AltaMira/ Rowman and Littlefield, 2005.

Stevens-Arroyo, Anthony M. "Latino Catholicism and the Eye of the Beholder: Notes towards a New Sociological Paradigm." *Latino Studies Journal* 6, no. 2 (May 1995): 22–55.

Taylor, Diana. *The Archive and the Repertoire: Performing Cultural Memory in the Americas*. Durham: Duke University Press, 2003.

Taylor, William B. "Mexico's Virgin of Guadalupe in the Seventeenth Century: Hagiography and Beyond." In *Colonial Saints: Discovering the Holy in the Americas, 1500–1800*, edited by Allan Greer and Jodi Bilinkoff, 277–98. New York: Routledge Falmer, 2003.

Thompson, Ginger. "In Mexico's Murders, Fury Is Aimed at Officials." *New York Times*, September 26, 2005.

Thompson, Paul. "Believe It or Not: Rethinking the Historical Interpretation of Memory." In *Memory and History: Essays on Recalling and Interpreting Experience*, edited by Jaclyn Jeffrey and Glenace Edwall, 1–13. Lanham, Md.: University Press of America, 1994.

Torres, Carlos Alberto. *The Church, Society, and Hegemony: A Critical Sociology of Religion in Latin America*, translated by Richard A. Young. Westport, Conn.: Praeger, 1992.

Torres, Lourdes. "The Construction of Self in U.S. Latina Autobiographies." In *Third World Women and the Politics of Feminism*, edited by Chandra Talpade Mohanty, Ann Russo, and Lourdes Torres, 271–87. Bloomington: Indiana University Press, 1991.

Trotter, Robert T., and Juan Antonio Chavira. *Curanderismo: Mexican American Folk Healing*. Athens: University of Georgia Press, 1997 [1981].

Trujillo, Carla, ed. *Living Chicana Theory*. Berkeley: Third Woman, 1998.

Turner, Kay. *Beautiful Necessity: The Art and Meaning of Women's Altars*. New York: Thames and Hudson, 1999.

Van Der Veer, Peter. "The Moral State: Religion, Nation, and the Empire in Victorian Britain and British India." In *Nation and Religion: Perspectives on Europe and Asia*, edited by Peter Van Der Veer and Hartmut Lehmann. Princeton: Princeton University Press, 1999.

Vanpool, Christine S., and Todd L. Vanpool, eds. *Religion in the Prehispanic Southwest*. Lanham, Md.: Rowman and Littlefield, 2006.

Vargas, Zaragosa. *Proletarians of the North: A History of Mexican Industrial Workers in Detroit and the Midwest, 1917–1933*. Berkeley: University of California Press, 1999.

Vasconcelos, José. *The Cosmic Race: A Bilingual Edition.* [The Cosmic Race/ La raza cósmica]. Trans. Didier T. Jaén. Baltimore: Johns Hopkins University Press, 1997 [1925].

Warner, R. Stephen. "Introduction: Immigration and Religious Communities in the United States." In *Gatherings in Diaspora: Religious Communities and the New Immigration,* edited by R. Stephen Warner and Judith G. Wittner, 3–34. Philadelphia: Temple University Press, 1998.

White, Hayden. *The Content of the Form: Narrative Discourse and the Historical Representation.* Baltimore: Johns Hopkins University Press, 1987.

Wilkinson, Joanne. Review of *Flower in the Skull. Booklist* 94, nos. 19–20 (June 1, 1998): 1719.

Wolfson, Elliot R. "Forms of Visionary Ascent as Ecstatic Experience in the Zoharic Literature." In *Gershom Scholem's Major Trends in Jewish Mysticism 50 Years After: Proceedings of the Sixth International Conference on the History of Jewish Mysticism,* edited by Peter Schäfer and Joseph Dan, 209–35. Tübingen: J. C. B. Mohr (Paul Siebeck), 1993.

Wuthnow, Robert. *After Heaven: Spirituality in America since the 1950s.* Berkeley: University of California Press, 1998.

Yarbro-Bejarano, Yvonne. "Gloria Anzaldúa's *Borderlands/La Frontera*: Cultural Studies, 'Difference,' and the Non-Unitary Subject." In *Contemporary American Women Writers: Gender, Class, Ethnicity,* edited by Lois Parkinson Zamora, 11–31. New York: Longman, 1998.

———. *The Wounded Heart: Writing on Cherríe Moraga.* Austin: University of Texas Press, 2001.

Young, Pamela Dickey. *Feminist Theology/Christian Theology: In Search of Method.* Minneapolis: Fortress, 1990.

Yúdice, George. "Testimonio and Postmodernism." In *The Real Thing: Testimonial Discourse and Latin America,* edited by Georg M. Gugelberger, 42–57. Durham: Duke University Press, 1996.

Zavella, Patricia. *Women's Work and Chicano Families: Cannery Workers of the Santa Clara Valley.* Ithaca, N.Y.: Cornell University Press, 1987.

Zimmerman, Marc. "Testimonio in Guatemala." In *The Real Thing: Testimonial Discourse and Latin America,* edited by Georg M. Gugelberger, 101–29. Durham: Duke University Press, 1996.

Zuniga, Bernice, and Terri Fout. "King on the Mountain: An El Paso Community College History Project." *Borderlands* 10 (spring 1992), 3.

INDEX

Boff, Clodovis, 88, 217–18 n. 151
Boff, Leonardo, 88, 126, 217–18 n. 151
Bolivia, 182
Book of Service: A Handbook for Servers
(fictional oral history), 43, 45, 51–52,
58
Borderlands/La Frontera (Anzaldúa):
as autohisteoría, 2, 19, 20; critics of,
5, 14; dynamicism of borders in, 13,
200–201 n. 26; frontera history in,
19–20; "The Homeland, Aztlán/El
otro México," 20–23; languages in,
20; lesbianism in, 5–6; memory in,
20–22, 184, 204 n. 50; mestiza consciousness in, 11–13; personal narratives in, 19–22, 204 n. 46; spirituality
in, 4, 199 n. 7; spiritual mestizaje in,
7, 13, 200–201 n. 26; testimonio in,
2, 19, 20
Brading, D. A., 83, 123
Brady, Mary Pat, 28, 102
Braziel, Jane Evans, 100
Bridge Called My Back, The
(ed. Anzaldúa), 9, 24, 69
Brooklyn, N.Y., 94, 117, 122–23, 124, 125,
126
Brooks, James F., 148
Brown Virgin. *See* Guadalupe
Broyles-González, Yolanda, 111
Bruce, Steve, 194
Buddhism, 90, 197, 198
Butler, Judith, 63, 64, 65, 73, 81, 213 n. 83

Camera Lucida (Barthes), 102, 105
Caminantes, 39
Campos, Eduardo, 121, 123, 127–28
Canclini, Néstor García, 86, 180, 182,
183, 217 n. 144, 219 n. 165, 219 n. 167,
232 n. 14

Canícula (Cantú): as autobioethnography, 95, 99; bodily sensations in,
97, 106–7; cotton picking in, 106–7;
Doña Carmen, 110, 111, 113, 114; la
frontera in, 100–102; heteronormativity and, 113–14; individual
memory in collective framework,
102–3; as narrative, 95, 219 n. 3; pairing of photographs and prose in, 102;
religious performance in, 107, 108,
109–11; sacred place in, 223 n. 47;
social space in, 108, 222 n. 39; spiritual community of women in, 110–13;
spiritual mestizaje in, 101; subversion
of, 112–13; time frame of, 193; transnationalism of, 95, 96, 100. *See also*
Photographs; Photography
Cantú, Norma Elia, 2, 35, 36
Carabajal, Julio and Mariana (fictional
characters), 144, 152, 160, 162–63,
164, 169, 173, 175–76, 227–28 n. 6
Carabajál de la Cueva y Vargas, Zacarías
(fictional character): family relations
of, 173; as healer, 144, 156; on Jewish
religious practice, 160; personality of,
172–73; on racial and religious mixture, 160; spiritual renewal of, 154,
155–57, 164–65, 229 n. 36
Carpentier, Alejo, 232 n. 11
Carrasco, David, 14, 58, 59
Casas Grandes: government suppression
of, 144, 157, 176, 190; growth of spirituality and, 161, 164; as social site,
157; spiritual renaissance at, 145, 153,
154, 155–57, 164, 229 n. 38
Castillo, Ana, 16–17, 31, 184, 224 n. 63
Castillo, Debra A., 102, 215 n. 103
Catholic Buddhism, 197, 198
Catholic Church: elitism in, 84; family

and, 110–11; female ordination and, 75, 87, 88, 89; feminist activism in, 87, 88–89; Hispanic links to, 97–98; liberation theology and, 68, 71, 75–76, 82, 88–89, 98, 201–3 n. 31, 217–18 n. 151, 220 n. 16; pious performance in, 48, 112; social and political involvement of, 87, 98, 174; women in, 16, 110–13. *See also* Guadalupe

Catholicism, 16, 200 n. 16; Catholic Buddhism, 197, 198; of Cesar Chávez, 197–98; childhood religious training and, 54–55, 107, 108, 110; churches of, 108; confession and, 206–8 n. 96; cross-border communities and, 108; curanderismo and, 224 n. 63; Eastern spiritual beliefs and, 41, 80, 89, 90, 91; in *Face of an Angel*, 54–55, 185; folk, 24–25; Hispanic women empowered within, 201–3 n. 31; mujerista theology and, 201–3 n. 31; in southwest United States, 161

Cetina Gutiérrez, Rita, 149

Chabram-Dernersesian, Angie, 216–17 n. 143

Chaparro, Mirna García, 120

Chávez, Cesar, 197–98

Chávez, Denise, 2, 59, 198, 213 n. 73

Chávez, Guadalupe, 123

Chavira, Juan Antonio, 223–24 n. 62

Chiapas, 121, 182

Chicana and Latina feminist theologians, 15, 201 n. 30, 201–3 n. 31, 228 n. 20

Chicana feminism, 5, 199–200 n. 11; multiple subject positions, 60; Pérez's decolonial history in, 150–51; publications of, 40; religion and, 40–41; spiritual communities created by, 17–18

Chicana Feminist Thought (García), 40

Chicanas, 62; in collective memory, 20–22, 184, 204 n. 50; empowerment of, 43, 50–51, 52, 53, 121; marginalization in labor force of, 49–53

Chicano/a identities: El Plan Espiritual de Aztlán, 12; hybridization of, 27–28; language in, 20; mestizaje, 11

Chicano/a literature: challenges to, 34–35, 195, 234 n. 34; development of, 40; dialectic of difference in, 147; religion in, 40–41; religious traditions of the Americas in, 158–59; writing La Lupe, 27, 114

Chicano/a movement, 12, 66; indigenous cultures in, 25; nativism of, 181; on use of mestizaje, 10–11

Child abuse, 64, 65–66, 78

Chile, 132

Chiri/Hummingbird (fictional character), 143, 163

Christianity: commitment to social justice in, 194, 196–97; hybrid spiritualities and, 42, 170, 197–98, 220 n. 11; indigenous beliefs and practices in, 15, 98, 110–11, 220 n. 11; indigenous rituals and, 110–11, 167; liberation theology and, 68, 71, 75–76, 82, 88–89, 98, 201–3 n. 31, 217–18 n. 151, 220 n. 16; mestizo, 220 n. 11; mysticism and, 156; popular religiosity and, 59, 94, 117, 122–26, 212–13 n. 66; religious performance in, 48, 112, 167

Christian Right, 194

Cihuacoatl (goddess), 24, 26

Cinematic testimonios. *See Flowers for Guadalupe*; *Señorita Extraviada*

Cisneros, Sandra, 27, 82–83, 198

Citizenship, 49–50, 231 n. 82

83–84, 216–17 nn. 143–44; as healing presence, 120; images in homes of
disappeared women of, 131, 134, 135,
137, 140; immigrant Mexican women
in Brooklyn and, 94, 117, 122–23, 124,
125, 126; indigenous goddesses and,
8, 24–26, 27, 31, 204 n. 46; interces-
sionary prayers to, 119; marathons
and, 97, 116; in mestiza feminist theology, 201–3 n. 31; as mother of the
poor, 84–85; as patroness of Mexico,
115; performance piece on, 31–32;
in poetry, 30–31; pre-Columbian
origins of rituals for, 116; reconciliation with, 28–30; retablos and, 122;
sacred visions of, 119; as sex goddess,
82–83; spiritual mestizaje represented
by, 8, 24–25, 201 n. 30, 201–3 n. 31;
Tonantzin seen in, 24, 31, 116, 117;
women's pilgrimages to, 94, 97, 116–17,
118, 126, 188; women's relay races and,
94, 110, 116, 117, 119, 120, 122, 126, 188;
women's self-knowledge and, 188. *See
also Flowers for Guadalupe*
Guadaña, María, 31
Guatemala, 140, 182
Gugelberger, Georg M., 206–8 n. 96
Guha, Ranajit, 181
Guillén, Nicolás, 233 n. 17
Gutiérrez, Gustavo, 126, 128
Gutiérrez-Jones, Carl, 179, 232–33 n. 16

Halbwachs, Maurice, 22, 23, 106, 226 n. 121
Hanh, Thich Nhat, 90
Hansen, Christian, 127
Hart, Janice, 104, 221 n. 29
Healing, 17, 42, 97, 111–12, 156, 183,
223–24 nn. 62–63
Hedges, Elaine, 44

Hernandez, Ester, 216–17 n. 143
Hernández, Guillermo, 46–47
Hinduism, 180–81
Hispanic popular religiosity, 94, 117,
122–26, 201 n. 30
Historical fiction. *See The Flower in the
Skull; Spirits of the Ordinary; Trea-
sures in Heaven*
Hite, Molly, 212 n. 59
Holler, Stephen C., 97–98
Home altars, 80, 82, 108, 131
Hondagneu-Sotelo, Pierrette, 49, 50
hooks, bell, 17
Hutcheon, Linda, 211 n. 35
Hybrid spiritualities, 42, 154–55, 163,
164–65, 170, 197–98, 220 n. 11

Imagination, 2, 199 n. 3
Immigrants, 50–51, 109, 122–25, 129,
226 n. 105
Incest taboo, 63–64
Indigenous communities: cultural in-
cursions in, 167–69; curanderismo
and, 17, 42, 97, 111–12, 156,
223–24 nn. 62–63
Indigenous goddesses, 8, 24–26, 27, 31,
204 n. 46
Indigenous spiritualities: curanderismo,
17, 42, 111–12, 156, 223–24 nn. 62–63;
Tarahumara, 151, 153, 154, 155, 159, 167.
See also Guadalupe
Interviews, with women, 94, 117, 118,
119–23, 125, 126, 134, 226 n. 117
Intimacy, 210 n. 19
Isasí-Díaz, Ada-María, 201–3 n. 31
Ixtacihuátl, 26

Jameson, Fredric, 190
Jara, René, 45, 210 nn. 19–20

Sexuality, 17, 21, 52; conventions of, 143, 171; discovery of sexual self, 82–83; of female goddesses, 26; in Jewish mystical tradition, 175, 231 n. 83; in Mexican indigenous past, 25; performance of, 56–57; production of, 63–64, 213 n. 83; reclamation of, 42; regulation of women's, 185–86; religion's determining of, 4; violence and, 47, 64, 65, 78, 93, 145, 214 n. 86; virgin-whore dichotomy and, 55

Sexual violence, 29–30, 47, 64, 65–66, 78, 214 n. 86

Shawcross, Nancy M., 105, 221–22 n. 32, 222 n. 34

Shea, Maureen F., 206–8 n. 96

Shelly (fictional character): exile of, 231 n. 75; family history of, 145–46, 151, 170, 172, 176; Opata roots of, 157, 170; sexual harassment of, 145, 172

Siempreviva (Mexican feminist organization), 149

Silence, imposed on women, 36, 44–46, 139–40, 186

Smith, Sidonie, 206 n. 94

Social sites of resistance. *See* Casas Grandes

Social space, 106, 222 n. 39

Soledad (fictional character), 41–42, 68, 69, 70, 73, 80–81, 87

Sommer, Doris, 33, 65, 206 n. 95, 206–8 n. 96

Sontag, Susan, 99

Soveida (fictional character): *Book of Service: A Handbook for Servers*, 43, 45, 51–52, 58; communities of working women and, 41–42, 43–44, 49–51, 57–58, 61; family nostalgia and, 47–48; feminist spirituality of,

66; marriage of, 66; mentors for, 41–42, 43–44, 49–50, 53; on regulation of the body, 186; religious upbringing of, 54–55; sense of self developed by, 54–56, 61, 64, 66; sexual violence in family of, 47, 64–66; silence imposed on, 44–45, 186; spiritual mestizaje of, 60, 61; spiritual renewal of, 41, 42; voiced narrative of, 43–44, 44–45, 46

Spain, Daphne, 41, 209 n. 7

Spirits of the Ordinary (Alcalá): book cover of, 153; Julio and Mariana Carabajal in, 144, 152, 160, 162–63, 164, 169, 173, 175–76, 227–28 n. 6; Crypto Jews in, 37–38, 143–44, 153, 160, 161, 164; cultural hybridity in, 164–65; freedom to engage in traditional rituals in, 156–58; gardens in, 162; gender conventions and sexual norms policed in, 171; gender identity discussed in, 152; as historical fiction, 35; Kabbalah in, 17, 144, 152–53, 154, 158, 171, 227–28 n. 6; love in, 166; Manzana in, 163, 171; Membrillo in, 163, 171; plot summary of, 143–44; religion in borderlands historical events in, 143–44; religious traditions in, 154–59; spiritual quests in, 152; timeframe of, 193. *See also* Casas Grandes

Spirituality, 3

Spiritual mestizaje, 1, 4, 98, 180; Catholic Buddhism and, 197, 198; conocimiento and, 9, 18, 23, 24; of Crypto Jews, 37–38, 143–44, 160, 161, 164; curanderismo and, 17, 42, 97, 111–12, 156, 223–24 nn. 62–63; demystification of religion and, 191; Eastern spiritual beliefs and, 41, 80, 89, 90, 91,

Theresa Delgadillo is an assistant professor of comparative studies, Ohio State University.

Library of Congress Cataloging-in-Publication Data
Delgadillo, Theresa
Spiritual mestizaje : religion, gender, race, and nation in
contemporary Chicana narrative / Theresa Delgadillo.
p. cm. — (Latin America otherwise)
ISBN 978-0-8223-5029-3 (cloth : alk. paper)
ISBN 978-0-8223-5046-0 (pbk. : alk. paper)
1. Anzaldúa, Gloria—Criticism and interpretation.
2. American literature—Mexican American authors—History
and criticism.   3. Mestizaje in literature.   4. Spirituality in
literature.   5. Gender identity in literature.   I. Title.
II. Series: Latin America otherwise.
PS153.M4D454 2011
810.9'86872—dc22   2011006369